THE STUDY OF
FUGUE

ALFRED MANN

Eastman School of Music
University of Rochester

DOVER PUBLICATIONS, INC., NEW YORK

Published in Canada by General Publishing Company, Ltd., 30 Lesmill Road, Don Mills, Toronto, Ontario.

Published in the United Kingdom by Constable and Company, Ltd., 10 Orange Street, London WC2H 7EG.

This Dover edition, first published in 1987, is a slightly enlarged and corrected republication of the work originally published by Rutgers University Press, New Brunswick, N.J., in 1958. In addition to the preface to the original edition, the present edition includes the preface written by the author for the 1965 paperbound edition published by W. W. Norton & Company, Inc., N.Y., and a new Preface to the Dover Edition and brief biography of the author. The present edition is published by special arrangement with Rutgers University Press, 109 Church Street, New Brunswick, N.J. 08901.

Manufactured in the United States of America
Dover Publications, Inc., 31 East 2nd Street, Mineola, N.Y. 11501

Library of Congress Cataloging-in-Publication Data

Mann, Alfred, 1917–
    The study of fugue.

    Reprint. Originally published: New York : Norton, 1965. With new note.
    Bibliography: p.
    Includes index.
    1. Fugue. I. Title.
ML448.M25 1987   781.4′2   87-6663
ISBN 0-486-25439-9 (pbk.)

Fugue is an adornment of music governed
by no other principles than those of good
taste. The general rules given here can therefore never in themselves lead to the perfection
of fugal art.

Jean Philippe Rameau

Preface to the Dover Edition
(1987)

Having gone through another hardcover printing since the paperback
editions of 1965 were issued in the United States and Canada, *The Study of
Fugue* is now given a new lease on life through a Dover Publications
paperback reprint—doubly gratifying to the author because, as in 1965,
he can report to the readers of the book new results of inquiry into the
history of fugal teaching. A facsimile edition of Fux's *Gradus ad Parnassum*
published in 1967 as Series VII, Volume 1, of *Johann Joseph Fux: Sämtliche
Werke* contains Haydn's comments on Fux's fugal teaching; and Series
VIII, Volume 2, of the *Neue Schubert-Ausgabe*, published in 1986, includes the full documentation of the historic lesson in fugue—long
believed lost, but rediscovered in 1968—that concluded Schubert's life-
work. The evidence that has thus come to light once again guides the
student of fugue from theory to practice—which was the original purpose of the book.

Several footnotes in the text refer to the author's translation of Fux's
Gradus as *Steps to Parnassus: The Study of Counterpoint*, a title that was
changed in 1965 to *The Study of Counterpoint: From Johann Joseph Fux's
Gradus ad Parnassum*.

A. M.

Contents

Preface to the Paperback Edition
(1965)

The first edition of the *Study of Fugue* was published in the United States in 1958 and was issued a year later under an English imprint. Two didactic works have since come to light that are of such importance to the historical account of fugal instruction that they should be brought to the attention of the reader of the present edition.

In December 1959 the late Erich Hertzmann, Professor of Musicology at Columbia University, presented a paper before the American Musicological Society in which he described the studies that the English organist and composer Thomas Attwood pursued under the guidance of Mozart from 1785 to 1787. The paper was published under the title "Mozart and Attwood" in Vol. XII, Nos. 2–3 of the *Journal of the American Musicological Society*. Publication of the entire volume containing the exercises written by Attwood and the assignments, notes, and corrections entered by Mozart was planned within the Complete Works of Mozart (*Neue Mozart-Ausgabe*) under the joint editorship of Cecil B. Oldman, the owner of the manuscript, and Prof. Hertzmann. After the death of Prof. Hertzmann in 1963, preparations for publication were completed by Daniel Heartz and the present writer, and the volume is in press. The discussion of counterpoint and fugue included in the Attwood papers is based to a large extent upon Fux's *Gradus ad Parnassum*, and Mozart's interpretation of Fux's instruction represents a hitherto unknown chapter of singular interest in the history of contrapuntal teaching.

The other work is formed by a group of Handel autographs preserved in the Fitzwilliam Museum in Cambridge, which the present writer discussed at the international musicological congress in Kassel in the fall of 1962 and which until that time had not been recognized as a course of instruction ("Händels Fugenlehre – ein unveröffentlichtes Manuskript" published in *Kongress-Bericht Kassel 1962* of the *Gesellschaft für Musikforschung*). The manuscript, probably first compiled by Handel in the 1720s for his pupil Princess Anne, daughter of George II, is more fully described in the *Händel-Jahrbuch 1964/65* and will be published as a volume of the Complete Works of Handel (*Hallische Händel-Ausgabe*). Handel's study of fugue leads from short examples of various imitative procedures (real and fugal answer, augmentation, diminution, stretto, and double exposition) to assignments and models for extended fugal structures. The most interesting portion of the manuscript is Handel's treatment of double fugue, which bears out the key position of his fugal writing between the stylistic trends of two eras briefly suggested on page 68, below.

In both cases, the manuscripts show direct connections to the masters' own works. The Attwood studies contain copies of canons by Mozart, among them K. 507, 508, 508a, 515b, and a reference to the parody of an academic fugal exposition in the finale of K. 522 (*Ein musikalischer Spass*). The Fitzwilliam autographs are in several instances related to portions from Handel's Harpsichord Lessons of 1720, the *Foundling Hospital Anthem*, *Samson*, and *Messiah*. Thus the student of fugue will find new sets of classical examples that enhance the significance of the instructive material they illustrate.

A. M.

Preface
(1958)

The term fugue holds a particular fascination for the student of music. It suggests the essence of polyphony, the most intricate expression of the complex language of Western music. Where did it originate, what is its true meaning?

As a rule, we associate this concept with the music of Bach, and we are apt to assume that several generations prepared the ground for what in his work became a final form not essentially changed since. In reality, it assumed an important role more than four hundred years earlier. These centuries of fugal history have been inadequately treated in our retrospective view. They have been crowded into a "pre-Bach" era, and although we have begun to discover their contrapuntal wealth, we are hesitant to recognize their claim to the "fugue proper."

Curiously, the name Bach has symbolized not only the beginning and end but also the perfection and imperfection of fugal art. We shall see that his fugal writing, cherished as the supreme model, has nevertheless been denounced as contrary to the rules. Theory and practice have fought bitterly. "There is probably no branch of musical composition in which theory is more widely, one might almost say hopelessly, at variance with practice," wrote the English theorist Ebenezer Prout in one of the last comprehensive textbooks on fugue (1891).

This divergence between theory and practice did not exist in earlier periods. The domains of teacher and composer, of didactic and creative thought, were joined rather than opposed. Theoretical works of lasting importance were published by such composers as Praetorius and Rameau, and such works as Bach's *Art of Fugue* and Schütz's *Geistliche Chormusik* were meant to serve for the instruction of the student of composition.

The modern conflict between theory and practice can only be resolved through historical study. A glance into musical history shows that the very concepts of theory and practice have changed, and that the study of fugue was once considered *musica activa* rather than *musica speculativa*: active practice rather than speculative theory. Through the perspective of history it becomes clear that the term fugue—like the terms sonata and concerto—held different meanings at different times, and that we fail to understand it if we speak of the "fugue proper."

The plan of this book is guided by a historical approach to the concepts and principles of fugue. Part One traces the study of fugue from its beginnings, and Part Two dwells on that phase of its history which produced its classical presentations. For this reason the reader may not want to observe the order of Parts One and Two. The teacher and student may want to go directly to the practical instruction of Part Two; but a particular aspect or problem of fugal technique may soon lead them back to Part One to determine its origin. The historian or theorist will want to give his attention primarily to Part One, yet in following the course of fugal history he, too, may turn to Part Two in order to participate actively once again in the ever fascinating problems of fugue. *The Study of Fugue* will fulfill its purpose if it can recall in some measure the integration of theory and practice that the past has known.

ALFRED MANN

Newark, New Jersey

Acknowledgments

This book owes its inception to my students at the Newark Colleges of Rutgers University. In search for a series of models that might serve as a practical introduction to the theory of fugue, we gathered around a copy of Fux's *Gradus ad Parnassum* to study the examples. As so often in its history, Fux's instruction provided the students with an immediate challenge and with fascinating tasks. From the discussion of the group grew the first English translation of Fux's study of fugue.

The larger plan of the book is indebted above all to the ever encouraging advice and decisive help of Paul Henry Lang, Professor of Musicology at Columbia University and editor of *The Musical Quarterly*. Together with my thanks to Professor Lang, I want to express my gratitude to Professors Douglas Moore, Erich Hertzmann, William J. Mitchell, and André von Gronicka of Columbia University, and to my colleagues Professors A. Kunrad Kvam, Remigio U. Pane, and Alice M. Pollin of Rutgers University for their kind and valuable suggestions; to Professor Randall Thompson of Harvard University, who first called my attention to the admirable teaching of Padre Martini; and to Professor Arthur Mendel of Princeton University, whose friendly reassurance aided the critical last steps towards publication.

My thanks go also to Miss Virgene Leverenz, Miss Evangeline Broderick, Mrs. Mary Lago, Mrs. Georgiana Pollak, Mr. Frank Dillingham, Mr. Fritz Rikko, and to the staff members of the music library of Columbia University and of the music division of the New York Public Library for many kindnesses; to the publishers W. W. Norton and G. Schirmer for permission to use my earlier translations (Fux's Study of Counterpoint and his Study of Fugue); to the staff of Rutgers University Press for their understanding and skillful cooperation; to Mr. Wolfgang Weissleder for his careful work on the musical examples; to Mr. Judd Woldin, who prepared the index; and finally to my wife, who translated the texts for the works by Johann Christoph Bach, Caldara, and Mozart, and whose help has guided every phase of the work on this book.

A. M.

Part One

THE STUDY OF FUGUE
IN HISTORICAL OUTLINE

I

Texture Versus Form

The rise of polyphony has been recognized as the most decisive phase in the history of Occidental music. The beginnings of polyphonic art, long buried in oblivion, are today a subject of intense study. Early traces are suspected in classical antiquity and in the less familiar past of Northern countries.[1] Yet, those beginnings were actually contained in all monophonic practice which involved the simultaneous use of different voice registers. The octave, fifth, and fourth, which mark the distances between vocal registers, have gradually emerged in musical knowledge as fundamental phenomena and thus as the basis of part writing.

The first documents of polyphonic practice and theory that have been preserved show the rule of these intervals in various styles of the medieval organum. The technique of part writing reached a considerable degree of melodic independence when contrary motion of different voices triumphed over direct and oblique motion, crystallizing in the style of the *discantus* the true spirit of polyphony.

Throughout the gradual process in which the elements of polyphonic practice unfolded, we can recognize the gains and setbacks characteristic of the contest between the old and the new. Each bold advance was eventually checked and followed by a consolidation of forces which made the newly won objective more clearly perceptible. The victory of the use of contrary motion was modified through the fact that this principle of part writing was at first ap-

[1] See C. Sachs, *The Rise of Music in the Ancient World*, pp. 256 f.; and P. H. Lang, *Music in Western Civilization*, p. 128.

3

plied to the narrow choice of perfect consonances. Connected in angular voice movements, they failed to provide early polyphony with an undisturbed melodic flow. As the tradition of essentially linear writing was restored, the actual conquest attained was the use of imperfect consonances. Although still considered "harsh to the ears,"[2] these new aids to polyphonic writing were now accepted.

A final reconciliation of the various polyphonic means was found when Western art music adopted and cultivated the technique of imitation, which had probably existed for many centuries in the improvisations of popular musicianship. The linear strength of monophony was not only regained, but it received a totally new meaning as different voices performed the same melodic line, although, through spaced entrances, they were more clearly distinguished than ever before. The older forms of polyphony had assumed their roles as components of a more complex system of part writing, serving as *motus rectus, obliquus,* and *contrarius.* Contrary motion remained the most important of the three, and the combination of the principles of contrary motion and imitation ensured a more definite balance of ascent and descent in the course of each melodic line than had been possible in monophonic music; for any ascending passage called for a descending continuation against the imitative entrance of the next part, just as any descending passage required an ascending continuation.[3]

This technique of imitation, which became the outstanding characteristic of the Renaissance style of composition, thus proved to be the ideal combination of likeness and diversity, the strongest form of polyphony. The fifteenth-century theorist Bartolomeo Ramos de Pareja described it in his *Musica practica* as *optimus organisandi modus*—the best manner of part writing—and added, "This manner is

---

[2] J. de Grocheo's description of the major third, in *Theoria, c.* 1300 (*SIM*, I, 80).

[3] The rule of contrary motion which John Cotton stated about 1100—"if the main voice is ascending, the accompanying voice should descend, and vice versa" (*Gerb. Script.*, II, 264)—was adopted for the imitative technique two centuries later by Walter Odington in his description of the *rondellus:* "What is sung in one part is repeated by the others in turn . . . the parts being so arranged that while one ascends the other descends" (*Couss. Script.*, I, 264). A similar widening of polyphonic concepts can be recognized in the expression *cantus contra cantum,* which Prosdocimus de Beldemandis uses a century after Odington in his discussion of the older term *contrapunctus* (*Couss. Script.*, III, 194). Odington's teaching proves insufficient, however, when it comes to the treatment of a third part which, as he says, should not ascend or descend simultaneously with one of the other parts—a rule which his own examples invalidate. It was revised by Franchino Gafori in his *Practica musica* (cf. p. 12, below).

called *fuga* by practicing musicians." A texture for Occidental music was found. Now began the search for its form. It is here that the study of fugue originates.

In several sources which antedate Ramos de Pareja's writing, the word *fuga* already appears as title or inscription to musical works. In one instance it is listed together with such forms of medieval music as the conductus and the motet. Thus from the earliest period of its use, the term fugue held the curious double meaning of texture and form or genre that has bedeviled musical theory ever since.

While the texture of music had developed an entirely new world of its own, the structure of music had followed lines well defined and prepared by the literary arts. One notable exception of an early form-giving element was the canon—in its original meaning the "precept indicating the composer's plan"; [4] but, in general, musical form was guided by the text. The dominant position of vocal performance, naturally established in the early phases of musical history, was increased through the influence of the Church, which directed all cultural activity. It had tied medieval music to the *Mot*—the sacred *Word*—as the pre-eminence of the term motet shows. With the decline of the Middle Ages new concepts, an *ars nova*, lent importance to musical practice beyond the domain of the Church, and musical forms began to lean more and more on secular texts and, eventually, in the greatest event of musical secularization, on the drama modeled on classical antiquity.

Yet the departure from liturgic forms and the renaissance of drama and dramatic music in the opera only served to strengthen the influential role of the text. The search for a form constructed with purely musical means was left to music which, in the words of the English composer and theorist Thomas Morley, was "made without a ditty" [5]—to instrumental music derived from modest idiomatic beginnings that lived on in the early toccata (overture) and in stylized dance movements. After a long apprenticeship in the subservient roles of accompanying, paraphrasing, varying, or prefacing vocal forms and dances, instrumental music gradually was raised to independent tasks. Its literature produced the new foils to vocal forms: the *canzona da sonare*, or song for instrumental performance; the ricercare

[4] J. Tinctoris, *Diffinitorium musicae*, c. 1475 (*Couss. Script.*, IV, 179).
[5] *A Plain and Easy Introduction to Practical Music*, 1597 (R. A. Harman ed., 1952, p. 296).

and the tiento, works whose titles describe the "searching" and the "tentative" groping for form; and the fantasia, the capriccio, and later the inventio, pieces in which the matter of musical structure was left entirely to the fancy, caprice, or invention of the composer. The search for form continued through the music of the Baroque until the Classic era found a final solution, and it ended in the triumph of instrumental music. Just as the "cantata" departed from the musical scene, the "sonata" had found its "form." [6]

This quest for musical structure was associated in all its phases with the term fugue, for originally or eventually this term served each of the forms mentioned. In its first meaning, it identified the canon, but it was to be used in turn for the motet and its instrumental descendants, the ricercare, tiento, and fantasia. It was applied to the core, and at times to the very essence, of the canzona, of the toccata, and of the overture (even as late as in Beethoven's Quartet Op. 133). It ruled the forms of the Baroque concerto and sonata, and eventually bequeathed the structural achievements which it had gathered during three centuries to the Classic sonata, yet retained its own life in the developmental technique, the "major element" that marked the "final decisive step" toward and beyond the Classic era. [7]

An understanding of the course that this search for musical form followed has grown only slowly. Fifty years ago, Vincent d'Indy placed before the musical scholars assembled at the third meeting of the International Music Society the question: "Can the epoch be determined in which the decline of the admirable form of the fugue occurred—a decline leading to a mere formula void of any artistic and musical interest—and can the first source of such treatment of the fugue be ascertained?" The chairman of the meeting, Johannes Wolf, stated that a direct answer could not be given since it would require a comprehensive discussion of the history of the fugue which was not as yet available.

This suggestion led to Joseph Maria Müller-Blattau's outline his-

---

[6] The music of the nineteenth century returned to a relative balance of vocal and instrumental forces. While the instrumental element extended its rule even into the opera (Wagner), and the song (Wolf), the vocal element, which had found its way into the symphony with Beethoven, resumed a decisive influence on instrumental music. It is interesting that the two terms which mark the extreme points of the evolution briefly outlined here are almost identical: *canzona da sonare* and *Lied ohne Worte*.

[7] P. H. Lang, *Music in Western Civilization*, pp. 629 f.

tory of fugue, *Grundzüge einer Geschichte der Fuge* (1923), a work which deals particularly with the formal and expressive aspects of fugal art. Although Müller-Blattau's careful account provides a new perspective against which d'Indy's question can be studied, it does not discuss the problem contained in the question itself. It fails to conclude that the eventful history of fugal writing never led to a definite form in the sense of a pattern, and that the very attempt to halt the evolution of fugal technique, freezing it into "the fugue," and this attempt only, represents decline and reduction to a mere formula.

A recent essay by Alberto Ghislanzoni, which follows the plan of Müller-Blattau's work, offers a solution to the problem by summarizing the ever-changing appearance of fugue in a comprehensive definition, expressed in one sentence, which is too unwieldy to serve its purpose.[8] A more concise and successful explanation is given by Manfred Bukofzer, who declares fugue neither a form nor a texture but a contrapuntal procedure.[9]

In answer to d'Indy's question, Müller-Blattau places the end of the fugue with Bach;[10] but surely we cannot consider any of the fugues in Mozart's instrumental and choral works or in Beethoven's piano sonatas and string quartets as works that represent "a decline leading to a mere formula void of any artistic and musical interest." Nevertheless, a significant difference between the fugues of Bach and

---

[8] "A musical work written for two or more parts—vocal or instrumental—which present initially a basic theme or subject melodically and rhythmically well defined and easily recognizable (or two or more such basic themes), restating this theme again and again at the fifth, at the fourth, or at some other diatonic or chromatic interval, and elaborating upon this theme and its various elements contrapuntally in a number of sections by use of augmentation or diminution (double, triple, quadruple note values, etc.; half, third, quarter note values, etc.), by use of contrary motion, reversion, suitable rhythmic changes, increasingly closer spacing of theme and answer (stretto or partial stretto), and by use of extended tones in the lower, upper, or middle voices (pedal points); all of this with the greatest possible freedom of melodic and rhythmic invention and without any particular limitations as to resulting harmonies, structural patterns, or tonal and modulatory progressions." ("La Genesi storica della fuga," *Rivista Musicale Italiana*, LIII [1951].)

[9] *Music in the Baroque Era*, pp. 361 ff. Cf. also S. Levarie, "Fugue and Form," a paper presented before the American Musicological Society in 1941; and H. T. David and A. Mendel, *The Bach Reader*, p. 30. Fugue was first discussed as "a texture the rules of which do not suffice to determine the shape of the composition as a whole" by D. F. Tovey in his article written for the eleventh edition of the *Encyclopaedia Britannica*.

[10] See also the earlier study by J. S. Shedlock, "The Evolution of Fugue," in *Proceedings of the Royal Musical Association*, 1896.

Beethoven is expressed in the qualifications that appear in Beethoven's fugue titles. Beethoven called the finale of his Sonata Op. 106 (Hammerklavier) *fuga con alcune licenze,* and his Quartet Op. 133 was published as *Grande Fugue tantôt libre, tantôt recherchée*—qualifications that we do not find in Bach's writing. Bach's use of the older term ricercare in his *Musical Offering* may be understood in the sense in which *recherchée* is used in Beethoven's Quartet Op. 133— as describing a highly elaborate example of fugal writing—but the *fugue libre* or *fuga con licenze* is foreign to Bach's style.

Ebenezer Prout's textbook *Fugue* (1891) shows in its opening sentence that the "licenses" in fugal writing had grown to incredible dimensions within a century. Prout quotes his colleagues as saying that "Bach is not a good model because he allows himself too many exceptions," and that "there is not a single correctly written fugue among Bach's 'Forty-Eight.'" With the premise of his work, namely to go "to the works of the great composers themselves," Prout draws unquestionably the right conclusion. Yet his aim to find by this method that which is "correct" shows that he is guided by a new concept, that of the "fugue without exceptions," which never existed in actual literature. Since the problems connected with this concept arise from the theory of music, not the music itself, we shall take for the present discussion a point of departure that differs from those of Müller-Blattau and Prout and direct our attention primarily to the writings of theorists—the works which represent the actual study of fugue.

Theoretical discussions, as a rule, present musical phenomena considerably later than they have appeared in practice, but their very purpose is to present them at a stage of development which permits precise formulation of rules and doctrines. A comparison of these first definitions and the changes to which they were subjected in the course of time will make it easier to determine where the study of fugue properly served to support and clarify its practice, and where it deviated from it, thereby creating an imaginary, unreal world of its own.

II

The Renaissance: Fugal Exposition

The Beginnings of Fugal Theory

The first known use of the term *fuga* in theoretical writings occurred in the *Speculum musicae* by Jacobus of Liège.[1] This work, written about 1330, holds a significant place as "the last great medieval treatise on music,"[2] a final summary that opened the road to musical theory in the modern sense. Although *fuga* is listed here among the chief vocal forms of the time, the mention of the term remains relatively isolated. The reason for this is doubtless to be found in the fact that the imitative technique was generally associated with secular music, far removed from the domain of sacred art, with which the writing of music theorists was primarily concerned. In the course of the fourteenth century, however, the secular technique of canonic imitation gained prominence and recognition in the *caccia* and the *rondellus*—canonic forms whose designations have come down in English usage as catch and round.[3] And the term *fuga* seems to have served for either of them.

[1] *Couss. Script.*, II, 395.

[2] P. H. Lang, *Music in Western Civilization*, p. 161.

[3] The term *caccia* (French *chace*, Spanish *caça*) designates, as a rule, works relating scenes of actual chasing or hunting, which were performed by two canonic voices moving above a free tenor part. The term *rondellus* (*rotundellus*, *rota*) described "the return of the melody into itself in the manner of a circle," as is stated in Grocheo's *Theoria*, which also relegates the *rondellus* to worldly festivities (*in festibus vulgarium laicorum*). The terms were subjected to various interpretations and acquired certain connotations in different periods. "Amongst early writers on music, the terms 'round' and 'catch' were synonymous, but at the present day the latter is generally understood to be what Hawkins (Vol. II) defines as that species of round 'wherein, to humor some conceit in the words, the melody is broken, and the sense interrupted in one part, and caught again or supplied by another.'" (*Grove's Dictionary*, 3d ed., 1946.)

In the Latin text of Jacobus, *fuga* evidently stands for *caccia*, its Italian equivalent, since in his enumerations of musical forms it is mentioned separately from the popular round (*cantilena vel rondellus*). On the other hand, two generations later, *fuga* appeared as the title for two- and three-part rounds by the minnesinger Oswald von Wolkenstein.[4] In the Trent Codices the term *fuga* is for the first time applied to both secular and sacred works: No. 62, *Chasse mois, je vois devant* (anonymous), and No. 911, *Et in terra ad modum tubae*, a portion of a Mass by Guillaume Dufay (the opening is given in Example 1). It is interesting that Dufay's *fuga* still contains the typical accompaniment of secular canons. The supporting *ostinato* fanfare (written "in trumpet style"), which foreshadows the bright orchestral Gloria settings of later periods, is similar to the *pes* of the famous Sumer Canon.

Ex. 1

The fusion of imitative style and sacred music was completed by the generation after Dufay (Ockeghem and Obrecht) and clearly borne out in the title *Missa ad Fugam* (Josquin des Prez and Palestrina). By what amounts to a reversal of history, imitation was to remain the characteristic of church music when secular influences threatened its traditions anew.

Whereas the term *fuga* served in its earliest use as a title for the accompanied canon and the round, it emerged in its first precise definition as the technique common to both: "the identity of rhythmic and melodic writing in various parts of a composition." This explanation is contained in the *Diffinitorium musicae*, the first musical dictionary in history, written about 1475 by the Flemish theorist Johannes Tinctoris.

Once the imitative technique was identified by the generic term

[4] *DTOe*, IX, 190, 191, 196.

fuga, it was also recognized as a means of artistic expression, for in his *Liber de arte contrapuncti* (1477), Tinctoris groups *fuga* with other devices that a composer may use in order to obtain musical variety—the final and most strongly emphasized rule in his teaching of counterpoint. Tinctoris adds that at times *fuga* can designate even an identity of pitch and spacing for successive entrances, giving a first suggestion of the distinction between free and strict imitation. With Tinctoris, then, fugue is acknowledged as a principle of composition. This principle assumes a significant position in the treatise of Bartolomeo Ramos de Pareja, less than a decade after Tinctoris. Ramos is the first to recommend the choice of perfect intervals, fourth, fifth, and octave, for imitative entrances—the intervals which we have encountered as basic elements from the very beginning of polyphonic writing. He introduces the musical usage of the verb *imitari* and applies it to both the strict and free repetition of interval progressions. But his most important remark lies in the suggestion that free writing be introduced in the imitative style whenever consistent imitation would result in difficulty. This principle of composition leads to the concept of fugue which was to gain greatest importance in the following centuries.

The emphasis upon free use of the imitative manner may seem surprising at a time which we customarily associate with contrapuntal art of amazing and mysterious strictness. Yet it is doubtless this free, non-canonic use of imitation on which the most significant achievements of the time are founded. The importance of Flemish contrapuntal skill is easily seen out of proportion—just as the complexity of its most famous example, the thirty-six-part canon *Deo Gratia* by Ockeghem, is easily overrated.[5]

The German theorist Adam von Fulda, a contemporary of Ramos, was one of the first to speak of the limited value of canonic artifices,[6] and his opinion was followed in the account of Ockeghem's and Josquin's work given half a century later by Heinrich Glarean.[7] The attitude which places freedom of imitative writing above strictness, expressed in theoretical discussions as early as this, was to remain

---

[5] Published in H. Riemann, *Handbuch der Musikgeschichte,* II, 237 ff. No more than half of the total number of voices are actually used together, and then only very briefly.

[6] *Musica,* 1490 (*Gerb. Script.,* III, 354).

[7] *Dodekachordon,* 1547 (*PGM,* XVI).

typical of theoretical thought, and we shall find it again and again as
the key to decisive advances in the study of fugue.

The growing importance of the imitative technique prompted
theorists after Ramos to subject some of the established principles
of contrapuntal practice to revisions. In his *Practica musica* (1496),
Franchino Gafori points out an inadequacy in the accepted code of
part writing. He examines the rule requiring different parts of a
composition to move in contrary motion and declares it "an arbitrary law." He states that direct motion, which is bound to arise in
the conduct of more than two parts, is often found in practice, and
that it becomes highly commendable when "the parts of a composition combine their equal motion in fugal manner."

Pietro Aron's *Toscanello in musica* (1523) challenges the fundamental procedure which had ruled polyphonic writing: the successive composition of different parts forming one work. Aron declares
this method obsolete since "it causes the parts to suffer" and says
that modern composers show better judgment because "they consider all parts together." [8]

Hugo Riemann has suggested that it was the increasing use of
the imitative technique, raising different voices of a composition to
equal importance, which caused Aron to take his stand.[9] Aron had
mentioned the *imitatio* or *fugatio* seven years earlier in his *Libri tres
de institutione harmonica.*[10] It becomes clear from his discussion in
the *Toscanello in musica* that he is aware of the complexity of the
new system which he advocates, and he concedes that it will be
easier for the student to gain his first experience writing part by
part. His choice for the beginning, however, is no longer necessarily
the tenor—the part that traditionally presented the cantus firmus or
cantus prius factus. He states that any part may be written first but
favors the soprano and bass. This shows that a new concept of harmony had begun to rule theoretical thinking. Gafori had characterized *harmonia* as the "sweet and congruous sonority" which arises

---

[8] The problems which the composer encounters in writing different parts of a work
successively are borne out by the typically disjunct melodic lines of the parts written
last: in three-part works of fifteenth-century music, the *contratenor,* and in compositions of a later period, often the *quinta vox* and *sexta vox.*

[9] *Geschichte der Musiktheorie,* p. 353.

[10] Ch. 52. Unlike Aron's later works, this first publication is still written in Latin.
The rise of fugal theory coincides with the appearance of modern languages in theoretical literature; both reflect the spirit of the Renaissance.

from the consonant combination of three tones, whereas Tinctoris, only twenty years earlier, had considered it synonymous with melody.[11]

This new orientation reveals also the impetus which polyphony had received through the rise of the keyboard technique. The art of improvising several voices simultaneously decisively influenced contrapuntal practice for centuries to come, and the combination of instrumental improvisation and virtuosity characterized the creative achievement of masters of fugal writing until Bach's time. The curiously one-sided appraisal that Bach's contemporaries accorded his work is perhaps more easily understood in view of this tradition.

The earliest instructions for the composition of organ works, in Konrad Paumann's *Fundamentum organisandi* (1452), do not include the use of the imitative technique. But Johannes Buchner's *Fundamentbuch* (*c.* 1525), in both letter and spirit a continuation of Paumann's work, contains a systematic exposition of the *ars fugandi* in tabular form.

A pupil of the great organ master Paul Hofhaimer, Buchner ably proves that the presentation of several imitative parts by a single performer has become an accepted accomplishment. His treatment of the fugal technique is shown in short three-part settings, as a rule in even note values, with which he explores all existing possibilities. Reasoning that the cantus firmus will begin with either an ascending or descending second, third, fourth, or fifth, he gives a separate example for each case.[12] The two imitative parts usually alternate entrances at the fourth and fifth, so that the third part enters at the octave of the first entrance. This order of entrances, however, is not yet observed as a definite principle; there is also the case in which two entrances at the fourth follow each other, causing the third part to enter at the seventh of the first entrance (Example 2). Buchner's examples are broken off once the third part is introduced or concluded by a cadence (Example 3). Similar tables deal with non-imitative elaborations of ascending, descending, or stationary cantus firmus beginnings.

[11] *Practica musica*, III, ch. 10; *Diffinitorium musicae* (*Couss. Script.*, IV, 185). Even Glarean used the term to denote a single melodic line: "recommendations for the invention of a *harmonia* or, as it is usually called, tenor" (*Dodekachordon*, Bk. II, ch. 39).

[12] The practice of the period considered skips beyond the fifth generally too large; cf. H. Glarean's statement in *Dodekachordon* (*PGM*, XVI, 20), which advises against the skip of the major sixth, though it admits that of the minor sixth "if properly used."

Ex. 2

Ex. 3

The discussion of the elements of composition which precedes these tables adds no further information to Buchner's fugal technique, but a number of his organ works, which appear at the end of his text, show it in practice. Possibly the best examples of organ composition that emanated from the Hofhaimer school, these works show an early culmination of the fugal style in instrumental writing. One of them, Buchner's setting of the sacred song *Maria zart*, is quoted in the collection of organ tablatures by his contemporary, Leonhard Kleber, as *fuga optima*.[13]

Elements of Fugal Technique:
Vicentino

Whereas the discussion of fugue is brief in all the early theoretical sources, by the middle of the sixteenth century it becomes much more extensive, and it is not unusual to find entire chapters given over to it. The first of these appears in Don Nicola Vicentino's sig-

[13] Cf. H. Loewenfeld, L. *Kleber und sein Orgeltabulaturbuch* (1897).

nificant work, *L'Antica Musica ridotta alla moderna prattica* (1555), and the discussion of fugue is by no means confined to this one chapter. Vicentino refers to it in many other instances, some of them particularly interesting for us because they contain comments on those aspects of fugal writing which had become trivial to the ears of the sixteenth-century master. In the choice of his title, in the very idea of proposing a blending of the styles of antiquity and modern times in musical practice, Vicentino appears as a genuine representative of the musical Renaissance, and he proves in his work that he can speak for his time with authority.

Along with musical phenomena of antiquity, such as the chromatic and enharmonic systems, Vicentino "reduces to modern practice" the technique of fugue. Interesting, first of all, is his stand on strict canonic writing and free imitation. Ramos had suggested free imitative writing as a matter of convenience. Vicentino relates this manner of imitation to the majority of known musical forms—among them the instrumental forms of the fantasia and canzona, which were beginning to assume an important role in the development of fugal technique—and he decidedly advises against the use of the strict canon.

Vicentino's new attitude toward free and canonic imitation is doubtless prompted by the fact that the role of the cantus firmus had greatly changed. Ramos had based the fugal technique on imitation of a cantus firmus, whereas Vicentino dismisses "the fugue that follows a cantus firmus" as "not modern." He then describes the desirable *modo moderno*. It requires first a certain choice of melodic material to be made within the cantus firmus. This choice is designated as *punto*, and it becomes the basis for imitation. Vicentino's important recommendation is that the imitation should take only its point of departure from the cantus firmus, and should no longer actually employ it; for, he says, the parts should "imitate each other, but not the cantus firmus." Thus Vicentino not only crystallizes the cantus firmus technique of the High Renaissance and the Baroque, but he also introduces with his term *punto* the modern concept of the theme. We shall encounter it again in Morley's term "point."

Vicentino's chapter on fugue contains a number of remarks pertaining to the nature of thematic material. He stresses the importance of the fact that the beginning of a fugue must be well written and that it should present a passage equally suited to all voices. He suggests that the composer distinguish between his fugal writing in Masses, motets, and madrigals, and, generally, in vocal and instrumental music. Although his recommendations give evidence of the greatly widened scope of the fugal technique, his actual instruction on the formation of fugal themes does not go far beyond the old rule for the composition of the *rondellus* given by Walter Odington.[14] He comments, however, on the length of the theme, which may vary from the equivalent of one half note to that of four whole notes; for the second entrance may occur after the corresponding number of rests.[15] He states that the delay of the second entrance should be no greater because "more than four rests would seem too many." The entrances should be spaced evenly and occur at metrically corresponding points, although for a special effect of surprise they may occur alternately on upbeats and downbeats—a rule which remained an issue of debate well into the eighteenth century.

Although Vicentino arrives at no choice of terms for theme and counterpart, he defines the two concepts clearly in a passage dealing with the use of the fugal principle in keyboard works. He suggests that the composer, having completed the initial imitative entrances, take the passage which has served as accompaniment to the theme and make it the basis for new imitative treatment, so that "he will always have material with which to compose without having to stop and reflect." This formulation of the basic rule for fugal improvisation anticipates later sixteenth-century discussions which deal with the improvisational technique at the keyboard more extensively.

Vicentino is emphatic in his criticism of devices which, in his opinion, characterize the imitative style of the *non moderni*. He rules out the use of alternating fifths and sixths in imitation as unimaginative, and he scorns the manner of imitation by which the skip of an ascending fourth is repeatedly followed by that of a descending third, pointing out that it means too many progressions from octaves to fifths, and vice versa.[16]

---

[14] "The original melody should be invented as well as possible" (*Couss. Script.*, I, 246). The same maxim is adopted by Simon Tunstede for the freely invented tenor of a conductus (*Couss. Script.*, IV, 294).

[15] "*Con un sospiro doppo, o con una pausa, o due, o tre, o quattro.*" This wording may be understood as describing lengths ranging from half a measure to four full measures of 4/4, for Vicentino shows in his examples that in his terminology the *sospiro* designates a half rest.

[16]

With Vicentino, it is understood that imitation should preferably occur at perfect intervals, but he adds that imitation at the unison and the octave does not lend enough variety to the composition and should thus be used only "in case of necessity." Therefore the intervals which he singles out as particularly suited for imitation are the fourth and fifth. According to Vicentino, these two intervals should be used alternately in an imitative setting of four voices; that is, the soprano and alto should be written in imitation at the fourth if the tenor and bass are written in imitation at the fifth, and vice versa.

This rule, which takes into consideration the uneven division of the octave, directs our attention to the most important point in Vicentino's discussion of fugue: The composer is asked to make a definite choice of a mode and to remain aware of the limitations of this mode throughout his fugal writing. Vicentino says, in fact, that for this reason the bass, or the parts that may take the place of the bass, should be treated with particular caution in imitative writing, "for those parts are the ones that determine the mode."

Here the Renaissance theorist acknowledges a complete break with the theoretical views of the Middle Ages. According to medieval theory, the technique of imitation, still restricted to secular forms, was entirely unrelated to the modal system which represented the heritage of sacred music.[17] The synthesis of fugal writing and modal theory in Vicentino's work was preceded by the reconciliation of modal theory with the tonalities of traditional Western secular music in Heinrich Glarean's *Dodekachordon*, published less than a decade earlier. This was the same work which contained the first account of canonic art in sacred music given in theoretical literature. The title of Glarean's work designates a new system of twelve modes, adding to the existing four authentic and four plagal modes the authentic and plagal versions of the major and minor genera. Actually, this reconciliation had begun when the modes—the theoretical basis of monophonic music—were first adapted to polyphony, and its effect was to be felt far beyond Glarean's writing. We can still recognize it in the flexible handling of accidentals in minor tonalities, which is reminiscent of the practice of *musica ficta;* moreover, our terminology itself, which has borrowed the term "tonal" from modal theory, designates major and minor as either

---

[17] Cf. J. de Grocheo, *Theoria* (*SIM*, I, 115): "Modes do not apply to secular music" —a tacit recognition of a system of modern, "secular" tonalities which is indicative of Grocheo's role as progressive spokesman for secular music.

modes or tonalities.[18] The specific principle which emerges from
Vicentino's theory of adapting the fugal technique to the modal
system has thus become known in our terminology as the tonal answer—obviously one of the most decisive events in the entire evolution of fugal writing.

Vicentino formulates this principle with the example of the counterfugue at the octave, in which the skip of a descending fifth is to
be answered with the skip of an ascending fourth, and vice versa, so
that the composition will not exceed the octave and thus the limits
of the mode. It is interesting that in its first mention the tonal answer
is linked to the counterfugue, for the exchange of the fourth and
fifth is thus explained through the process of inversion, which with
Vicentino's contemporary, Gioseffo Zarlino, became the basis for the
system of dual harmony.

Inversion plays a prominent part in Vicentino's writing, for the
counterfugue, or fugue by inverted motion, as well as invertible
counterpoint, is mentioned here for the first time.[19] Their place in
contrapuntal theory is fully established by Zarlino.

Ex. 4   Counterfugue

Throughout his discussion, Vicentino is true to his role as advocate of a new style, fully aware of his mission of innovator. Indicative of his stand is his concern for a clear presentation of the text in
vocal music. He seems far ahead of his time when he speaks of a
carefully concerted accompaniment, and in his rules for fugal writing the treatment of the text—even a distinction between Latin and
Italian prosody—holds an important place. He feels that the understanding of the text is assured in polyphony up to four parts. For
composition in five and more parts, he recommends the frequent use
of rests and unisons, although, he says, "even here a fugal texture
should be maintained."

[18] The terms "modal" and "tonal" were originally synonymous (cf. J. J. Fux's discussion on Fugues in General, p. 80, below), though it must be borne in mind that in
earlier medieval theory "modal" referred exclusively to rhythmic patterns.
[19] The two different ways in which the principle of inversion is applied in these
two cases were eventually distinguished as melodic inversion and harmonic inversion.

Establishment of Fugal Terminology: Zarlino

Vicentino's work appeared three years before Gioseffo Zarlino's famous *Istitutioni harmoniche*. It anticipated important aspects of Zarlino's teaching and on some points, such as the definition of the tonal answer, had clearly gone beyond it. Yet it remained for Zarlino, Vicentino's fellow student under Adrian Willaert, to synthesize all earlier theoretical studies and to create a definite basis for a system of musical theory in the modern sense.

We find in Zarlino's comprehensive treatment of fugue the foundation of a new terminology. He is the first to distinguish between fugue (*fuga, consequenza, reditta*) and imitation (*imitatione*). Entrances at the perfect intervals of unison, fourth, fifth, and octave are now the only ones recognized as constituting a fugue; entrances at all other intervals are called imitation. Zarlino carefully separates the term canon from either, quoting it in Greek in order to stress the original meaning of the word, which, as he says, is beginning to be confused with the term fugue by "musicians of lesser intelligence."

Equally important is Zarlino's use of the words *guida* and *consequente* as definite terms; however, he still uses them to designate the opening and answering voices in their entirety, not the opening and answering statements.[20] Similarly, the term *soggetto*, which gains considerable prominence in Zarlino's writing, refers to a complete part, as a rule the tenor.[21] Its function is still close to that of the cantus firmus. Zarlino's own definition describes the *soggetto* as a pre-existing melody. This melody may have been "invented by the composer beforehand"; thus it is to be understood as a part written earlier than the other parts (*cantus prius factus*), not as a

---

[20] The terms were translated to *dux* and *comes* in the *Melopoeia sive melodiae condendae ratio* (1592), a condensed paraphrase of Zarlino's work by Seth Calvisius, cantor at St. Thomas's in Leipzig. Calvisius transformed Zarlino's scholarly treatise into a practical, concise text aiming at popular instruction rather than erudite discussion. Although his version presents a useful summary of Zarlino's teaching, it ignores one of the most important ideas Zarlino had contributed to the study of fugue: the distinction between fugue and imitation.

[21] Zarlino's terminology is doubtless derived from Willaert's instruction. The words *guida* and *suggietto* [*sic*] are used also, though not consistently, in Vicentino's work. For the use of the term *consequentia*, cf. Padre Martini's comment in his discussion of the Seven-Part Fugue, pp. 303 f., below.

theme. This meaning is apparent in some of Zarlino's three-part examples in which the melodic line of the *soggetto* bears no relation to the imitative parts (*guida* and *consequente*) written upon this *soggetto*.

Ex. 5

In a separate chapter, however, the musical usage of the term *thema* is introduced in Zarlino's work.[22] It arises in the discussion of the *replica*, a term which Zarlino uses generally as a synonym for the fugal procedure and specifically for the repetition of a melodic pattern within a contrapuntal part. The phenomenon of melodic repetition had undergone a number of different considerations in contrapuntal theory. The basic rule, stated long before Zarlino and accepted by many theorists after him, denounces melodic repetition as *monotonia* which tends to impede the free flow of the vocal line. The fifteenth-century theorist Guilelmus Monachus had pointed out that such melodic "reiteration" might exist in the cantus firmus, but he advised the composer to use all the more care in avoiding it in the contrapuntal part to be written upon such a cantus firmus.[23] Tinctoris, introducing the term *redicta* for melodic repetition, follows the earlier rule but adds that the *redicta* may be tolerated when it is used for a special effect of imitating the sound of bells or of horns (*tubae*). This first acknowledgment of melodic repetition is particularly interesting because it is thus linked to the *pes* technique of the canon; in fact, a motif identical with that of the tenor *ad modum tubae* in Dufay's *fuga, Et in terra* (Example 1) is found in one of the examples which Tinctoris quotes (Example 6). It is used by Tinctoris as *redicta* in the tenor part, above which two higher parts move in free imitation.

Ex. 6

[22] Orig. ed., Pt. III, ch. 55.   [23] *Couss. Script.*, III, 291.

In Zarlino's teaching, the use of repeated melodic patterns enters free contrapuntal writing and is considerably broadened in scope. After explaining the danger of monotony, Zarlino states that a *replica* used intentionally rather than incidentally "may be acceptable and even desirable . . . provided it is subjected to certain changes," for example the change from breves to semibreves or minims, or the change from rhythmically even passages to syncopations.

It is highly significant that Zarlino designates the melodic line which is repeated in a carefully planned and varied manner with the term *thema*, for we can recognize here the first discussion of a working procedure which fugal practice was to raise to utmost importance. It is here still limited by the restrictions resulting from the use of a pre-existing part. Zarlino is therefore bound to consider the thematically written counterpoint a *contrappunto con obbligo* (counterpoint with obligatory melodic repetition), but it is evident from his examples that this obligatory repetition is now no longer based on such short, stereotyped patterns as were used by Tinctoris.

Ex. 7

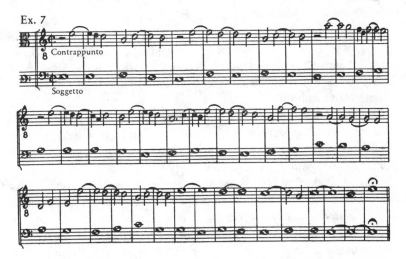

The three terms which Zarlino employs to describe this procedure, *replica*, *pertinacia*, and *thema*, actually outline the course that leads from casual repetition through the use of brief *ostinato* statements to the choice of a determining melodic phrase that requires both originality of invention and flexibility of treatment. In an example in which the parts are not distinguished as subject and counterpoint but simply as upper part and lower part, Zarlino distributes the free treatment of several themes over both parts and thus presents the first theoretical discussion of the ricercare technique.

Ex. 8

Zarlino admits the difficulty of composing a thematic counterpoint but says that consistency in using the theme justifies various licenses in part writing and that a composition in which this difficulty is mastered is much to be preferred to one "without difficulty," no matter how smoothly written.

In addition, Zarlino formulates an important general rule concerning the melodic passage which becomes subject to repetition through fugal treatment. He comments on the practice of maintaining small distances between fugal entrances—a practice which Vicentino had recommended—and points out that although narrow spacing may strengthen the intelligibility of fugal entrances, it will necessarily limit their originality: "At present it is hardly possible to find an instance of fugal writing that has not been used a thousand million times by other composers." Vicentino had expressed a similar concern—"of common fugues the world is full"; but it was Zarlino who first related the problem of stereotyped patterns to the distance between imitative entrances and who urged the composer to increase this distance. We may see in this argument the first step toward the idea of the fugue on a single, highly individual theme which began to play an important role in the writings of later theorists.

In his fundamental distinction between fugue and imitation, however, Zarlino appears as a systematic rather than progressive theorist, for there is no indication in his text that it is a tendency toward tonal orientation which prompts him to single out entrances at the unison, fourth, fifth, and octave as the only true fugal entrances. According to Zarlino, the essential difference between fugue and imitation lies merely in the degree of accuracy with which interval progressions are maintained. If the sequence of intervals in one part is only generally followed in another part, Zarlino speaks of imitation; if the repetition of interval progressions is exact to the point of maintaining half- and whole-tone steps—and this is possible only with entrances at perfect intervals—Zarlino speaks of fugue. We must assume that it is for this reason that he ignores the tonal answer, which, by his classification, is no different from any other imitation and has no place in fugues.

Aside from the general distinction as to imitative strictness which is expressed in these two categories, Zarlino establishes a distinction between strict and free species (*ligate* and *sciolte*) in both fugue and imitation. Strict are the canonic imitation and fugue in which "the parts can be written in one." Thus the case in which all interval progressions are maintained in imitation, although their major and minor forms are interchanged, is considered strict imitation; its notation can still be given in one part. It occurs in canons at any but the perfect intervals, whereas canons at perfect intervals are considered strict fugues. If half- and whole-tone relationships and the major and minor forms of other intervals are strictly observed for only part of the composition, Zarlino speaks of a mixture of strict imitation and fugue, although, he adds, it is commonly called fugue.

Free are those instances of imitation and fugue in which the canonic repetition rules the beginning, but in which the remaining part of the composition is written according to "whatever the composer likes best." As Zarlino's examples show, the composer's free choice is guided not merely by fluent contrapuntal invention but also by thematic treatment of suitable melodic lines (see p. 24).

This free continuation of the imitative setting, which Ramos had mentioned and which Vicentino had recommended, is now recognized as an essential part of imitation or fugue. The mixture of free fugue and free imitation emerges from Zarlino's writing as the basis for all further developments in the history of fugue.

With similar thoroughness, Zarlino discusses imitation and fugue

Ex. 9

Free Fugues

by contrary motion [24] and the technique of double counterpoint. Zarlino considers imitation by contrary motion a highly important device because he feels that it supplies the imitative technique with much-needed variety, and he asks the student to regard this manner of composition "not with scorn but rather with affection." His distinction according to strict interval relationships was maintained longer in this category of fugal writing than in all others.[25]

Double counterpoint assumes in Zarlino's teaching a definite function as "an ingenious kind of composition which can be performed in different ways by exchanging the parts"; in Vicentino's writing the presentation of this technique was still mingled with canonic instructions, since he applied it to a "fugue between a part

[24] Zarlino calls the fugue by contrary motion (counterfugue) *fuga per arsin et thesin,* applying "arsis" and "thesis" to the raising and lowering of the melodic line. The same term was used later to designate the fugue in contrary rhythm (cf. Marpurg on Imitation and Fugue in General, p. 158, below).

[25] See the mention of Bononcini's discussion of melodic inversion in the next chapter.

written above and a part written below the cantus firmus." Zarlino's instruction in double counterpoint has remained virtually unchanged, although its importance in fugal writing was first fully recognized by students of the Zarlino school more than a century after the appearance of the *Istitutioni harmoniche*.

Interesting, finally, is the fact that the chapters on fugue and imitation are presented together with the discussion of cadences. From the combination of these musical concepts was to grow one of the chief principles of musical construction. Zarlino takes up cadences and fugue without relation to each other but considers both of paramount importance. Cadences are "the most necessary part of harmonies." Fugue, however, has become indispensable as a means of composition, for even "when there remains nothing in a composition that could be subject to criticism, when it is free from any error and shows nothing but refinement, beauty, and sweetness of harmony, it would still lack a certain element of grace and distinction if it did not contain what is by now universally known and practiced—the process which arises when the parts form a fugue."

The Last Renaissance Theorists

Zarlino's teaching became the basis for the majority of theoretical discussions of fugue by later writers. Much of his text was literally adopted, much was translated and paraphrased.[26] The most important single force in the propagation of Zarlino's work, however, was in the teaching of his great pupil Jan Pieterszoon Sweelinck. Through Sweelinck, the Zarlino tradition was handed down to a host of eminent seventeenth-century musicians, among them Samuel Scheidt, Heinrich Scheidemann, and Jacob Praetorius. Once again, we observe that the study of fugue is perpetuated by organ masters. But before we turn to the teaching of Sweelinck and his students we

[26] E.g., S. Calvisius, *Melopoeia* (see note 20, above). Other notable works based on Zarlino's text are *Il Compendio della musica* (1588; dedicated to Zarlino) by Orazio Tigrini; *L'Arte del contrappunto* (1586-1589) by Giovanni Maria Artusi; *Il Transilvano* (Pt. II, 1609) by the Zarlino pupil Girolamo Diruta; and the *Prattica di musica* (Pt. II, 1622) by Lodovico Zacconi. Zacconi's work stands out among the writings of Zarlino's followers since it contains important new ideas (cf. pp. 34, 37, below).

should direct our attention to some of the works written by theorists closer to Zarlino's own generation.

Valuable remarks are contained in a work dealing with the technique of instrumental improvisation, the *Arte de tañer fantasía* (1565) by Fray Tomás de Santa María. Improvisation is here discussed as part of the instruction not only for organists but for players of all chordal instruments. The work, to which Otto Kinkeldey has drawn attention in his *Orgel und Klavier in der Musik des 16. Jahrhunderts* (1910), was published in two volumes. The first volume presents the technical aspects of instrumental performance; the second deals with the invention and performance of fantasias proper.

Santa María's work shows that the use of the fugal technique had gained considerable importance in instrumental improvisation.[27] In his chapter on the improvisational use of the *fuga*, he mentions two methods of treating a theme (*invención*) in imitative entrances of two parts. According to the first method, the theme is presented in its entirety in the opening part before the answering part begins. In this case, the opening part is to form a passage which will be well suited as an accompaniment when the theme is taken up in the anwering part. According to the other method, the answering part is introduced before the opening part has completed the theme. These remarks show that the author is referring to extended thematic passages and that the placing of imitative entrances has become a matter of considerable concern. The proper placing of entrances, in fact, is singled out by Santa María as the most intricate as well as the most beautiful device in music.

In Santa María's writing we also find a definite relationship established between thematic entrances and cadences. The student is asked to determine whether a thematic entrance occurs in conjunction with a cadence, and if so, whether it occurs before, in, or after a cadence. In his instructions for fantasias in more than two parts Santa María suggests that one pair of voices may enter while the other pair forms a cadence, and he shows how entrances in various cadences may be handled (Example 11).

[27] Cf. the tests for applicants to the post of organist at St. Mark's in Venice (O. Kinkeldey, p. 136). It is interesting that the third edition of Zarlino's *Istitutioni harmoniche*, which appeared eleven years after the second (unaltered) edition and eight years after Santa María's work, contains an added chapter dealing with the improvisation of fugal counterpoint.

Ex. 11   Fantasia

One further important step in fugal construction is suggested in Santa María's discussion of fantasias in four parts. He states that a new thematic passage (*passo*) should be introduced after all four voices have entered, or else that the original passage should be used again.

This tendency toward the use of a single theme is even more clearly formulated in Pietro Ponzio's *Raggionamenti di musica* (1588), the first work which mentions the ricercare and its recurring, exploring use of the fugal principle: "It is possible to repeat the same melodic invention (*inventio*) two, three, or four times in different ways, as we find in the *ricercari* by Jaches Buus, Annibale Padovano, Claudio Merulo, and Luzzasco Luzzaschi. . . . The same theme (*soggetto*) may be followed from the beginning to the end of a composition, or, if the composer does not want to use it throughout, he may turn to a new one and repeat this as often as he wishes."

Ponzio explains that he is thinking in terms of extended thematic material. He states that "the melodic invention should be long and the parts should be well spaced," and gives an example to illustrate these points (Example 12). It is now no longer the mere process of imitation but the theme itself which should be "clearly perceptible to the listener." Ponzio emphasizes that for this reason the first appearance of the theme should be entirely unaccompanied. On the other hand, he anticipates the situation in which the composer might present two themes simultaneously—a thought which was to gain importance in the theoretical writings of the next generation.

Ex. 12

A comprehensive account showing how the concept of the fugal theme had changed in the course of the sixteenth century appeared in Thomas Morley's *Plain and Easy Introduction to Practical Music* (1597). "Indeed it is true, that the nearer the following part be unto the leading, the better the fugue is perceived and the more plainly discerned, and therefore did the musicians strive to bring in their points the soonest they could, but the continuation of that nearness caused them fall into such common manner of composing that all their points were brought in after one sort . . . therefore we must give the fugue some more scope to come in and by that means we shall show some variety which cannot the other way be shown." [28] The example that Morley gives for widely spaced fugal entrances shows in itself the range of possibilities he discusses (Example 13).[29]

[28] R. A. Harman ed. (1952), p. 265.

[29] It was not until almost a century later that the relative values of widely spaced entrances in the fugal exposition and narrowly spaced entrances in the fugal stretto were clearly distinguished; see Bononcini's and Berardi's discussions of the stretto technique, pp. 43, 45 f., below.

Ex. 13

Morley's work, written in the classical form of the dialogue, contains a number of the keenest observations on the imitative technique to be found in his time. Morley assigns the extended theme a definite function. "These maintaining of long points, either foreright or revert, are very good in Motets and all other kind of grave music." We also encounter here the suggestion that rests—especially those of rhythmically uneven length—be used in order to lend prominence to the return of a thematic passage. "The odd rest giveth an unspeakable grace to the point," for ". . . it is supposed that when a man keepeth long silence and then beginneth to speak, he will speak to the purpose."

Morley makes the composer realize that the importance which is thus attributed to the thematic material calls for a new attitude in choosing a theme, for a conscientious and highly disciplined working procedure. "When he hath once set down a point, though it be right, yet ought he not to rest there, but should rather look more earnestly how he may bring it more artificially about." This admonition given by the master in Morley's text is interrupted by the remark of the student, "By that means he may scrape out that which is good and bring in that which will be worse"; to which the master answers, "It may be that he will do so at the first, but afterwards, when he hath discretion to discern the goodness of one point above another, he will take the best and leave the worst."

His detailed discussion of the fugal theme prompts Morley finally to weigh the merits of such musical variety as will naturally arise from the use of several themes against that which the composer's inventive mind, set to the task, may draw from a single theme. Morley declares the monothematic principle a characteristic of Northern music and the use of several themes a stylistic property of the South. "The Italians and other strangers are greatly to be commended who, taking any point in hand, will not stand long upon it but will take the best of it and so away to another, whereas by the contrary we are so tedious that of one point we will make as much as may serve for a whole song, which, though it show great art in variety, yet is it more than needeth." It is interesting that Morley's own stand is taken against his countrymen, because it reflects a typical tendency which he himself criticizes,[30] and it shows Morley as a musician at heart still devoted to the Renaissance madrigal and its principle of composition by which "no point is long stayed upon, but once or twice driven through all the parts, and sometimes reverted, and so to the close, then taking another. . . . In this kind," Morley writes, "our age excelleth."

[30] "Such be the new-fangled opinions of our countrymen who will highly esteem whatsoever cometh from beyond the seas (and specially from Italy), be it never so simple, condemning that which is done at home though it be never so excellent" (commenting upon the English predilection for Italian secular music).

III

The Baroque: Fugal Development

Growth of Formal Concepts

Morley's work concludes the fugal theory of the sixteenth century and marks the transition to a new epoch. If we review the fugal theory of the Renaissance, we find that it traces techniques of composition from the strict canonic to the free imitative manner and finally to the harmonically oriented fugal treatment of a theme. The procedure of the tonal answer, although not fully discussed, is described in Morley's text: "This [the answer] riseth five notes and the plain song [the theme] riseth but four" (Example 14). And it

Ex. 14

etc.

is accepted as typical for the fugue: "Although it rise five notes yet it is the point, for if it were in *Canon* we might not rise one note higher, nor descend one note lower than the plain song did, but in fugues we are not so straitly bound."

Thus the fugal teaching of the Renaissance assembles all the elements of the fugal exposition; and although in this period *fuga* designates the imitative or canonic manner as well as individual compositions in which this manner is applied, the term refers in its strict theoretical sense to a fugal exposition within a work. This meaning is evident from Ponzio's references to fugues at the beginning and in other parts of the composition. And it is evident from Vicentino's recommendation that the composer should end a composition, if possible, with the same fugue with which he began—a remark which in itself suggests the very beginning of a larger fugal structure.

Whereas sixteenth-century theory was not, on the whole, concerned with the form of a fugal setting beyond its exposition, the theorists of the seventeenth century attached considerable importance to the matter of fugal structure. Their attitude is representative of the period in which fugal writing began to free itself from the guidance of cantus firmus and verbal text. We can recognize a point of departure in Morley's discussion of the fantasy, the "most principal and chiefest kind of music which is made without a ditty." Morley says here that "a musician taketh a point at his pleasure and wresteth and turneth it as he list, making either much or little of it as shall seem best in his own conceit"; and he adds that "in this may more art be shown than in any other music because the composer is tied to nothing." What to do with this newly won freedom of instrumental music was to become the essence of the study of fugue in the Baroque.

It is characteristic that the discussion of fugue in the *Rules for Composing* (*c.* 1610) by the English composer Giovanni Coperario is entitled "How to Maintain a Fugue." Coperario, a master of the string fantasy ("who by the way was plain Cooper but affected an Italian termination"[1]), deals with the technique of connecting expositions of different themes as well as successive expositions of the same theme. The "maintaining of a fugue" is here still equal in meaning to the "maintaining of a point"—a wording which is also used by Morley to describe the recurrence of a theme within and beyond the initial exposition. In commenting upon the restatement of a theme in a second exposition, Coperario repeats almost literally Morley's advice: "if you will twice use the fugue in all the parts . . . you must observe that your part may rest before his coming in with the fugue, which is a great grace to a part, and to the fugue."

Although Coperario still expresses a general preference for the use of short themes and close entrances, he formulates an important new principle for the handling of extended thematic material: "If a point be long . . . you must invent another point to go with him.

[1] R. North, *The Musical Grammarian*, p. 28.

Then you must frame two parts in such sort, that so soon as shall be possible to bring in your other two resting parts." This remark shows a notable departure from Morley's text, even though Morley had declared that "two or three several points going together is the most artificial kind of composing that hitherto hath been invented." Coperario not only suggests the norm of two themes but also begins to distinguish their relative importance as theme and countertheme. For a fugue written in this manner he introduces the term double fugue and adds: "This fashion of maintaining double fugues is most used of excellent authors for in single fugues there can no such great art be shewed, but only in the invention thereof."

Ex. 15 Double Fugue

Whereas in Coperario's text the term fugue still stands for fugal exposition, it assumes a new meaning in the *Musices poeticae prae-ceptiones,* published by his contemporary Johannes Nucius. *Fuga* is here mentioned together with the term repetitio (the recurrence of a melodic passage), yet distinguished from it as "the frequent and definite recurrence of the same theme (*thema*) in various parts which follow each other in spaced entrances." This explanation, which forms part of the author's description of the doctrine of figures,[2] is grouped together with definitions of several other terms, such as climax and complexio, which reflect a new scope of structural planning.

The description of the climax, a device of part writing intended to heighten the listener's anticipation of the end of a composition, is reminiscent of Morley's "coming to a close . . . when a fugue which hath been in the same song handled is drawn out to make the close in binding wise." The description of the complexio systema-

---

[2] Cf. M. Bukofzer, *Music in the Baroque Era,* p. 388.

tizes Vicentino's remarks suggesting that the restatement of the beginning should form the end of the work.

Since the structural thinking which this discussion implies raises the importance of the opening theme, it becomes doubly meaningful that Nucius is the first to relate the term *thema* directly to the term *fuga*. In fact, the monothematic principle is clearly pronounced in a work which was published in the same year as that by Nucius—Pietro Cerone's encyclopedic *El Melopeo y maestro*. Morley had characterized the fantasy as a piece of music in which the composer should as much as possible "insist in following the point," but Cerone's discussion of the *ricercario o tiento* formulates this thought in the categorical statement that "the true tiento is based on one theme only."

A similar principle appears a decade later in the writing of Lodovico Zacconi, the outstanding master of the *contrappunto a mente* (freely improvised counterpoint), who asks the student to limit himself to the use of only one cantus firmus in all his exercises until he has fully exhausted its possibilities—a principle which eventually ruled the entire plan of Bach's *Art of Fugue*. This imposed limitation called for a more clearly directed creative effort, a more intense use of musical imagination. Cerone, using the terms *thema*, *subjecto*, and *invención* synonymously, stresses the use of original thematic material (*invención propia*). Though his explanations follow, for the most part, Ponzio's rules for the composition of the ricercare, he shows with one brief but ingenious addition, almost literally drawn from Zarlino's text, that now not only the *thema* but also the significance which this term is given in Zarlino's discussion has been linked to fugue: "The same theme may be followed from the beginning to the end of the composition, provided it is subjected to rhythmic changes and different manners of accompaniment."

The term *thema*, as well as the meaning of *fuga*, is quoted from Nucius's work in the *Syntagma musicum* (Vol. III, 1619) of Michael Praetorius, but the "treatment of a good fugue" is given here a much more eloquent and significant description. Praetorius explains that it entails a process of "searching in all possible manner and with particular diligence and thought how it may be joined, entwined, and woven together, and by direct and inverted, ordinary and unusual, entrances, connected and carried to the end." His wording anticipates in name and spirit the technique of *Durch-*

führung (development), a technique which the concentration on a single theme was bound to produce.

Praetorius uses the word ricercare both as a term for this technique and as a synonym for *fuga*, although *fuga* appears in his text also in its older, narrower sense of fugal exposition. His explanation shows the decline of the purely improvisational concept of fugal construction represented by the early term fantasia. His own description of the fantasia, a composition in which the composer "drifts according to his whim" from one fugue to another, follows closely and at times literally that given by Morley and shows the affinity of ricercare and fantasia. Yet Praetorius restricts the domain of the fantasia, since he refers to it as *Capriccio* or *Phantasia subitanea*—a composition formed by instantaneous improvisation.

On the other hand, a composition based on a clearly discernible structural plan emerges in Praetorius's description of the canzona, for which he quotes the manner of Giovanni Gabrieli's works as model. He explains that in the canzona "short fugues" and "good fantasies" are combined in such a manner that in order to form the conclusion "the first fugue is usually restated at the end." Thus the earlier theoretical suggestions of a larger form are for the first time integrated in a cycle of fugal exposition, development, and restatement. Nevertheless, the fugal character of the canzona is clearly recognizable as an element of procedure rather than of form. The formal organization of the canzona points in a different direction, toward a new goal, not to be fully realized for more than a century but revealed by the very name of the *canzona da sonare*—the sonata. The fantasia and ricercare are in Praetorius's text first assigned to a "development" function within this larger frame of musical form, a function in which they were to be fully absorbed, just as the earliest forms of polyphony had once been absorbed as components of the *optimus organisandi modus*.

Whereas Praetorius uses ricercare as a synonym for *fuga*, the term is used interchangeably with tiento in the *Melopeo* by Cerone. The word tiento is perhaps the most interesting among those which the declining Renaissance had applied to fugal construction, for the literal meaning, "the touch of a blind person," recalls a host of early organ masters who both by technical ability and vivid imagination may have surpassed other architects of musical form because they were, like the legendary first great epic poet, stricken with blindness.[3] Cerone emphasizes that the tiento is intended for keyboard performance and, like Ponzio, mentions as models of the form the works of the same Italian masters whom Vincenzo Galilei in his *Dialogo* (1581) had singled out for their excellence as keyboard players and contrapuntists. Morley had mentioned a similar consideration in his description of the fantasy: "This kind of music is with them who practice instruments of parts, in greatest use, but for voices it is but seldom used"; and Praetorius applies the instrumental character to the fugue in general, saying that "proper fugues may contain no text." In this respect *canzona da sonare* may be understood as the most comprehensive term for the new fugal forms. Praetorius describes its instrumental idiom by saying that the canzona moves "with many black notes, briskly, lively, and fast." In the *Tabulaturbuch* of the German keyboard composer Bernhard Schmid (1607), the term canzona is used synonymously with fugue.

Progress of Harmonic Thought: The Sweelinck School

While the term *fuga* came to be applied more and more to the growing instrumental forms, the term canon was gradually limited to the shorter *fuga ligata*, which had remained essentially vocal and in which imitation at the fifth was less strongly favored than in the *fuga sciolta*. Morley speaks of the "canon in that sense as we commonly take it . . . being many parts in one"; and Cerone, as the first of several theorists, goes to some length to refute the derivation *canon a canendo* (that canon comes from the Latin, to sing). Thus we must gather that the original meaning of the term was no longer generally understood, although Zarlino's attempt to preserve it had found its way into the various adaptations and translations of his text.

In Silvero Picerli's *Specchio di musica* (1630), the word canon in its literal meaning—rule, precept—no longer serves for an inscription

[3] Some famous blind organists were Francesco Landino, Antonio Squarcialupi, Konrad Paumann, Arnold Schlick, Francisco Salinas, and the great master of the tiento, Antonio de Cabezón. Also, Miguel de Fuenllana, in whose writing the tiento is applied to the vihuela, was blind.

explaining the manner in which the different voices follow each other; instead, it signifies the opening voice in its entirety. It is this opening part which is to be observed as a "canon." Thus the modern usage of the term is established. Nevertheless, the use of the term *fuga* in the meaning of consistently strict imitation was retained for a considerable time, and the confusion which was bound to arise from the coexistence of the old and new terminology is mentioned by Marin Mersenne in his *Harmonie universelle* (1636), though dismissed as a mere play on words.

Mersenne's discussion of the canon is based, for the most part, on Cerone's text, to which he refers the reader. But it introduces a term which was to assume importance in later theoretical works: the *point d'orgue*. It is used here in the sense of the *fermata* designating the closing tone of a canonic voice—the tone which in a more complex fugal setting was to provide extended support for the final statement of the theme as its harmonic basis.

As the changed meaning of the term canon began to acquire currency, Zarlino's classification of free and strict fugues (*fughe ligate* and *sciolte*), although quoted throughout the seventeenth century, lost its validity and gave way to distinctions between strict and free fugal treatment governed by new criteria. Zacconi's *Prattica di musica* introduced within the category of the *fuga sciolta* the types of *fuga propria* or *naturale* and *fuga accidentale*—a differentiation based on the strict observance of thematic material and actually replacing Zarlino's distinction between *fuga sciolta* and *imitatione sciolta*. Almost the same terminology, however, was to denote within a short time the difference between fugal writing with and without proper observance of the tonality.

This change is indicative of the progress of harmonic thought in the musical practice and theory of the Baroque. Commenting on the unusual amount of freedom which the composer was given in writing fantasies, Morley had made one notable exception: ". . . and this kind will bear any allowances . . . except changing the air and leaving the key, which in Fantasie may never be suffered." [4] Yet, this hint toward tonal unity of the extended form marks the final point in Morley's teaching. To the student's question, "Have you no general rule to be given for an instruction for keeping of the key," the master replies, "No, for it must proceed only of the judgment of the composer." Praetorius, adapting Morley's description of the

[4] Morley explains that by "air" he means that "which the antiquity termed 'Modi.'"

fantasy, introduces a small though significant change: "Modus and aria should not be exceeded to too great an extent." Thus he offers a first suggestion of the possibility of modulation within a widened frame of consistent tonality.

By the middle of the century, the new concepts of tonality began to occupy the most prominent place in the study of fugue. The first theoretical discussion which is determined by this attitude is the *Tractatus compositionis augmentatus* (*c.* 1650) by Christoph Bernhard, a disciple of Schütz.[5]

In Bernhard's work, the study of fugue forms part of a new interpretation of modal theory which approaches the system of major and minor tonalities. He adopts the mode based on C as the first, "since all others follow its model in their perfect cadences." Bernhard explains that he deviates from the traditional arrangement of modes in which the mode on D is the first. With his discussion of modes, he continues the work begun a century earlier by Glarean, whose theory he endorses with the words: "Suffice it to say that there are twelve modes, no more, no less."

Bernhard's discussion includes the procedures of transposition and modulation (*transpositio modorum* and *extensio* or *alteratio modorum*). The *transpositio modorum* in Bernhard's text normally designates the shift to the upper fifth or the lower fourth, more rarely that to the upper or lower second [6] or other intervals. Modulation is described as *extensio modorum* if it is followed by a return to the original mode, and as *alteratio modorum* if it is not followed by such a return. The mention of the *extensio* and *alteratio modorum* is preceded, however, by that of the *consociatio* and *aequatio*

---

[5] Bernhard's work (written in German, despite its Latin title) has been newly edited in J. M. Müller-Blattau's *Die Kompositionslehre Heinrich Schützens in der Fassung seines Schülers Christoph Bernhard.* Müller-Blattau dates the work at 1649 or 1650— the time when Bernhard was first mentioned as chapelsinger under Schütz in Dresden. He points out that Schütz had described in the preface to his *Geistliche Chormusik* (1648) a plan of studies in composition close to that followed in Bernhard's work and that Schütz had expressed the hope that a manual of instruction based on this plan might be published in the German language by a competent author before long. Müller-Blattau's assumption has recently been declared untenable by B. Grusnick (article on Bernhard in *Musik in Geschichte und Gegenwart*), who suggests that Schütz referred to a work by Marco Scacchi and mentions 1657 as a possible date for Bernhard's work.

[6] It is interesting that Bernhard calls the latter transposition *durus in durum*, thus turning the traditional hexachordal designation into the modern German terminology.

modorum—the different manners of arranging fugal entrances according to the nature of the mode.

The *consociatio modorum* is a combination of corresponding authentic and plagal modes in neighboring voices through which the presentation of a fugal theme is bound to "exchange the fourth for a fifth and the fifth for a fourth." It is an ingenious interpretation of the tonal answer based on the characteristically polyphonic concept that different voices of the same composition are ruled by different modes—a concept which is also represented in the writing of Glarean and Zarlino. Bernhard explains that the *consociatio modorum* applies above all to fugal subjects which do not exceed the range of a fourth or fifth and move in "comfortable skips."

In the *aequatio modorum*, Bernhard describes the procedure of the real answer which "equalizes" the melodic pattern of consecutive fugal entrances in order to preserve their characteristic intervals. It is to be used with fugal subjects that move by step rather than by skip. In comparing the *consociatio* and *aequatio modorum*, Bernhard establishes an important rule for the disposition of the extended fugal structure. He assigns the *consociatio modorum* to the harmonically decisive beginning of a work—a principle from which the composer should "not easily deviate." The *aequatio modorum* is to be used "more often in the middle than in the beginning"; and it is significant that Bernhard describes this, the melodically faithful imitation, as better suited to later sections of the work because it is "less strict."

For the categories that he establishes, Bernhard quotes examples of Palestrina's and his own writing (Examples 16 to 19).

Consociatio Modorum

Ex. 16   G. P. da Palestrina

Me - - di - ta - bar in ___ etc.

Me - di - ta - bar in ___ man-da - tis etc.

Ex. 17   Christoph Bernhard

Aequatio Modorum

Ex. 18   G. P. da Palestrina

Ex. 19   Christoph Bernhard

In the remaining chapters dealing with the fugal technique, Bernhard lists the different forms of direct, inverted, and rhythmically altered imitation. His discussion shows that a new terminology and a new, harmonic orientation of canonic writing have come into existence, for he speaks of concluded and perpetual, of closed and open versions of canonic settings. Nevertheless, the term *fuga* is still used in the sense of canonic imitation in Bernhard's writing; in fact, one *fuga perpetua* quoted by Bernhard reappears a century later among Antonio Caldara's numerous canons.

Although Bernhard's work doubtless reflects the instruction of Heinrich Schütz, his earlier studies with the Sweelinck student, Paul Siefert, link his work to the Sweelinck tradition. And it is in the writings of the Sweelinck School that the new aspects of fugal theory, which appear in Bernhard's work, are taken up and more fully discussed.

The teaching of the Sweelinck School, which reflects the influence of Sweelinck's own works as much as that of his instruction, has been preserved in manuscripts by Jacob Praetorius, a direct pupil of Sweelinck, and by Matthias Weckmann and Jan Adams Reinken, both students of Praetorius. All three manuscripts are included in Sweelinck's collected works (Vol. X). The study of fugue is presented by Reinken, whose signature appears at the end of his manuscript with the date 1670—exactly half a century before the aged master met J. S. Bach and recognized in him the great heir of the polyphonic tradition of the Renaissance.[7]

Reinken's notes are casually compiled; nevertheless, they show clearly the new organization of fugal teaching. His discussion opens with a careful explanation of the tonal answer, and the relationship between tonality and fugal writing is here for the first time defined in a plan outlining the entire structure of a work. Using the *primus tonus* as an example, Reinken assigns the first full cadence of a fugue to the tonic d, the next to the dominant a, and the third to the tone of the relative major, f. Reinken refers to these cadences as regular or proper cadences and states that they should be the first to be used. Other cadences, especially imperfect cadences, may be used in later portions of the fugue, but the proper cadences "should be preferred and used above all." Reinken emphasizes, however, that his order of proper cadences is not to be taken as an inflexible rule, quoting the instance in which the first full cadence occurs at the dominant, "which is also found with good musicians."

Thus Reinken acknowledges and systematizes a cycle of modulations which had long been the subject of bold experiments. A notable instance is found in the *Fuga suavissima* by Charles Luython, a contemporary and compatriot of Sweelinck's. Luython's work[8] is doubly interesting as an example of a harmonically progressive structure, since we know from a careful account by Praetorius[9] that Luython used a specially constructed harpsichord, a *clavicymbalum universale* or *perfectum* in which he had seven keys added to the twelve keys of each octave in order to obtain a pure chromatic scale. A century later, in Bach's fugal writing, we find modulations

[7] Cf. the obituary of Bach from Lorenz Christoph Mizler's *Musikalische Bibliothek* (1754): "About the year 1722, he made a journey to Hamburg and was heard for more than two hours on the fine organ of the Catherinen-Kirche before the Magistrate and many other distinguished persons of the town, to their general astonishment. The aged organist of this church, Jan Adams Reinken, who was at that time nearly a hundred years old, listened to him with particular pleasure. Bach, at the request of those present, performed extempore the chorale *An Wasserflüssen Babylon* at great length (for almost a half-hour) and in different ways, just as the better organists of Hamburg in the past had been used to do at the Saturday vespers. Particularly on this, Reinken made Bach the following compliment: 'I thought that this art was dead, but I see that in you it still lives.'" (H. T. David and A. Mendel, *The Bach Reader*, p. 219.) Bach's meeting with Reinken actually took place in November, 1720 (cf. *The Bach Reader*, pp. 79–81).

[8] Edited in A. G. Ritter, *Zur Geschichte des Orgelspiels* (1884), II.

[9] *Syntagma musicum*, II, 634.

extending beyond that from tonic to dominant even in the initial exposition. The harmonic territory, which seventeenth-century fugal practice and theory explored, was fully conquered once the invention of equal temperament had been generally adopted—an achievement historically marked by Bach's forty-eight preludes and fugues.

With the larger scope of Reinken's fugal structure, the stretto technique, which he calls *ins kurtze imitiren,* begins to assume meaning as a special device of fugal writing, and Reinken recommends it to the student as particularly good discipline. In his examples he shows instances of imitation in which similar themes are answered after a full measure, a half measure, and a quarter measure.

Ex. 20

Larger dimensions are also implied in Reinken's new definition of the double fugue (*contrafuga*—fugue with a countersubject), in which two or more themes are "not continually treated together, but also separately, one after the other, then at times together and against each other, which shows much greater mastery." Reinken advises the composer to distinguish different themes carefully one from another by using skips or rests or by placing a slow, singable melodic line against passages in sixteenths or thirty-seconds, and he stresses the role that the technique of double counterpoint plays in the composition of double fugues.

The combination of Reinken's remarks about the organization of thematic entrances in the double fugue and those about the order of

modulations suggests a complex fugal structure which again anticipates an important characteristic of the Classic sonata: the introduction of a second theme on the dominant.

Re-evaluation of Fugal Terminology

In the two decades following Reinken's discussion, two Italian
theoretical works stand out as important contributions to the study
of fugue: Giovanni Maria Bononcini's *Musico prattico* (1673) and
Angelo Berardi's *Documenti armonici* (1681). Both are firmly based
on Zarlino's teachings, yet both reflect in many details the experience
gained by several generations of Zarlino and Sweelinck students.

Bononcini suggests a function for the stretto technique, which
had appeared as a new concept in Reinken's writing. By way of
general advice rather than definite rule, Bononcini states that close
entrances of fugal parts should be avoided at the beginning of the
composition and postponed to later portions where the listener—
sufficiently familiar with the thematic material—will more readily
understand a complex texture of imitative voices.

The freedom of harmonic thinking that is expressed in Reinken's
disposition of tonalities within a fugue is shown also in a new species of canonic writing which Bononcini mentions: the *canon per
tonos*, a "canon which rises a whole-tone step above its beginning
with each new return."

The most interesting aspect of Bononcini's writing, however, is
his new use of the term *fuga regolare*. After paying obeisance to the
Zarlino tradition by defining the *fuga propria* or *regolare* as the one
in which the sequence of half- and whole-tone steps is strictly observed, Bononcini makes a comment which, in effect, reverses the
terminology he accepts. He mentions that certain types of fugues,
though not based on strict observance of half- and whole-tone progressions, are nevertheless to be considered regular fugues because
they are contained within the octave of the key (*tuono*). Thus the
term *fuga regolare* is for the first time assigned to the tonal fugue—
the fugue based on the tonal answer (Example 21).

Ex. 21   Fuga regolare

The confusion which Bononcini creates in presenting criteria by which to judge the *fuga regolare* is understandable. Faithful observance of interval progressions was one of the most striking means fugal theory had found in accounting for the tonic-dominant relationship of theme and answer. Ramos de Pareja had established the choice of perfect intervals for fugal entrances, and Vicentino had established the preference of alternating entrances at the fifth and fourth, but Zarlino had formulated the law to which these fugal answers were necessarily subjected: exactness of melodic imitation. It seemed indeed difficult to reconcile such exactness with the considerable melodic inaccuracy of the tonal answer. Bononcini is the first to come to grips with this problem. His ambiguous definition of the *fuga regolare* marks the transition from the old to the new age—from theoretical ideas favoring melodic consistency to those favoring harmonic consistency as determining that which is "regular."

Zarlino's theory is applied directly, on the other hand, in Bononcini's discussion of the manners of melodic inversion, for he distinguishes free from diatonically strict inversion. As model for the strictly inverted melodic line, he uses the ascending and descending forms of the Dorian scale (Example 22). The system and terminology he thus established were adapted and propagated in Fux's *Gradus ad Parnassum* (1725), and retained validity well into the nineteenth century.[10]

Ex. 22

The *fuga reale*, the counterpart of Bononcini's *fuga regolare*, appears in Berardi's *Documenti armonici*. Reale refers in this usage merely to the melodic formation of the fugal answer; it holds no

[10] Cf. E. F. Richter, *Lehrbuch der Fuge* (1859), p. 8.

other significance. In fact, the meaning of the word "real" stands curiously against that of the word "regular" in the fugal theory of the period. It becomes clear from Berardi's writing that the "real fugue" is by now considered rather an exceptional, not a "regular," occurrence; for, as Berardi points out, it is not adapted to the key structure which "cannot be formed by either two fifths or two fourths."

The discussion of fugue occupies a considerable portion of Berardi's work. The *fuga reale* is only one of numerous kinds that he lists and describes. Most of them are not presented as categories in the true sense but rather as instances of fugal writing in which a special device of contrapuntal technique is applied for the sake of training: for example, the *fuga variabile*, a fugue the texture of which may be varied by omitting one of the voices; or the *fuga ingegnosa* or *artificiale*, a fugue in which by ingenious or artificial rules certain tones, rests, or progressions are to be avoided. Of particular interest, however, is the *fuga reditta*, in which successive entrances, emphasized by either strictly canonic or stretto imitation, are used as a conclusion.

Ex. 23 Fuga reditta

Here Berardi's work carries the discussion of the stretto beyond the point reached in Bononcini's text, and it marks the first instance in which a definite preference is stated for placing the stretto at the end of the fugue in order to let the most highly intensified treatment of the theme serve for an effect of finality. "Some have used such passages at the beginning or in the middle of the work. But I feel it is better to use them at the end: All's well that ends well."

While the procedure of melodic inversion was standardized in Bononcini's work, Berardi introduced a conclusive method for harmonic inversion. He explains double counterpoint in his *Documenti armonici*, and again in his *Raggionamenti musicali* (1687), through a double row of numbers well known to the student of theory ever since. The arrangement by which Berardi combines rising and falling series of numbers is similar to the cross design of ascending and descending scales Bononcini uses in his explanation of the melodic inversion. Indeed, both reflect the same spirit and foreshadow the formulation of the theory of harmony which was fully achieved half a century later in Jean Philippe Rameau's *Traité de l'harmonie*.

With the acceptance of the term *fuga reale*, as distinguished from *fuga propria* or *regolare*, Zarlino's original distinction between fugue and imitation had all but lost its meaning. By the end of the seventeenth century it had become evident that the domains of fugue and imitation needed redefining. This task was taken on by an author of unquestionable authority—Henry Purcell.

In 1694, a year before his death, Purcell was asked to revise John Playford's *Introduction to the Skill of Music* for a twelfth edition. The third part of the work, almost entirely rewritten by Purcell in the process, contains a concise study of fugue—an illuminating summary of the ideas with which fugal writing was viewed as the music of the Baroque entered its final phase. Purcell recognized that fugue and imitation no longer held equal importance, as all theoretical discussions following Zarlino had maintained. Consequently, he subordinated one term to the other, calling imitation a "diminutive sort of Fugeing" which is accomplished "in some few Notes as you find occasion" and not necessarily introduced with successive entrances, as Purcell's example shows (Example 24).

Even more significant is the fact that the term fugue itself is subordinated in Purcell's text to another term. After having given a full

Ex. 24 Imitation

description of simple and double fugues and the various contrapuntal devices used in connection with them, Purcell states: "Most of these different sorts of Fugeing are used in Sonatas, the chiefest instrumental music now in request, where you will find Double and Treble Fugues, also reverted and augmented. . . ." It is characteristic that Purcell uses the verbal form "fugeing" in the same sense as the noun "fuge." Adopting a term which earlier English theorists had used synonymously with "fugeing," he entitles his essay on fugal theory *Of Fuge, or Pointing;* and when he speaks, for instance, of a "Double Fuge in three parts," it is once again apparent that the term denotes merely a procedure according to which the composition is written.

The manner in which Purcell relates the term fugue to the sonata recalls the manner in which Morley, a hundred years earlier, had related "pointing" to the fantasy; in fact, the wording is almost the same—"the chiefest instrumental music now in request" has taken the place of "the chiefest kind of music without a ditty." One form is based upon the use of a "point" which the composer "wresteth and turneth as he list"; the other uses "most of these different sorts of Fugeing." Thus fugue served merely as an agent between two manifestations of musical form that had carried the concept of instrumental structure from an early exploratory phase to maturity. Purcell's statement is all the more striking since it guides the view a century ahead as easily as a century back. It can be applied to the use of the fugal procedure in the Classic sonata as much as to its use in the church and chamber sonata of Purcell's time.

The fact that a musician of supreme judgment and vision speaks from these lines is expressed also in the freedom which Purcell's instruction recommends. He suggests that "you are left to your pleasure" in choosing the themes for the exposition of a double fugue, so that for the third entrance which follows the introduction of theme and countertheme "you may as well answer the second as first, according as you find it smoothest to your Air and most regular to your design." Nevertheless, in his own example for the

distribution of subjects in a triple fugue, a strictly regular pattern
for the succession of thematic statements is presented with perfect
ease.

Ex. 25   Triple Fugue

His principle—to write "with a great deal of Art mixed with good
Air, which is the perfection of a master"—is as delightfully phrased
as it is ever valid as a motto for the study of composition.

Toward the end of the seventeenth century, the purpose of theoretical writings had become more and more to summarize, review,
and re-evaluate. It is the time of the first historical essays on music,
whose new critical attitude affects, together with other aspects of
music, the theory of fugue. In Giovanni Andrea Bontempi's *Historia musica*, published in 1695—one year after Purcell's edition of
the *Introduction to the Skill of Music*—it is the term fugue itself
which is subjected to scrutiny and revision. Bontempi uses the terminology and the definitions of Zarlino, but he extends this traditional discussion of fugue by a weighty paragraph.

He asserts that the terms *fuga* and *reditta* are of little practical use.
Reditta is dismissed as a "barbaric term" because it is neither Latin
nor Greek nor good Italian; and *fuga* is judged unsuitable as a term
"since it does not signify anything but the act of pursuit itself"—a
fascinating statement which links the view of one of the earliest
musical historians to that of modern scholarship. Obviously, judging
from his vantage point, Bontempi could not take the fugal works of
the High Baroque into consideration; nor did he have to take issue
with the theoretical literature that attempted to reduce fugues to
examples of a regular form. Although he tries to relegate the term
fuga entirely to those "semicontrapuntists" whose compositions dis-
solve after one or two thematic statements into a "state of rapid
flight in which our ears cannot catch up with them," his definition

of the term remains sound. It opens a historical perspective which explains the use of the same word as a name for the brief canon, the elaborate chorale fantasy, or the extensive concerto movement.

Reconciliation of Linear and Vertical Concepts: Rameau

The first thorough discussion of fugal theory written after the turn of the century is contained in Johann Gottfried Walther's essay on composition (1708). Walther, a friend and relative of Bach, with whom he doubtless exchanged views on contrapuntal problems,[11] presents a summary of the writings of the seventeenth century, but draws information above all from the works by Bernhard, Reinken, and Bononcini.

The term that assumes the most important place in this review is *repercussio*, a term which had undergone considerable change in usage. Earlier theorists had applied it to the characteristic "repercussion" in Gregorian psalmody, the inexorable return of the melody to the modal dominant which served as tone of recitation. Hence *repercussio* was accepted as designation for the reciting tone itself. Seventeenth-century theory, with its growing awareness of tonal functions, reassigned the term to the process by which a musical thought was carried beyond the dominant, back to the tonic. Thus it first appeared in fugal theory as a term for the thematic statement that would drive back, return, the tonal answer. Later it served for the regular return of theme and answer—the exposition—or even for the return of the exposition, the second or counterexposition. This use of the term resembles its first application, for it describes the return of the theme on the dominant.

Walther's own definition, given in his *Musikalisches Lexikon*, which appeared in print twenty-five years after his synopsis of fugal

---

[11] Walther was town organist in Weimar, and a close association between Walther and Bach began when Bach took up duties at the Weimar court in 1708—the same year in which Walther's manuscript was completed. In acquainting Bach with the interesting collections of double counterpoint examples by the Schütz pupil Johann Theile, Walther may have given a first suggestion for the plan of the *Art of Fugue*. Cf. H. T. David and A. Mendel, *The Bach Reader*, pp. 28, 64 f.

theory had been written, presents *repercussio* clearly as the essence of the tonal fugue—the recurring exchange of fourths and fifths. Yet the German and Italian terminology on which Walther's writing is based remains awkward compared to that of his French contemporaries.

German and Italian theorists—still guided by melodic concepts—continued to describe the harmonic functions of fugal entrances in terms of modal progressions; however, the French composer and theorist Guillaume Gabriel Nivers had used the terms *finale* and *dominante* for the tones of fugal entrances in his *Traité de la composition* as early 1667. The term *dominante*, the key word of harmonic thought and the modern equivalent for the early meaning of *repercussio*, had gained currency in France much earlier than in the other European countries (it appeared first in the *Institution harmonique* by Salomon de Caus, 1615). And it is to France that we must turn for a final explanation, based on harmonic concepts, which fully clarifies the difference between fugue and imitation.

"Since authors who have written on fugue have neglected these observations, it will not be improper to show what experience has taught us on this subject."

When Jean Philippe Rameau wrote these words to preface the discussion of fugal technique contained in the final chapter of his *Traité d'harmonie* (1722), he must have been aware of the significance of his contribution to the study of fugue. Renouncing the confusing fugal terminology of the seventeenth century, he restored the categoric distinction between fugue and imitation but replaced the purely melodic criteria of Zarlino's days with new criteria based on the very theory of harmony which he had established in his *Traité*. Thus he fully substantiated the explanation Purcell had suggested. He applied the term imitation only to the casual application of the imitative manner, which "holds no particular merit worthy of our attention," and reserved the unqualified term fugue for the harmonically oriented imitative manner, to be treated both "with more circumspection and according to given rules."

The rules which Rameau sets up are the first in fugal theory which deal systematically with both beginning and end of thematic entrances. They outline a strict correspondence of tonic and dominant functions for theme and answer and thus reinterpret the melodic inaccuracy of the tonal answer as harmonic accuracy and logic.

The harmonic rules for theme and answer are supported by rhythmic and metric rules. The last note of the theme should be on the downbeat,[12] whereas the beginning of the theme might occur on any beat. Excepted is the case in which the theme reaches a feminine ending—an observation that suggests the ever-present influence of literary art on French music. With his remarks concerning the metric norm of the theme, Rameau revives one of the first rules of fugal theory: "The theme of a fugue should cover at least a half measure; if it comprises more than four measures, the answer should begin in the fourth." Vicentino's wording suggested the same metric proportions; however, the old precept is now interpreted in a totally new light: Rameau states his preference for introducing the answer before the end of the theme has been reached. Thus he welcomes the extended theme provided it does not remain unaccompanied for its entire length. A similar thought was anticipated—though expressed in less detail—by Bononcini, who suggested that the composer be careful not to delay the fugal answer too long "since one voice alone offers no harmony." [13]

On the other hand, the harmonic considerations expressed in Rameau's rules are not limited to the fugal exposition. In his discussion of double fugues he mentions the case in which all parts are brought to a halt before the introduction of a new theme. Such a caesura should not be emphasized by a full cadence but should rather occur on a deceptive cadence. Yet if a full cadence is to be used, it should be in a key other than the original. He reminds the composer that the theme must be exactly transposed when it appears by way of modulation. But he recommends the frequent use of inversion—"the essence of all harmonic variety."

We are dealing here with a new system of rules governing the composition of fugues. It reappears in the writing of Marpurg, who spent several years under the influence of Rameau in Paris; and it was to be adopted and paraphrased in a multitude of theoretical works during the next two centuries. It is no mere coincidence that

---

[12] Rameau extends the meaning of this term to the third beat of a 4/4 measure.

[13] Rameau's rule shows the concern of the harmonist about proper accompaniment for any melodic line. In the practice of the time it was actually applied to the introduction of subject and countersubject in the double fugue rather than to the spacing of theme and answer.

the first theorist to define fugue in this manner was the one who formulated the principles of harmony, for aside from the regular repetition of the same theme in different parts, the only "regularity" in a fugal composition rests on harmonic planning. The theory of the Baroque thus completed the reconciliation of linear and vertical concepts inherent in fugal writing from its beginning. Yet the eminence of Rameau's discussion of fugue is founded not so much on his rules as on broader principles by which he subjects their application to the composer's judgment and separates those aspects of fugal technique that normally follow rules from those that invariably defy them.

Like other Baroque theorists, Rameau is aware of the structural progress of fugal writing, but he is emphatic about the fact that fugal structure cannot be bound by rules. Rather, he discusses its origin, recalling the difference in structural planning (*dessein*) in vocal and instrumental music—the former guided by the text, the latter by musical imagination alone (*bon goût ou la fantaisie*)—and to the latter he relates imitation and fugue.

We are again reminded of Morley, of his characterization of the textless fantasy which will "bear any allowances" except that it must follow the considerations of the key. It is in this respect that progress in fugal theory had been made, for Morley had as yet no "general rule for keeping of the key." The rule was found, but beyond it lay the domain of fugal art that, as Rameau says, "cannot be reduced to rules." It was the tonal basis of fugue which had been determined—not its form.

"It is true that perfect knowledge of harmony opens the roads we should take, but the choice of roads is left to our discretion." This opening of Rameau's final paragraph is to be understood, not as an exhortation of a general nature, but as a deliberate statement distinguishing that which the student of fugue can gather through the study of a book of instruction from that which he should learn through an experience much more far-reaching and complex. The words from Rameau's text quoted in the epigraph of this book characterize an attitude toward the study of fugue which is bound to retain ultimate validity.

IV

The Classic Summaries

The decisive contributions of Baroque theory were completed. What was left to be done was to present the accumulated body of theory in a comprehensive synthesis of fugal teaching. This appeared in the *Gradus ad Parnassum* by Johann Josef Fux (1725), which confirmed the victory of the tonal fugue yet reconciled it with the traditional theoretical concepts that had guided the study of fugue from its beginning.

Fux is the first theorist who approaches the study of counterpoint and fugue with sound didactic organization as well as genuine historical perception. He recognized a basic conflict which Rameau had only touched upon when he mentioned the necessity of letting the bass use the same melodic progressions as the other parts. Since Fux, the contrapuntist, raised the equality of parts to the most important principle of his teaching, he turned, more consciously than any theorist before him, from the basso continuo practice of his age and adopted for his instruction the style of another period—a style that had served the ultimate ideal of balanced part writing.[1] For this reason Fux chose Palestrina as model, allotting him the role of the master in the time-honored classical dialogue form in which his work is cast.

[1] Fux's decision was foreshadowed in the plan which Schütz had followed in publishing his *Geistliche Chormusik*. Schütz wrote in his preface: "Since there is no doubt among well-trained musicians that . . . one cannot take up and master other species of composition without sufficient experience in the style without basso continuo. . . . I have been tempted to undertake a small work without basso continuo myself, in order to encourage some composers, especially those in this country, to postpone their attempts in the concerted style until they have cracked this hard nut, in whose kernel is to be found the proper foundation of good counterpoint."

This choice explains his retention of the modes, the theoretical basis of Palestrina's music. Indeed, in this presentation, Glarean's six authentic scales offered Fux's student both a melodic-linear wealth which his own time had lost and the harmonic organization which it had conquered; studying the structure of the six basic modes and the essential intervals and cadences, he learned to understand the harmonic aspects of fugue while perceiving its melodic and linear aspects far more consciously than the limitation to two modes—major and minor—would allow.

The logic of Fux's decision has been misconstrued as often as his profound judgment has been understood. Yet to followers and critics alike, his work has become the "Bible of Counterpoint" [2]— the manual of polyphonic art which has not been replaced by a work of equal stature. Written at the dawn of a new era, it opens the series of Classical presentations of the study of fugue which were to become definitive.

Fux's work was preceded and followed by publications of the prolific "spectator in music," Johann Mattheson.[3] A spirited scholar and critic, Mattheson subjected much of the available literature on fugue to comment and explanation. In his chef-d'oeuvre, *Der voll-kommene Kapellmeister* (1739), he quotes the definitions given by his "esteemed friend" J. G. Walther, and corrects those given by his French colleague Sébastien de Brossard in the *Dictionnaire de musique* (1703). He introduces a diagram for the construction of the tonal answer similar to Bononcini's and Berardi's schemes for the use of inversion and double counterpoint. He was the first to publish Bernhard's terms *consociatio* and *aequatio modorum* and to add a related term, *conciliatio modorum*, designating a codetta or transitional passage which may be used to "reconcile" the end of the theme to the beginning of the answer.

A considerable portion of Mattheson's text is based on Rameau's writing. Yet, though Mattheson's discussion of fugue moves on fa-

---

[2] C. Sachs, *The Commonwealth of Art*, p. 225.

[3] See B. C. Cannon, *Johann Mattheson, Spectator in Music*. The work includes a brief account of Mattheson's and Fux's controversial correspondence dealing with the modal system. Fux's position, however, is not fully clarified, since his term "modulation" is interpreted in the modern meaning, whereas it should be understood as standing for "melody," a true derivative of *modus*—in the sense of melodic patterns determined by a modal scale. This explains why Fux maintained that all possibilities of modulation were contained in the six modes and why he saw no reason to establish a system of "twenty-four new modes."

miliar ground, it is guided by a spirit markedly different from that of earlier theoretical works. Mattheson is the first author who does not address his instruction to the "young composer" but rather to the "professional and amateur"—*Kenner und Liebhaber*. Mattheson's intention is clearly stated in a remark with which he shortens the discussion of fugue in his first musical treatise, *Das neueröffnete Orchestre* (1713): "My purpose, however, is not so much to train the composer as to offer my help to the amateur who wishes to form a judgment of things musical but needs no *mysteria* of this kind." This attitude prevails in Mattheson's writing, and even in the *Vollkommene Kapellmeister*, a work expressly dealing with the professional qualifications of conductors, Mattheson directs his observations on fugue to the *Fugen-Liebhaber und -Kenner*.

Consequently, Mattheson's efforts are concentrated on systematizing and rationalizing the principles of fugue writing. He counts the thematic statements of a fugue in an attempt to set up a ratio between frequency of entrances and the basic tempo of the composition. He states that a fugue should be written in duple meter since it requires a "certain element of seriousness" which is not to be found in the "light, skipping motion" of triple meter. Associating the fugal technique with the conservative style of sacred music rather than with the secular *style galant* of his own time, Mattheson links fugal writing to the time signature which he believes to be the older of the two accepted basic meters. It is significant that it is a historical error which furnishes the basis for this rule—doubtless one of the first strikingly arbitrary rules of fugal theory.

Mattheson's approach to fugal instruction was obviously prompted by the increasing lay interest in the art of music. The new situation of musical practice with which he was confronted is easily understood from his mention of the music lover who plays a fugue well but does not know of what it consists. Yet, addressing primarily the connoisseur rather than the creative artist, Mattheson's writing introduced a critical change in the teaching of composition—a change from living music to an inanimate subject. It was bound to prepare the ground for theoretical literature which taught "a métier, not an art." [4]

Thus musical theory of this period was occupied in discovering incongruities between fugal tradition and eighteenth-century styles—

[4] Cf. P. H. Lang, *Music in Western Civilization*, pp. 973 f.

leading to totally different consequences in Fux's and Mattheson's teaching. During the same time musical practice produced the great artistic summaries of fugal technique in Bach's *Well-Tempered Clavier, Musical Offering,* and *Art of Fugue.* Amid these momentous circumstances appeared the first monograph on fugue—Friedrich Wilhelm Marpurg's *Abhandlung von der Fuge* (1753–1754).

Under the immediate impression of Bach's work, Marpurg tried to define its principles in terms of contemporaneous theory, adopting Rameau's rules and absorbing most of Mattheson's discussion. The foundation of Marpurg's writing explains both its strength and weakness. Rameau's rules provide Marpurg with convincing arguments, but the heritage of Mattheson's instruction grows in Marpurg's writing to a system that threatens to freeze into rules what Rameau had decidedly left to the composer's judgment.

Like Mattheson, who had related the term fugue to the unempeded linear flow of contrapuntal voices (a "fleeing" from perfect cadences), Marpurg is concerned with the fact that a fugue cannot be explained in terms of a formal pattern of sections into which "a musical work is normally divided." Nevertheless, he tries to gather the "characteristic elements" of fugal writing into a precise fugal structure. Essentially, these characteristic elements are the elements of exposition and development which had served all phases of instrumental form governed by the fugal procedure and which the practice of Marpurg's time began to absorb into the form of the Classic sonata. For such a fugal structure he revives the term "regular fugue." In its new meaning, however, the term designates no longer merely a tonal fugue but rather a formal fugue. Deriving a model of fugal construction from the "proper arrangement" of the characteristic elements, Marpurg declares the fugal procedure itself a form. Thus he presents a summary of regular and irregular forms—a step which proved to be of singular consequence.

The concept of a "regular" fugue form has never completely disappeared from fugal theory since Marpurg, although all theorists who followed Marpurg in discussing Bach's fugal work were eventually faced with the fact that it comprises a multitude of forms written in fugal manner—and that it is this manner, not a structural pattern, which Bach's fugues have in common. In Marpurg's own text the "regular" fugue competes with the "strict" fugue, the "ordinary" fugue or "natural" fugue, and the "conventional" fugue.

The system of fugal forms which Marpurg erects leads necessarily to contradictions. He lists various classes of fugues, only to admit in a more detailed discussion that in practice most of them do not appear as independent categories.

Even though Marpurg shows in his discussion of the qualities of the fugal theme that he is aware of the fact that rules should remain subject to the composer's choice, he states in the same context: "It will always be best, however, to take the rule literally." Thus, in Marpurg's text, the student of fugue is almost entirely bound by rules. Marpurg, like Mattheson, refers to "rules of the old masters" which are not actually stated in any of the older theoretical works; and in Marpurg's text we encounter for the first time the case of a rule forbidding a progression "even though examples of this sort are found in the writings of the great masters."

In spite of its shortcomings, this fugal theory of the Age of Reason remains one of the most remarkable accomplishments in the study of fugue. More important than the diligence with which Marpurg gathered and revised the available material for a first book on fugal technique is his endeavor to present the tradition of this technique from a modern point of view. The principles of vocal polyphony which govern Fux's work are completely replaced by those of a new instrumental practice. The meaningful limitations of vocal performance are purposely disregarded, the soprano clef is for the most part replaced by the G clef, and the majority of the examples are written in keyboard score. Rather than using examples of his own writing, Marpurg quotes and analyzes portions from existing literature. With the thorough discussion of complete works, especially those by Bach, he approaches the method of Padre Martini. The other examples are fragments, but they are carefully gathered from a variety of outstanding works that connect the tradition of the Renaissance with the Rococo.

Unlike Fux, who gave his student a manual (*Manuductio*) to "guide him by the hand" in exploring the fugal technique, Marpurg wrote a treatise (*Abhandlung*) which places this technique before the student as a finished theory. His presentation of fugue has influenced didactic literature ever since.

The fugal theory of the Classic era is almost entirely covered by the various editions of Fux's and Marpurg's texts. Fux's original

Latin edition was followed by editions in German (1742), Italian (1761), French (1763), and English (1791). Marpurg's original edition was followed by an edition in French (1756), a second German edition (1806), and a revised version by Simon Sechter (*c.* 1850).

A synthesis of Fux's and Marpurg's works appeared in the *Gründliche Anweisung zur Komposition* (1790) by Johann Georg Albrechtsberger, a friend of Haydn and teacher of Beethoven. Marpurg's modern approach to fugal theory was paralleled in Albrechtsberger's work, for his discussion presents the study of both counterpoint and fugue in terms of the accepted harmonic practice of his time. In fact, Albrechtsberger's *Anweisung* may be considered the last theoretical work in which the heritage of contrapuntal technique was successfully reconciled with actual compositional needs of his day.

Albrechtsberger leads the student from strict to free contrapuntal writing, supporting the didactic reason for this distinction with practical considerations. Pointing out that compositions without instrumental accompaniment are required for use during Lent, he trains the student in a strict vocal style without recourse to complicated progressions or instrumental idioms. The expressive possibilities of the free style are reserved for other works, especially those to be used in concert and opera.

Albrechtsberger uses the means of composition which emanate from the training in these two styles with keen judgment. The fugal exposition, for instance, remains to him a purely polyphonic procedure not to be weakened by interpolated modulations. Thus, he rejects the use of a connecting passage between theme and answer that Mattheson had recommended, and he shows the student how a fresher and more transparent change of tonality can be achieved by letting the end of a statement on the tonic coincide with the beginning of a statement on the dominant. In the progress of a fugal composition, on the other hand, Albrechtsberger suggests a more liberal use of modulation to "distant keys" than his predecessors, and he condemns the use of sequential modulations through the circle of fifths as "obsolete and trivial."

Yet, fugue appears primarily as a species of church music in Albrechtsberger's discussion. In the general musical practice of his time, the appreciation of fugal technique had reached its lowest ebb.

It is revealing that Bach's eminent pupil Johann Philipp Kirnberger includes no fugal instruction in his work on counterpoint. Kirnberger's *Kunst des reinen Satzes* (1774), which was compiled with the intention "to reduce the method of the late J. S. Bach to principles," contains a thorough discussion of contrapuntal theory, based on harmonic progressions, but it does not present the weightiest part of his master's teaching.[5] In the same year, however, appeared the most representative work of a totally different school of contrapuntal theory, the *Esemplare o sia saggio fondamentale prattico di contrappunto* by Giambattista Martini.

Padre Martini, the teacher of Johann Christian Bach and Mozart, held an unequaled position of authority among eighteenth-century theorists. The admiration and irreproachable respect that this "Padre di tutti i Maestri"[6] commanded can doubtless be attributed to the fact that he was the only one among his colleagues who combined competent judgment in the art of composition with a thorough knowledge of the history of music.

Martini singled out the cardinal point of Fux's teaching, the return to the era of Palestrina, and made the object of his work a searching discussion of this style, presenting only complete works and limiting his text modestly to introductions and annotations. Although his first concern is to offer the student authentic examples of the polyphonic art represented by Palestrina's generation, he quotes the works of numerous composers, ranging from Willaert to Scarlatti, and the writings of theorists from Tinctoris to Marpurg. Thus he assumes a completely modern attitude of instruction in composition. Dismissing the concept of a set fugal structure, he teaches the student of fugue by means of an anthology which includes examples of madrigals, accompanied canons, and various other forms of fugal art.

As for the didactic method, Martini subscribed to Fux's *Gradus*. He said to Abbé Vogler, his pupil: "We have no system other than

---

[5] As Kirnberger himself confirms, Bach's teaching moved step by step to fugal writing. J. N. Forkel in his biography of Bach (1802) adds that whenever a student was sufficiently prepared, Bach "took up the doctrine of fugues and made a beginning with those in two parts, etc." (quoted in H. T. David and A. Mendel, *The Bach Reader*, p. 329).

[6] K. D. von Dittersdorf, *Lebensbeschreibung*, p. 110.

that of Fux." [7] In fact, Martini seems to have inherited his determination to adhere to Fux's method, and even the outline of his own work, from his teacher Giacomo Antonio Perti. Leonida Busi mentions in his biography of Martini the plan of an unpublished *Esemplare* by Perti, with which the author supplied a choice of valid examples to guide the student of Fux in furthering his contrapuntal skill. [8] When ultimately he adapted Perti's plan in an extensive work combining historical and critical commentary with contrapuntal analysis, Martini emerged as the central figure of a group of theorists devoted to the same method of teaching.

At first, as Willi Reich has pointed out in a dissertation dealing with Martini's teaching (1934), Martini apparently underestimated the work involved in preparing a collection of this kind and rather considered it a task to be entrusted to a diligent student. Thus Martini encouraged his pupil Giuseppe Paolucci in a plan to publish notes gathered during Paolucci's studies under him, together with a number of examples chosen from the wealth of Martini's library. Paolucci's work, *Arte prattica di contrappunto*, prefaced by formal recommendations from Martini and his eminent colleague Vallotti, [9] appeared in three parts (1765–1772). Yet, once Paolucci's book was completed, Martini seems to have realized that only a work of considerably wider didactic and historical scope could give a true presentation of his method of teaching. Thus he decided to interrupt the work on his *Storia della musica* to prepare his own practical essay on counterpoint. The first volume of his *Esemplare* appeared in 1774 and the second, devoted to fugal counterpoint in particular, in 1775.

Another book which followed the same plan was published by Luigi Antonio Sabbatini, also a student of Martini, and an apprentice and successor to Vallotti. In his *Trattato sopra le fughe musicali* (1802), Sabbatini adopted the form of Martini's *Esemplare* in order to present the models Vallotti had used in teaching.

However, not all students of this school followed Martini's teaching implicitly. Abbé Vogler—like Sabbatini, a pupil of Vallotti and Martini—rejected all existing manners of contrapuntal instruction, including Kirnberger's presentation of Bach's teaching, and tried to

[7] G. J. Vogler, *Choral-System*, p. 6.

[8] *Il Padre G. B. Martini* (1891), p. 117.

[9] Francesco Antonio Vallotti (1697–1780), organist and chapelmaster in Padua. Giuseppe Tartini, with whom Vallotti shared musical duties at the church of St. Antonio, referred to Vallotti as the most outstanding Italian organist of his time.

replace them with a new method of coordinating melodies derived from harmonic analysis (*Gesangs-Verbindungs-Lehre*). He suggested that this approach to contrapuntal theory would turn study into play since the student himself could devise the tabulations (*Tabellen*) which were to guide his work. While seeking freedom, his plan obviously leads to arbitrary restrictions—the blemish that marred almost all theoretical discussions of the Romantic era. It is characteristic that Vogler's brief discussion of fugal theory, published in 1811 as introduction to a planned larger work and combining "mathematic, rhetoric, logic, and esthetic aspects of fugue," bears the title *System für den Fugenbau*—a system for the construction of fugues.

V

Textbook Versus History

The nineteenth century produced no work in which Martini's teaching was continued. Joseph-François Fétis, one of the ablest musical scholars of the nineteenth century, aimed in his *Traité de la fugue et du contrepoint* (1824) at a decidedly different mode of instruction.

Reviewing the history of contrapuntal teaching in the preface to his work, Fétis points out that a gap exists between the contrapuntal instruction of, on the one hand, Fux and the Italian theorists, who adopt the linear principle of the modes (*la tonalité de plain chant*), and, on the other, that of the recent German theorists, Marpurg, Kirnberger, and Albrechtsberger, who tend toward a more instrumental style. He proposes to fill this gap with a "book which will avoid the pitfalls of too liberal a training by applying the strictness of rules to modern tonality." Yet this plan leads to a compromise which relates the student's work neither to a true account of contrapuntal traditions nor to the music of his own time. Written specifically for the classes at the young Paris Conservatoire, the *Traité* opens the series of modern textbooks on fugue—works which offer a thoroughly organized course of training but, having lost the connection with both past and present, move in a musical no man's land.

That fugue was beginning to be looked upon as a purely theoretical exercise is borne out by the writing of Fétis's colleagues at the Conservatoire. Anton Reicha calls fugue "une production scientifique" in his *Traité de haute composition* (1824–1826),[1] and Luigi

---

[1] Reicha had introduced his fugal instruction with "thirty-six keyboard fugues written according to a new system." His system suggested fugal answers at all intervals and was meant to widen the possibilities of modulation, but it remained, like Vogler's system, without practical or theoretical consequence.

Cherubini's *Cours de contrepoint et de fugue* (actually compiled from his instruction by J. F. Halévy) describes the transformation from the living to the academic fugue with these words: "Such as it exists at the present day, fugue is the complement of counterpoint. It ought to include not only all the resources which are furnished by the study of the different species of counterpoint, but also many other artifices peculiar to itself. . . ."[2]

A counterpart to the fugal instruction at the Paris Conservatoire appeared a few decades later in the publications of teachers at the Conservatory of Leipzig, although these works show greater concern over the difference between theoretical and practical music. Ernst Friedrich Richter, one of the founding members of the Conservatory of Leipzig, speaks of the necessity of mastering an "abstract form . . . which possibly cannot be traced to any of the existing fugues."[3] And Salomon Jadassohn, one of Richter's successors, refers to works of the old masters and of contemporary composers which are not written according to the rules that the "true fugue" would require. His explanation of this conflict defends the theoretical concept of the fugue: "These works are not actually fugues, nor were they meant to be such."[4]

Adopting a principle diametrically opposed to that of Martini's teaching, these authors tended to reject works from the great literature of fugal writing as "irregular" and not suited to serve as models for instruction. This point of view is stressed in Theodor Weinlig's *Anleitung zur Fuge*, also published in Leipzig (1845), in which the writer states the need for using his own examples, since they are best suited to illustrate his points and contain "nothing that might confuse or divert the student."

The work which shows the most extreme attempt to prove that there is a "regular" fugue form is the *Lehrbuch der Tonsetzkunst* (1832–1842) by Johann Anton André, the author whom Ebenezer Prout quotes as condemning Bach's "exceptions." André opens his presentation of fugal theory with a discussion of the origin of the term fugue. He claims that all accepted derivations are erroneous and that "fugue" is to be related solely to the German word *Fug* (rule, regularity). According to André, therefore, the term designates a piece of music subjected to rules and regularity. André goes to some

[2] Quoted from J. A. Hamilton's translation, *Cherubini's Course of Counterpoint and Fugue*, pp. 285 f.
[3] *Lehrbuch der Fuge* (1859), p. 111.
[4] *Lehre vom Canon und von der Fuge* (1884), p. 202.

length in refuting the derivation from the Latin or Italian *fuga*. He admits that some fugues are "fast, and even scrambled," but—not realizing that he is trying to replace one wrong interpretation with another—attributes this impression to the nature of instrumental performance rather than to the character of fugue itself, which, he assumes, is "stately and serious."

It seems important to follow André's confused argument as far as this because the last point links his writing to that of an earlier theorist, Mattheson, whom he quotes in the same context. Here, as in Mattheson's text, false conclusions arise from insufficient or misinterpreted historical information. In order to prove his contention, André discusses brief portions from the works of several theorists. He mentions the *diffinitiones* of Tinctoris, then turns to a quotation from Nucius in Athanasius Kircher's *Musurgia universalis* (1650) and a few examples contained in Kircher's work; the next two references are taken from Brossard's and Walther's dictionaries; and the last two theorists included in André's account are Zarlino and Bononcini.

At a few points André disputes the terminology of the earlier works, but obviously none of them serves his purpose since they use the Latin or Italian term *fuga*. His mention of Tinctoris, however, is preceded by quotations from the works of two medieval German authors—Notker Labeo (d. 1022), the first theorist to write in German,[5] and the minnesinger Walther von der Vogelweide (*c.* 1170–*c.* 1230). He admits that the word *fuogi*, as used by Notker, yields hardly any evidence that can be related to the later term. But he conjectures that Walther means by *fuoge* a well-regulated piece of music, since he decries the unruly songs of the declining courtly art as *ungefuege* (adjective) and *Unfuoge* (noun). Recognizing the weakness of the proof he has offered, André concludes his introductory remarks by gathering some justification of their hypothetical nature from the opening of the *Fugen-Betrachtungen* by the eighteenth-century theorist Joseph Riepel [6]—a passage so extraordinary in the history of fugal theory that we quote it in full:

> *Student:* I hope that you have fared well. Above all, I wish to ask you who was the first man to show his skill in setting a fugue? Under what circumstances? Where? And at what time?
> *Master:* I do not know.

[5] Three tracts by Notker Labeo are published in *Gerb. Script.*, I.
[6] Cf. W. Twittenhoff, *Die musikalischen Schriften Joseph Riepels*.

Student: Was this manner of music not practiced as early as the time of King David and King Solomon?

Master: I do not know.

Student: What is the origin of the name fugue?

Master: I do not know.

Student: Then you know nothing indeed; but how is it. . . .

Master: I can tell you no more than what I have heard, read, and tried myself. What I know of the fugue you shall learn now and then proceed from there. . . .

As we have seen, lack of historical orientation marked the beginning of the separation between theory and living music. The confusion of nineteenth-century theory proved that historical perspective had become an indispensable attribute of authoritative teaching.

The direct imparting of current principles of composition, which had marked the master-artisan relationship in the days of Morley and Sweelinck, was irrevocably gone. The great creative men of the century had little direct influence upon the teaching of composition. Their views on fugue, though often illuminating, could not in themselves correct the errors of the textbooks nor dispel their influence upon the student and general public. Here, too, the "growing cleavage between artist and public" to which Alfred Einstein draws attention [7] had become obvious. The study of composition was necessarily concerned with a tradition much more complex than that with which earlier periods had dealt, and, as first recognized by Mattheson, it was taken up by a much more diversified body of students.

In order to recognize the components of this large heritage, the nineteenth-century student had to travel into the history of the eighteenth, seventeenth, and sixteenth centuries and interpret the highest attainments of the past as illustrations of different disciplines of composition eventually labeled as counterpoint, harmony, form, and orchestration. The didactic device of dividing the study of composition into a study of different styles had been first suggested by Schütz. Fux's work marked the beginnings of its practical presentation, but Martini was the first to show that such dipping into the musical past required sure guidance. The fate of nineteenth-century theory was determined by the fact that the historians of the time did not rise to this task.

The impressive achievements which accompanied the progress of

[7] *Music in the Romantic Era,* p. 37.

musical scholarship had no direct bearing upon the teaching of composition, although they included monumental editions of early theoretical works (begun in 1784 by a friend of Martini's, the Abbot Martin Gerbert, and continued a century later by Edmond Henri de Coussemaker), as well as the first history of musical theory, Hugo Riemann's *Geschichte der Musik-Theorie* (1898).

The writings by Hugo Riemann give a particularly convincing illustration of the separation of the two fields, for here we find outstanding accomplishments in critical scholarship next to highly arbitrary hypotheses in practical instruction. Riemann sanctioned earlier theoretical endeavors to restrict the fugal structure by declaring fugue a tripartite form. His fugal instruction as presented in his *Lehrbuch des Kontrapunkts* (1888), *Katechismus der Fuge* (1890–1891), and *Grosse Kompositionslehre* (1902) is in part based upon the writings of Adolf Bernhard Marx, the first music historian appointed to the faculty of the University in Berlin. Marx, in his *Lehre von der musikalischen Komposition* (1837–1847, later revised by Riemann), discusses the structural regularity of fugal form thoroughly, but his theory is reduced to more definite terms by Riemann, who applies to the combination of theme and answer the norm of an eight-measure period which he considers basic for all music. He admits that "a diversity of complications" might alter, or, rather, obscure the norm. Thus he explains the form of Bach's fugues through extensions, contractions, elisions, and appendages which assume well-nigh incredible proportions.

A particular problem of this theory lies in the fact that formal analysis is substituted for stylistic analysis. Riemann carries to the extreme a theoretical attitude which we can begin to distinguish in Marpurg's writing: the tendency to explain the music of the Baroque in terms of the Classic era. Marpurg, however, judged from a proximity which admitted no perspective; his treatise was published within two years after the appearance of Bach's *Art of Fugue*. Moreover, he wrote at a time when the stylistic trends of the Classic era were not yet fully established.

The same tendency to interpret in terms of form rather than style may also explain the predicament of nineteenth-century theorists who judged the fugues of the Classic masters by standards of the Baroque and thus considered them no "proper" fugues. The origin of this opinion can be traced to Marpurg's distinction between Bach's "strict fugues"—works dominated in true Baroque fashion by the restriction to one "affection" treated in relentless continuity—and Handel's "free fugues"—works which approach the Classic principle of thematic dualism. Marpurg's new use of the Renaissance terms *fuga ligata* (*obbligata* in Marpurg's text) and *fuga sciolta* have logic and meaning in this context, but this meaning is lost once the designation "strict fugue" is reinterpreted as "proper" or "true" fugue.

Simon Sechter's revised edition of Marpurg's work contains an analysis of the final movement of Mozart's Jupiter Symphony [8] which may serve as an illustration of such reinterpretation. Although Sechter recognizes the adaptation of the fugal procedure to the Classic form, he searches throughout Mozart's finale for the "actual fugue" (*eigentliche Fuge*). He points out suggestions of it in various portions of the movement and finally arrives at a thematic entrance which, according to his analysis, marks the point where the fugue really begins—but this real beginning occurs near the middle of the coda.

Sechter's discussion forms the basis for an analysis of the same work in Johann Christian Lobe's *Lehrbuch der musikalischen Komposition* (Vol. III, 1855)—another work which furnished basic ideas for Riemann's fugal instruction. Lobe, however, advocates the exclusive validity of the Baroque fugue with more consistency than Sechter. He establishes the term *metrum*—a regular rhythmic motion—as a standard by which to judge the fugue. He tries to remove all obstacles that might interfere with the uninterrupted uniformity of the *metrum*. Thus he states: "My theory recognizes no answer, no exposition, no development." Yet the style Lobe is trying to recapture no longer agrees with the practice of his time. He admits that the fugal writing which he teaches can be produced only after "painstaking computations" (*mühsame Vorausberechnungen*), and though his theory is presented as a quasi-abstract of Bach's principles, the norm which it upholds offers no explanations for Bach's own "irregular" fugal writing—such as the fugal expositions in the *Et resurrexit* (B Minor Mass), which, like expositions of Classic themes, are supported by a "drum bass" accompaniment; or the *Confiteor* from the same work, in which a double fugue written upon an

---

[8] Published also separately in an edition by Friedrich Eckstein, *Das Finale von W. A. Mozarts Jupiter-Symphonie*, 1923.

independent basso continuo surrounds a Renaissance *fuga ligata* on a Gregorian cantus firmus.

Ebenezer Prout, while describing Lobe's theory as "too revolutionary," adopted his point of view and reformulated it in the maxim of his teaching. "Whatever Bach does systematically . . . is the correct thing for the student to do." Though meant to supplant the textbook rules, this principle itself assumes textbook rigidity. Maintained in numerous didactic and analytic works of the twentieth century, the "fetishistic absolutism for Bach"[9] was extended to all contrapuntal theory with the premise on which Ernst Kurth based his work: "The study of counterpoint cannot be separated from Bach's style."[10]

The exclusive correctness of Bach's fugal style is still affirmed by Charles Sanford Terry: "The fugue was a contrapuntal soulless exercise" until Bach had "expounded it by rule and example."[11] And Terry's statement, in turn, serves as point of departure for a book by George Oldroyd, *The Technique and Spirit of the Fugue*, which, although subtitled "an historical study," continues the textbook tradition in such characteristic chapter headings and subheadings as "The Second Middle-Entry Section" and "Does the Pedal Note Count as a Strand?"

A more sensitive attitude is taken in Quincy Porter's recent *Study of Fugal Writing*, "a method by which a student may discover for himself . . . the principles and restrictions of Bach's fugal style" so that he may learn how to write fugues "which might (to speak optimistically) have pleased the great master if they had been written by one of his pupils."

An admittedly strict textbook approach, on the other hand, has continued in numerous books which added to the *Musterfuge* of German nineteenth-century theorists the *fugue d'école*, discussed in the *Traité de la fugue* by André Gédalge (1901), and the *examination fugue*, discussed in *Studies in Fugue* by C. H. Kitson (1922). Kitson quotes brief excerpts from the works of nineteenth- and eighteenth-century masters, but the only complete works which he presents as models of fugal writing are a number of fugues submitted

---

[9] A. Ghislanzoni, "La Genesi storica della fuga," *Rivista Musicale Italiana*, LIII (1951), p. 137.
[10] *Grundlagen des linearen Kontrapunkts* (1911), preface, p. ix.
[11] *Bach, the Historical Approach* (1930), p. 12.

by examinees for music degrees at Oxford during the first decade of the twentieth century. In the explanations with which Kitson sets them up as standards, the stubbornness of this system of fugal instruction may very well have found its final expression: ". . . the student would be ill-advised to take the first fugue of the Forty-Eight as a model for examination work. Its imitation would afford him no opportunity of showing his command of some of the main features of fugal construction. This fugue contains no episodes. . . . Neither is the second fugue of the Forty-Eight a good model for examination work, for it contains no stretto. Most examination fugues are specially designed, so that the student may employ this device. Other fugues are obviously far too long to serve as models for the purpose in view. The examples in this book do not pretend to vie with those that may be seen in the classics. They are merely an attempt to illustrate the requirements of an examination. . . ."

Alfred Einstein has pointed out that the first scholarly editions of early theoretical writings (Gerbert's *Scriptores*) were guided by an essentially antiquarian interest, whereas their continuation (Coussemaker's *Scriptores*) was undertaken in a spirit of creative scholarship.[12] Two years before Coussemaker's series, however, appeared a scholarly work which concerned itself with the theory of the past for a completely practical reason: Heinrich Bellermann's *Kontrapunkt* (1862), a book in which critical history and textbook instruction were combined for the first time.

Unlike other nineteenth-century theorists who had drawn on Fux's work, Bellermann restored the modal teaching of Fux and presented an account of his study of counterpoint and fugue with several introductory sections which open a new historical perspective for the instruction contained in his work. Bellermann's volume was followed by several similar publications, including Michael Haller's *Kompositionslehre für den polyphonen Kirchengesang* (1891), and Wilhelm Hohn's *Der Kontrapunkt Palestrinas und seiner Zeitgenossen* (1918); but it found its most significant continuation in Knud Jeppesen's *Counterpoint* (1931), which presents Fux's teaching in a revision based on extensive studies of the Palestrina style.[13] Jeppesen's work is

---

[12] *Music in the Romantic Era*, p. 354.

[13] Mention should be made of R. O. Morris, *Contrapuntal Technique in the Sixteenth Century*, and H. Schenker, *Neue musikalische Theorien und Phantasien*, Vol. II, two significant works which follow the tradition of Fux's teaching but adhere less strictly to his method than the works listed above.

limited to the study of counterpoint (a brief section dealing with the vocal fugue appears only as appendix), but it is introduced by a new, concise history of contrapuntal teaching to which the present survey is indebted in plan and method.

Whereas the practical instruction in Bellermann's and Jeppesen's works paraphrases Fux's writing, the text of Fux's own study of counterpoint was restored in German and English translations by the present writer (1938, 1943) with commentary to allow a comparison between the original wording and revisions—especially those made by Haydn, Mozart, and Beethoven in their study or instruction. A number of similar editions which have appeared during the past decade have helped to prove that much is to be gained from a direct didactic use of the classic theoretical sources. Such publications as William Mitchell's edition of C. P. E. Bach's *Essay on the True Art of Playing Keyboard Instruments* (1949), R. Alec Harman's edition of Morley's *Plain and Easy Introduction to Practical Music* (1952), and David D. Boyden's edition of Francesco Geminiani's *Art of Playing on the Violin* (1952) have assumed a dual role as contributions to musical scholarship and as presentations of practical texts whose fresh pedagogical strength guides the student authoritatively to the outstanding phases of our musical heritage. For this reason, the account of fugal history given here is followed by a selection of texts from those works which precede the epoch of conventional instruction and present the study of fugue in its historic summaries.

*
* *

The evolution of fugal theory spans six centuries. It shows that remarkable changes have occurred in the concepts of fugal writing. Nevertheless, a line of continuous development can be clearly distinguished which gives the term *fuga* or its equivalents in the modern languages, a consistent meaning throughout its history. The perspective of this history will help the student of music to appreciate the intricate task of understanding the meaning of the term and of grasping its relationship to other musical concepts.

It has become evident that the term fugue does not apply to a form, as does, for instance, the term minuet. It denotes something structurally less concrete. Nor does the term merely apply to a texture, as does, for instance, the term counterpoint. From the very beginning of its use, it has denoted something structurally more concrete.

The earliest meaning of *fuga*—the canon—came to be interpreted by the theory of the Renaissance as a procedure of musical composition by which a theme is stated and restated. While, in the progress of Renaissance theory, the strict identity of the voices was readily relaxed and the free continuation of a fugal setting accepted and even given preference, the rules for the thematic statements were more carefully defined and treated with increasing strictness. Statement and restatement had to be spaced by the intervals of perfect consonances and a new distinction separated this, the fugal exposition, from imitation. Thus the fugal exposition gradually gained a thematic as well as a harmonic meaning which was to extend over the entire structure of a musical work.

The theory of the Baroque took over from the Renaissance the term fugue in the meaning of thematic exposition and widened it to thematic development. It introduced the principle of thematic dualism and the balance of tonalities within an extended musical structure.

With the establishment of harmonic theory, the terms imitation, canon, and fugue found their final distinction. Imitation remained the general term for the casual application of the imitative manner, and canon remained the term for the strict application of this manner; but the term fugue designated the sum of procedures by which the imitative manner was used in order to state and restate, tonally establish, develop, and re-establish thematic material.

The theory of fugue which created the concepts of theme, exposition, and development reflects step by step the evolution of musical form. In fact, it provides a new mirror for the development of Western music from the single vocal line to the complex orchestral score, and it is to be considered a catechism of the discipline of composition in general rather than the study of one particular type of composition. Thus the art of writing music will by necessity always return to the study of fugue.

Part Two

THE STUDY OF FUGUE
IN CLASSIC TEXTS

I

Johann Josef Fux

Fux as Disciple of Palestrina

The original version of Johann Josef Fux's *Gradus ad Parnassum*, written in Latin, appeared in 1725, published at imperial expense. It sold out within a year, and entered upon a history unparalleled in the literature of musical theory. Translated by Bach's pupil Lorenz Christoph Mizler, "under the very eyes of Bach as it were," [1] and paraphrased in abstracts by Haydn and Beethoven, the *Gradus ad Parnassum* became the classical manual of composition. Although two centuries of use subjected Fux's text to countless changes, the original, in modern translation, still served Richard Strauss and Paul Hindemith in their teaching.

Fux published his work in two volumes. The first volume, *pars speculativa*, is actually no more than an introduction dealing with the mathematical operations traditionally used to explain the nature of intervals and scales. As the author notes in his preface, it is kept "as brief as possible." The second, considerably larger, volume, *pars activa*, contains the study of counterpoint and the study of fugue. A few short chapters given to a discussion of the system of church modes and of different stylistic trends of Fux's time conclude the book.

Fux's study of fugue is less well known than his study of counterpoint; but it is his fugal instruction which he himself describes as the

[1] Philipp Spitta, *J. S. Bach*, p. 125.

most important aspect of his work. Again and again he points out that the contrapuntal training that precedes the study of fugue should not be considered an end in itself. He subordinates the simple exercises to florid counterpoint—a free combination of rhythmic values which still follows strict rules governing the use of dissonances. This, in turn, serves to prepare the student for the time "when the restraints of the cantus firmus are removed, and he, released from his fetters, so to speak . . . can write free compositions"—the time when he embarks upon the study of fugue. Yet, in this new freedom, the student is not left altogether without guidance. In the imitative setting, his own invention serves as a cantus firmus from measure to measure, each new idea forming the basis for the next. This process determines the logical place of fugue in Fux's teaching of composition.

Fux's method of graded progress—expressed in the title of the work—is a method of increasing gradually the possibilities open to the student, and thus the problems confronting him. It is decisively strengthened by the fact that Fux bases his discussion of fugue, as well as that of counterpoint, on the church modes.

The stand that Fux takes in turning to the modes is entirely practical, for the study of fugue is not preceded but rather followed by a formal explanation of the modal system in his text. At the outset the student is merely asked to build simple tone progressions by consistent use of the "natural tones." The use of sharps and flats is limited to those instances in which they help to form a cadence or to avoid a tritone. This restriction necessarily places particular emphasis on the melodic element through the various uses of the natural half-tone step, to which Fux refers as *mi fa*.[2]

Thus Fux develops the student's ability with respect to melodic invention before admitting a more complex and conscious use of harmonic means. He asks him to stay within the limits of the diatonic system and to save the advantages of the mixed system—combining diatonic and chromatic progressions—for the time when he has fully mastered the principles of fugal technique.

The return to the modal style and its strict treatment of consonances and dissonances, melody and rhythm, is explained by Fux as

[2] This designation arises from the combination of syllable names from the three traditional six tone rows—the *hexachordum durum* starting on g, the *hexachordum molle* starting on f, and the *hexachordum naturale* starting on c.

a matter of his own deep indebtedness. In his preface he attributes all that he knows in the art of composition to "the glorious light of music from Praeneste—Palestrina—whose memory I shall never cease to cherish with the feeling of profound reverence."

The ideal that Palestrina's style represents to Fux is an ideal of sacred music, and its choice reminds us of the inscription *Soli Deo Gloria*, which the works of Fux's time bear. The quest of musical excellence was to him a quest of an adequate expression of divine worship. "Since God is the highest perfection, the harmony composed for his praise should follow the strictest rules that perfection can claim, as far as human imperfection can realize them," writes Fux. But a particularly remarkable quality of Fux's work lies in the fact that this artistic integrity was paired with the historical and pedagogical discernment that prompted him to choose sixteenth-century polyphony as the ultimate standard of musical strictness and purity. Thus, in adopting the classical form of the dialogue for the lessons of the *Gradus*, Fux declared himself (Josephus) the student of Palestrina (Aloysius); and when, at the end of the book, master and student analyze portions of Fux's masses, it is as though Fux wanted to submit his own works to the judgment of the "prince of sacred music."

Some parts of the discussion between Aloysius and Josephus, especially the beginning and the ending, are doubtless reminiscences of scenes between Fux and his own students. In fact, the account that Fux's younger contemporary, Ignaz Jacob Holzbauer, gives of a visit to Fux almost literally retells the opening conversation from the *Gradus*.[3] But in the essence of his work, Fux appears as Josephus—the student—for Fux truly realized that teaching means to impart learning and that in order to assume his role as interpreter of the past, the teacher himself must assume the role of disciple.

The modern reader will find beneath the quaint language of the dialogue a refreshing pedagogical understanding and a superb mastery of the subject. The authority of Fux's *Gradus* is expressed in the fact that it is "that book through which all celebrated masters have learned composition,"[4] but the wisdom of Fux's teaching speaks to us directly from his work even when we are not aware of its history.

[3] See L. Ritter von Köchel, *J. J. Fux*, pp. 263 f.
[4] J. Habert, *DTOe*, I, ix.

From *Gradus ad Parnassum*

A Lesson on Imitation

Aloysius. I should like to instruct you now in the art of imitation and fugue.

Let us leave the restrictions that the use of the cantus firmus, or given melody, imposes and begin free composition in two parts with a Lesson on Imitation.

Imitation arises when one part follows another, after a number of rests, forming the same intervals with which the first part began and without any regard for the scale or mode in which these parts move or for the position of whole- and half-tone steps. This can occur at the unison, second, third, fourth, fifth, sixth, seventh, or octave, as can be seen from the following examples:

Ex. 26   Imitation at the unison

Josephus. From this first example I gather that not all notes of the part that enters first are to be taken over in the following part.

Aloysius. Yes, that would be the function of a canon, not of imitation. Here it is enough if a few notes follow those of the opening part.

Ex. 27   Imitation at the second

Ex. 28 Imitation at the third

Ex. 29 Imitation at the fourth

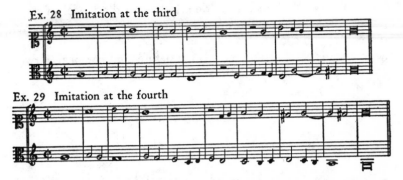

Josephus. It seems that the last example begins in C and ends in G.

Aloysius. Have you already forgotten that I said the imitation should not be made subject to any consideration of mode? It is sufficient if the imitating part follows in the footsteps of the preceding part, whatever the mode. Besides, imitation is used not only in the beginning of the composition but also later, where the restrictions of the mode play a less important role.

Ex. 30 Imitation at the fifth

Ex. 31 Imitation at the sixth

Ex. 32 Imitation at the seventh

Ex. 33 Imitation at the octave

Aloysius. Now spend a little time following the model of these examples. Take a succession of notes made up of whatever interval progressions you choose. Then add another part, write a new melodic line in counterpoint to the one written before, and complete a two-part setting, keeping in mind the rules of good, singable writing.

Fugues in General

Aloysius. Fugue takes its name from the words *fugere* and *fugare*—to flee and to pursue—a derivation confirmed by a number of eminent authors. When one part flees, pursued by another, this is actually nothing but what has been explained as imitation. Therefore another definition is needed that will distinguish fugue from imitation.

A fugue arises when a succession of notes in one part is taken over in another part, with due regard for the mode, and especially for the position of whole- and half-tone steps. To understand this definition fully, we shall need to know what is meant by the term mode. By mode I mean that which has often been called "tone." But obviously it is better to say the first mode or the second mode, than the first tone or the second tone, in order to avoid confusion with the tone step and the half-tone step—the intervals represented by the ratios 9:8 and 10:9—for which the same term is used. Since the matter of modes is highly intricate and not easily understood by the novice, I think that we shall be content with discussing only what is needed for our present purposes and postpone a fuller explanation until later.

A mode is comprised of a series of intervals, contained within the limits of an octave, in which the half-tone steps are irregularly placed. The word mode appears in the famous lines of Horace:

> All things are subject to a mode, a mean,
> Beyond the limits of which they cannot rightly exist.*

Since the placing of the half-tone steps occurs in six different manners, we shall have to specify six modes, shown in the following octave rows on the tones d, e, f, g, a, c.

* *Satires,* Bk. I, 1, vs. 106.

Ex. 34

If you count each mode from the first note, you will find the half-tone steps in six different places. This difference in placing is indicated by the black notes. For the time being, we need not consider which of these modes should rightfully be the first, second, third, and so on, but we may count them in the order in which they appear here.

A mode is further characterized by the fourth and fifth which make up its octave. According to the limits set by these intervals, fugal themes will have to be arranged.

Ex. 35

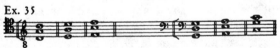

If the first part uses the skip of a fifth, the following part must use the skip of a fourth, in order not to exceed the limits of the mode or octave, and vice versa:

Ex. 36

This restriction does not apply to imitation, where it is in order to repeat the same steps or skips.

Ex. 37

Finally, the voices of a fugue cannot start at intervals other than those that constitute a mode, that is, intervals other than the unison, octave, and fifth; whereas imitation, as has been said, may occur at any interval.

Josephus. I think I have understood all that you have said about modes, imitation, and fugue. But I should like to ask that you teach me about the choice of themes and about the ways in which fugues have to be arranged and carried through, for I have often heard that the study of fugue is not known to all masters of the art of music.

Aloysius. That is true. Oratory on this subject is more common than knowledge. Therefore I want you to have all the explanations so that nothing about which you have inquired will remain obscure.

From what we have said before, it is clear that there are six different modes. It is for this reason that a theme will have to be adapted properly to each mode. You can gather from this that a theme that is suited to the first mode will not be suited to the second, third, fourth, fifth, or sixth modes because of the position of whole- and half-tone steps, which is different in each mode. Let me show you this with an example.

Ex. 38

re fa mi re

This theme is formed by the same whole- and half-tone steps, as it appears again at the fifth in the following part:

Ex. 39

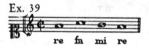

re fa mi re

This use of the subject would not be possible in any of the other modes. Let us see the mode of A, *la, mi, re*,* which in even distribution comes closest to the mode of D, *la, sol, re*.

Ex. 40

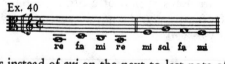

re fa mi re   mi sol fa mi

Here *fa* occurs instead of *mi* on the next-to-last note of the part that is following, and the position of the whole- and half-tone steps is inverted. The arrangement of the subject could not be as in the first part, except through the use of a sharp for the next-to-last note:

Ex. 41

* The traditional use of several syllables for the same tone according to its position in the different hexachords.

This, however, is not to be used in the diatonic system with which we are now dealing. We should avoid the use of any sharps or flats in our subjects, for otherwise we would never fully understand the true nature of the modes.

Fugues in Two Parts

Aloysius. I shall teach you first how to write simple two-part fugues. Choose a subject consisting of a few notes which is suited to the mode in which you intend to work. Place those notes in the part with which you have decided to start. Then, if nothing has to be altered because of the mode, use the same succession of notes in the following part which enters at the fourth or fifth.* Meanwhile, form a counterpoint with the part in which you began, using any free succession of notes, as you have learned in florid counterpoint. After a short continuation of the melodic figures, arrange the parts so that you can bring about the first cadence, at the fifth of the mode. Then resume the theme; as a rule, this is done in the part with which you started, but on a tone other than that which you used before. Mark this entrance with a full- or half-measure rest or by a large skip without a rest. The other part might, after a rest, enter before the theme in the preceding part is finished. Following this, let the parts move freely for a short distance and then form a second cadence at the third of the mode. Finally, placing the subject in either part, let the other part follow with the subject directly in the next measure if this is possible, and thus, locking the two parts as closely as possible, complete the fugue with a cadence on the final of the mode.

Josephus. I remember that you said a little while ago . . .

Aloysius. Let us postpone your question, for your uncertainty may be clarified by an example. I shall take the subject we have used before in discussing the nature of the modes and write a fugue on it in the manner prescribed. With this as a model before you, the road for your own work will be cleared.

---

* The fourth below or the fifth above (see Examples 44 and 45).

Ex. 42. Fugue for two voices — Cadence at the fifth — Cadence at the third

You see here the theme employed in the soprano at the fifth of the mode as soon as it is finished in the alto. Meanwhile the alto moves in florid counterpoint until the theme is finished in the soprano. A short continuation in both parts leads to a cadence on the fifth of the mode. After that, you see the subject repeated below in the alto at the fifth of the mode, without a previous rest since this entrance is accomplished by skip—whereas the soprano follows here earlier than before,* namely when the subject has reached its third measure, while the alto moves freely. After the subject is finished in the soprano and after a short continuation in both parts, you see the second cadence formed at the third of the mode. Finally, you find the subject taken up in the alto and the subject also introduced immediately in the next measure by the soprano and then the end formed by the cadence on the final of the mode. If you follow this simple example and apply it to the other modes, you need have no doubt that you will gradually acquire a fuller mastery of fugue.

Josephus. I see that in this fugue sharps and flats are used, notwithstanding the rule that they should not be employed in the diatonic system.

Aloysius. Those rules are to be understood for the themes, where only natural half-tone steps are to be used, without sharps or flats, so

---

* Fux adopts the practice of the Renaissance masters which generously admits rhythmic changes in imitative entrances. Later theorists held more strictly to the rule of rhythmic imitation (cf. Albrechtsberger's comment below Example 199).

that the nature and characteristics of the modes may be realized. It is different in the free continuation of the composition where the use of sharps and flats is not only allowed but even needed in order to avoid the harsh relation of *mi* against *fa* which usually arises in the following manner:

Ex. 43

Now let us turn to the question you meant to ask before.

Josephus. In distinguishing fugue from imitation you said that in a fugue the part entering later could begin only on the fifth, octave, or unison. But afterwards, when you taught me how to write a fugue, you mentioned also the fourth.

Aloysius. In the first instance we were reckoning from the fundamental tone,

Ex. 44

with which the fourth actually is not formed. In the second instance, however, the fundamental tone does not appear, and we are reckoning from the part above.

Ex. 45

Yet, even in this case the tone a could be called the fifth because the fundamental tone **d** is to be understood below it. Thus, in the following example the second part is to be judged as entering at the fifth.

Ex. 46

Josephus. How does it happen that the note values of the theme are somewhat changed at the end of the fugue?

Aloysius. I should like to say not only that it is permissible to tie the otherwise free notes at times but also that this lends to the composition a particular charm. Such a division may even be necessary where several parts using the subject and entering closely one after the other cannot otherwise be combined. Now try to take up the next mode yourself. Choose a subject suited to this and no other mode, and try to write a fugue using the preceding example as a model. Observe, however, the following difference: In the mode we used before, and in all other modes, the first cadence was formed at the fifth, whereas in this mode it has to be formed at the sixth. With the addition of a third voice, which would require the major third, the progression would otherwise become too alien to the mode, and the bad relation of *mi* against *fa*, arising from the combination with f, bound to follow soon afterward, would offend the ear. See the example:

Ex. 47

Now that all you need seems to have been discussed, you should be ready to go to work.

Josephus. Let me ask you again, Master, not to be displeased if I do not succeed in this first attempt.

Aloysius. Have no fear. You know that I shall be patient and that I am aware of the difficulties this study presents to the novice.

Ex. 48 Fugue in E

Josephus. I was sure that this subject would not be suited to any other mode in the diatonic system, and I am anxious to know from you if its treatment is satisfactory.

Aloysius. In inventing your subject you have shown excellent judgment, Josephus, and in treating it, such skill as could hardly be expected from a student; you give promise of extraordinary progress in this art. Now go ahead to the mode of F and to the remaining modes.

Ex. 49 Fugue in F

Ex. 50 Fugue in G

Josephus. I was somewhat hesitant in writing the second cadence, wondering whether it should be done in this or in the following manner:

Ex. 51

Aloysius. This cadence, which requires two sharps, or even three if a third part is added, departs too much from the natural tones of the mode. It would be more suitable for one of the transposed modes, of which we shall speak later. The cadence using the seventh and sixth, which you wrote, is therefore correct. Now let us go ahead to the mode of A, the fifth in the order we have adopted. Since this mode differs somewhat from the others, I shall give you an example for it.

Ex. 52

Josephus. I understand why you used a skip in the second part, going from the first note to the second note. The effect of *fa* on the second note * could not have been expressed otherwise. But I do not

---

* I.e., the half-tone step from the second note to the third.

know why, after the first cadence, you resumed the subject on the tone b *mi,* an entrance that does not seem properly suited to the mode.

Aloysius. It was necessary since the lower part has the tone e. This tone excludes the possibility of an entrance on a, which would be dissonant with the e below. Yet such a device will not detract from the quality of the composition. On the contrary, it contributes to it if it occurs in the middle of the fugue, because the formation of the subject becomes more nearly consistent through such an adjustment. It is different in the beginning of a fugue, where the character of the mode and the requirement of choosing the proper tone for the entrance of the subject, of which we have spoken before, must be observed strictly.

Josephus. I find great difficulty in placing the entrances of the subject more and more closely together, and it seems to me that subjects will have to be specially chosen with this in mind.

Aloysius. That is right. We have to try out the subjects first and examine their possibilities for such treatment. Therefore we shall have to think carefully before making a definite choice.

As for the rest, you will perhaps hear some people ridicule and criticize these subjects as being too simple and unimaginative. I do not want to deny that, in a way, this is true. But we are concerned here, not with the finesse of invention, but rather with the true nature of the modes of the diatonic system—a system that has narrow limits indeed. Greater opportunity to let our thoughts run free and capture more interesting themes will arise when we admit the use of the mixed system, of which we have spoken at length in the first part of this work. Now go ahead to the last mode, C.

Ex. 53

This work may serve as a general outline and may be understood as the vestibule through which entrance to fugal art may be gained. Just as the art of painting cannot be acquired without a thorough study of drawing, so it is necessary, for a full mastery of fugue, to do many exercises according to this prescribed form, which I should like to recommend to you to be taken up again and again.

Josephus. It seems to me that the diatonic system offers too few and inadequate possibilities and therefore leads necessarily to poor invention.

Aloysius. Doubtless it is more limited than the mixed system and does not open such a wide field for the imagination, but since it is best suited for learning the nature and characteristics of the modes, it becomes indispensable for acquiring the ability to write in a pure, unaccompanied style. Actually it is quite stimulating, since it offers a good deal of variety through the necessity of inventing different kinds of subjects. Let us leave the further study of two-part writing to your own work and proceed to fugues in three parts.

Fugues in Three Parts

Aloysius. I assume that you know the principles of three-part writing—with or without cantus firmus—from what has been said before.* The most important consideration in dealing with three parts is to obtain perfect triads. Now we shall have to see what plan should be followed and what practices should be observed in writing a three-part fugue. What has been said about two-part fugue applies here up to the point where the third part is to enter. This entrance

---

* In his introduction to three-part counterpoint, Fux stresses the fact that "three-part composition is the most perfect of all" because it admits complete triads, the addition of more voices merely resulting in doublings.

should occur when the subject has appeared in the two other parts, either with or without a short free continuation, whatever the nature of the parts admits or demands, and whatever the careful judgment of the composer dictates. In order that the introduction of the third part will not seem indistinct or lacking a full harmonic sound, we must try to accomplish it by a perfect triad or by a tied dissonance (which is an even better solution).*

Josephus. Which of the two preceding parts should the third part follow, insofar as the interval on which the entrance occurs is concerned?

Aloysius. As a rule, it should follow the one in which the subject first appeared. This will assure greater variety—a very important consideration. Yet, if the arrangement of the part seems to suggest the entrance at another interval, you may follow your own judgment and make the necessary adjustment to the rule.

Josephus. Is a similar change possible in using the cadences that you mentioned in the discussion of two-part writing?

Aloysius. By no means. In fact we should avoid any formal or perfect cadence (a cadence requiring a major third †) that cannot be made to coincide with a thematic entrance. On the other hand, if there is a possibility of introducing the subject, not only the fifth or third but also any other interval not leading too far away from the mode can serve for both perfect and deceptive cadences.

Josephus. What, Kind Master, do you mean by a deceptive cadence?

Aloysius. You know that the formal or perfect cadence leads from a major third into an octave. The deceptive cadence uses a minor third instead of a major third and, avoiding the full close which the ear expects, deceives the listener. For this reason it has been named *inganno*—deception—by the Italians.

Ex. 54 Perfect cadence   Deceptive cadence   Deceptive cadence

* The tied dissonance is characterized as "one of the chief excellences of composition" by Fux, because it enhances the following consonance and distinguishes the voice movements (*Steps to Parnassus: The Study of Counterpoint*, p. 102). Fux recommends its use again at the end of this discussion.

† The leading tone.

The perfect cadence can also be avoided by keeping the major third in the upper part and letting the lower part abandon the octave and assume another consonance.

Ex. 55

This can be done much better with a larger number of voices.

Ex. 56 In three voices   In four voices

Let us see how a perfect cadence can be used even at an unusual interval when a thematic entrance occurs, as in the following use of our theme:

Ex. 57

This example shows that the perfect cadence can occur on the first note of the theme and illustrates how the other parts should be handled. Now let us see the cadence on the second note of the theme.

Ex. 58

So much for the perfect cadence in thematic entrances. Now I shall show you how the perfect cadences that we have seen in thematic entrances should be avoided. This can be done with the help of the lowest part, even if the major third is used. Let us take the subject that we used for our first two-part fugue.

Ex. 59

Josephus. Why did you admit the frequent use of cadences in two-part writing, yet restrict their use here in three-part writing?

Aloysius. You will realize that the cadences we used in two-part writing were essentially different from perfect cadences. They were formed with the resolution of a seventh to a sixth or of a second to a third and did not produce the effect of complete rest. If we follow this thought further, we shall see that the cadences formed with the resolution of the seventh to the sixth or of the second to the third might be regarded as preparatory to full cadences, rather than as full cadences in themselves, for full cadences are actually formed with the addition of a third part, though without any other change.

Ex. 60

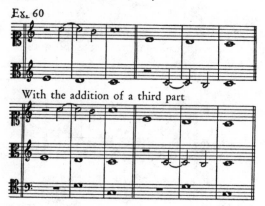

With the addition of a third part

Josephus. I hope, Dear Master, that you will not mind my numerous little questions, which must seem quite annoying to you.

Aloysius. Not at all. I am anxious to see removed the stumbling block that I know has proved disastrous to so many masters of this art.

Josephus. Why should a perfect cadence be acceptable when there is a thematic entrance, yet be avoided when there is none?

Aloysius. The perfect cadence conveys complete rest. For this reason it should be used only at the very end or whenever a section of the work is ended and a new subject assumed. If, on the other hand, a thematic entrance appears together with the perfect cadence, this detracts from the feeling of rest, helps to maintain the continuous flow that should prevail in such a composition, and indicates that the end has not yet been reached.

Josephus. Now with this question solved, and with the knowledge of all that has been discussed, I believe I might be ready to begin writing three-part fugues.

Aloysius. Yes, you are. Yet I should like to show you first how the lowest part will have to be arranged if the other two parts descend by successive sevenths resolving to sixths, or by seconds resolving to thirds. This will greatly help your facility in writing.

Ex. 61

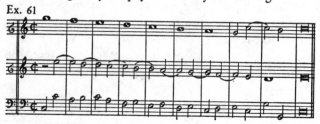

Ex. 62

These examples show how fifths and sixths may be used in direct succession * and, in the upper parts, how the sevenths must be resolved to sixths and the seconds to thirds. Similarly, fourths would have to be resolved to fifths. With the help of such passages you will find that writing will become easier in any voice, whether or not you are dealing with a thematic entrance, and that you will be in a better position to prepare the way for the entrance of the theme. Let us go ahead, then, take the subjects that we have used before in two-part writing, and treat them in three voices. I shall give you the first example, which you may follow in the other modes.

Ex. 63 Fugue in D for three voices

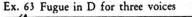

---

* The only two consonances that allow conjunct motion in the setting of two notes against one. With the use of these two intervals, the moving voice is therefore not committed to the resolution of a dissonance; it is free to enter and continue in any direction and to pursue an independent course. Fux recommends this use of fifth and sixth again in the discussion of the following example.

There is no difference between the beginning of this fugue and that in two voices up to the entrance of the third part, where the upper voices are written in counterpoint and adapted in a singable manner to the theme. The alto then repeats the theme, entering at an interval other than the one used at its first entrance, while the lowest part moves freely. During this time the soprano pauses and prepares for its new entrance, which follows at an interval other than the one this part used before. This entrance occurs on a strong dissonance, which helps to point out the presence of the theme, and a final cadence is avoided through the use of a minor sixth. Observe that the alto pauses for three measures as soon as it has presented the subject. This happens for two reasons: The soprano has come so close to the lowest part that between them there would not be enough space for the alto; and the alto is to re-enter shortly with the theme. I should also like to mention that this alto entrance occurs while the intervals of fifth and sixth are used, for this manner of entrance strengthens the writing considerably. Notice furthermore the entrance of the tenor soon after this, and the melodic lines above it.

Josephus. This entrance of the tenor does not seem to be written according to the prescribed manner, for it is accomplished neither by a complete triad nor by a tied dissonance but only through a combination of a sixth and an octave.

Aloysius. I am extremely happy to see that nothing escapes you. But you must realize that in writing this entrance we followed our own choice rather than rules. Besides, the first note of the theme carries here much less weight since it is only a half note, and the sixth above it is in itself strong and easily heard. Thus it marks the beginning of the theme clearly and makes up for the incomplete chord. Does this answer your question fully?

Josephus. It does indeed.

Aloysius. Let us go ahead with our discussion of this fugue. Notice the accompanying lines above this thematic entrance and their continuation, which, as you see, leads the upper parts to a cadence in F. The effect of this cadence is lessened, however, through the thematic entrance of the tenor immediately after the rests. Then, with a slight change of the note values, so that each part may enter with the subject in successive measures, the fugue is ended with a final cadence.

Josephus. From your example and from what has been said, I gather that a rest should never be used unless it is immediately followed by an entrance of the theme.

Aloysius. Yes, it is necessary after a rest to introduce either the old subject or some new subject, which must then be taken up also by the other parts, if you do not want to make yourself open to the reproving words of the gospel of St. Matthew (22:12): "Friend, how camest thou in hither not having a wedding garment?"

Now try your hand at the mode of E and write a three-part fugue in this or a similar manner. Do not hesitate to form a cadence at any interval as long as there is an opportunity of introducing the subject at the same time. It will be helpful for your work if you have an example of the final cadence in this mode before you start, since it is different from those in other modes.

Ex. 64

Ex. 65   Fugue in E for three voices

Josephus. Not without concern, Esteemed Master, do I submit this fugue to you, for I am afraid that you will find more cadences on the tone a than should be used.

Aloysius. Do not worry, Josephus, I shall certainly not reprove you. You have shown surprising skill for a novice in handling your theme and adapting your writing to the mode. As for frequent cadences on the tone a, they were caused by the nature of the theme. Yet this does not impair the effect of variety, because the cadences appear changed in every instance with the use of different tones. And if there seems to be a certain lack of agility and progress in the composition, this must be attributed to the restrictions of the diatonic system and especially to the inflexibility of this mode. I want to commend you, however, for your fine melodic writing, in which each voice, unhindered by the others, moves with perfect ease. Now go ahead to the mode of F and to the remaining modes.

Ex. 66 Fugue in F for three voices

Josephus. I am tempted to flatter myself that this fugue turned out quite well, unless you find fault with the melodic turn I combined with the subject at its second entrance in the upper voice.

Aloysius. On the contrary, I feel that this device is very ingeniously used. As long as all elements of the composition are subject to the limitations of the diatonic system and of the mode, and have to follow a rather conventional course, it is obvious that any originality in the treatment of the theme can be achieved only through means of this kind. I am also glad to notice that the thematic entrances always occur at the right time and are accompanied according to the rules of counterpoint. Now go ahead to the mode of G.

Ex. 67   Fugue in G for three voices

Ex. 68 Fugue in A for three voices

Ex. 69 Fugue in C for three voices

Aloysius. I am gratified to see not only that you have made a start in this practical study of fugue, but that you have already made considerable progress, as is shown by your writing. All parts move beautifully, pause for the right time, and enter again at the right place. You seem to need nothing else in this field of composition except a little more facility, which you will acquire with time and practice. Take care, however, to make use of tied notes in one or another part as often as it is possible. It is astonishing how much advantage can be gained through this device throughout the course of the composition, since almost every part is distinguished from the others in its movement and becomes thus more easily comprehensible. This consideration holds not only here but in any style of composition. Finally, since triplicity expresses perfection, I should like to urge you to devote yourself to this study again and again so that you will realize how much help and facility it can afford you in writing for more than three voices. Now let us proceed to four-part writing.

Fugues in Four Parts

Aloysius. In an earlier section * we have fully discussed what the function of the fourth part is and what place it should occupy in the complete setting, all of which I am sure is sufficiently familiar to you. Now it will have to be explained how the fourth part in a fugue should join the other three parts. Although it seems as though it might be left to the good judgment of the composer to decide how the combination of voices will sound best and move with grace and variety, a rule is usually adopted by which the entrance of the soprano corresponds to that of the tenor and the entrance of the alto to that of the bass.

Now that you are dealing with a greater number of parts, you should take special care not to crowd them too closely together; otherwise one part might deprive another of the possibility of moving freely. Just as a person walking through a dense crowd would be pushed from left, right, and front, and would hardly manage to make his way through, so it happens in a composition where one voice stands in the way of another and has no space in which to unfold. Any possibility for a well-rounded sound would thus be lost. You will therefore have to be very careful to avoid this danger.

Josephus. What remedy would there be if such a situation were to arise unforeseen?

Aloysius. Either you would have to change the entire setting or place a rest in that part which could only be forced in, and later—whenever the opportunity arose—let it re-enter with the theme. But

* *Steps to Parnassus: The Study of Counterpoint,* Pt. III, ch. I.

preferably plan ahead so cautiously that you will not regret later
what you have set out to do. It is better not to infringe upon the laws,
for this will inevitably mean seeking a remedy after matters have
gone wrong. For this reason it is important when dealing with any
one voice to be aware of the others and not to allow some voices so
much space or opportunity to sound well that there is none left for
the others.

I shall now give you an example which you might study and imitate. The theme and other material of the first three-part fugue will
be used here up to the point where the fourth part enters.

Ex. 70

Josephus. There seems to be little difference between the writing in this and in the three-part fugue. I see the four parts are rarely combined, except at the end, for another part usually stops when the fourth part enters.

Aloysius. The similarity of which you speak results from the use of the same theme; and the fact that the theme is treated in this four-part fugue almost in the same manner in which it was treated in three voices is meant to make it easier for you to become familiar with four-part writing. It is for the same reason that I stressed the importance of three-part writing to you a short while ago. Do not be surprised that the four parts rarely appear together. Aside from what I said before, namely that we should not force a part where there is insufficient space, it is not required in four-part writing that there always be complete four-part chords. It is perfectly adequate if just three parts move while the fourth rests in order to resume the subject later. Then the four-part sound might be somewhat prolonged by following up the end of the theme with a melodic continuation of a few notes. I shall let you work out the subjects in the other modes in similar fashion.

Ex. 71

Johann Josef Fux

Ex. 72 Fugue in F for four voices

Aloysius. I believe that you have done enough work following this practical method, and your examples, which are ably written, seem to prove it. We might leave the remaining modes to you to take up by yourself and use the time to proceed to fugues with several themes. Since this cannot be done without a knowledge of double counterpoint, we shall have to discuss this first.

Double Counterpoint

Aloysius. The term double counterpoint designates an ingenious manner of composition, the parts of which may be interchanged so that, by inversion, what was an upper part becomes a lower part. This technique evidently receives its name from the fact that it produces a duality of melodic lines which are different in register but, except for their inversion, show no change. You will soon realize how exceedingly useful this contrapuntal device is in any kind of composition, especially in a fugue where several themes are to be combined. For this reason we shall discuss and explain it fully.

A number of species of this kind of composition are often mentioned, such as double counterpoint at the third, fourth, fifth, sixth, octave, tenth, twelfth, and so forth. Disregarding those that either are confined within too narrow a space, and therefore of little use, or are too close in character to others, we shall concern ourselves only with those that are more commonly used and of greater importance in composing. These are counterpoint at the octave, tenth, and twelfth, each of which admits the shifting of one of two parts from its original position to another, as long as the use of certain consonances and dissonances—depending on their particular characteristics—is avoided.

Before we begin to study these species of counterpoint, some preliminary remarks should be made. In using several subjects, it should be observed first of all that they must show different movement in order to be easily distinguished. This can be achieved through variety in note values—giving one subject larger and the other smaller values, so that the difference will be more clearly perceived and confusion will be avoided. Second, the subjects are to be so placed that they do not begin at the same time. Rather it is necessary that one of them enter later, after a number of rests. Third, they must not exceed the interval limits that will be prescribed below for each species of double counterpoint. If all of this is understood, let us make a beginning with the counterpoint at the octave, which is the easiest and most frequently used.

Double counterpoint at the octave is a kind of composition so arranged that the transposition of either of two parts to the higher or lower octave will result in a changed harmonic sound, though this still conforms to the rules of good writing. To make this possible, you must be sure, Josephus, that the fifth is avoided, that no progression by skip into the octave occurs, and that the writing is contained within the limits of the octave. The following table of numbers may serve to clarify these points and to show where the inversion will turn consonance into dissonance.

1	2	3	4	5	6	7	8
8	7	6	5	4	3	2	1

It is evident that the unison becomes an octave by inversion; that the inverted second becomes a seventh; that the third becomes a sixth;

the fifth, a fourth, and so on. From this it is easily understood why, in this species of counterpoint, the fifth is forbidden; by inversion, it would become a dissonance, namely a fourth.*

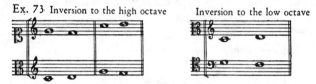

Ex. 73 Inversion to the high octave   Inversion to the low octave

With a tie, however, it can be used.

Ex. 74   Inversion

Josephus. I believe I have understood all that has been said so far. But it has not been explained why the progression by skip into an octave is forbidden and why the limits of the octave should not be exceeded. May I ask you, Venerable Master, to do this now. Since I have often heard this species of counterpoint mentioned with greatest praise, I am very anxious to see it used in some practical examples.

Aloysius. I shall explain without delay. The table of numbers given above makes it clear that the octave becomes a unison by inversion. The unison, however, should not be approached by skip, except in a final cadence, as has been mentioned before. See the example:

Ex. 75   Inversion

You will also do well to avoid the octave on a strong beat, since, by inversion, it will become a unison, which, as we have said, should

* Fux considers the fourth a dissonance whenever the lower of the two tones forming the interval serves at the same time as fundamental tone—which is invariably the case in two-part writing. This definition is adopted in all the theoretical discussions based on Fux—among them those by Haydn, Mozart, and Beethoven. The distinction between the fourth in two-part writing and in writing for more than two parts is founded on a tradition of contrapuntal theory reaching back to the thirteenth century (the English theorist Anonymous IV, *Couss. Script.*, I). On the other hand, theorists favoring vertical harmonic concepts, like Zarlino and Rameau, have considered the fourth always a consonance.

not be used except in a syncopation. The limits of the octave are not to be exceeded, because the function of double counterpoint is to produce a different harmonic sound through inversion. If, however, the limits of the octave are exceeded, the same harmonic sound will result, even though the compound consonances are changed to simple consonances, and inversion will result not in different but only in differently placed intervals:

Ex. 76

Here you see that the tenth, or compound third, becomes a simple third by inversion; the ninth, or compound second, becomes a simple second, and so forth. There is no difference between compound and simple intervals, however, except for that of register.

Josephus. Since I believe I have understood all you have said, I should like to ask you not to postpone the examples any longer.

Aloysius. Here, then, is the first example, which is subjected to the melodic line of a cantus firmus.

Ex. 77

An example without the restraint of a cantus firmus follows:

Ex. 78

Inversion

From these examples, we can gather that the inversion will infallibly work, and that it will by necessity work in accordance with the rules of good writing if all that has been mentioned is observed. In such an example as the first, the setting can even be read in three parts—the third part being added through the inversion of the counterpoint at the tenth below—provided that each downbeat is approached by contrary or oblique motion.

Ex. 79

Here the beginning of each measure is reached by contrary or oblique motion. For this reason the example can be turned into a three-part setting by transcribing the counterpoint note by note to the tenth below.

Ex. 80

Josephus. I am amazed at this device of counterpoint, and I am most anxious to learn how it is to be applied.

Aloysius. I shall do as you wish, although I had planned to discuss first the other species of double counterpoint. I shall take up the theme of the first fugue, in the first mode, and, combining it with a countersubject, shall show you how this can be carried through the entire fugue.

Ex. 81 Four-part fugue written with the use of a countersubject in double counterpoint at the octave

Here, then, is the use of double counterpoint and the practical example you wanted. Observe first that the countersubject begins after a half-measure rest at the unison in order to appear later, through the inversion of the subjects, at the octave, as may be seen at *1.*, *2.*, *3.*, *4.*, and *5.* The countersubject is used at times in the outer voices and at times in an inner voice, always answering the principal subject at the octave and always producing a new harmonic sound through the inversion.

Josephus. Where the *N.B.* is marked, the unison seems to be inverted to the fifteenth, not to the octave.

Aloysius. As we have said before, compound intervals are to be judged as simple intervals, insofar as their use here is concerned. For this reason a similar transposition is at times purposely used in order to give space to the middle parts.

Notice furthermore the play of the voices at *6.*, where the principal subject does not appear and, for the sake of variety, only the countersubject is used and led into a stretto passage.

Josephus. I am intrigued by this combination of the voices. But would it not have been possible to form this stretto passage and introduce the final cadence while using both themes?

Aloysius. It would have been possible if some of the note values had been changed, for example:

Ex. 82

Observe the *N.B.* Here, instead of two whole notes, appear two quarters which normally could not have been used. This makes it possible for the tenor and the bass to enter when the theme has reached its third measure. A change of note values applied for this reason is not only permissible but will be considered much to the composer's credit. Such flexibility should be accepted for the sake of double counterpoint, since this technique, applied to suitable themes, is of such considerable help in the writing of fugues. It is now your task, Josephus, to take up in the same manner the fugues in the remaining modes. For the sake of variety, however, the countersubject should not always be introduced in this particular way, namely during the first measure of the principal subject. According to the nature of this subject, the countersubject might enter in the second or third measure. You will see this in the following beginning of a fugue in the second mode, which you may complete.

Ex. 83

I should like you to bring to me this fugue and fugues in the other modes written out with the use of properly invented countersubjects.

Josephus. Is there nothing else that should be especially observed in this kind of composition?

Aloysius. Whatever else there is may be gathered from what has been said about the simple fugues and about the general rules of counterpoint. Particular attention should be paid, however, to the manner in which the melodic line is to be adapted to each mode owing to the varying positions of the half-tone steps, as I imagine you know from what has been said on several earlier occasions. Now let us leave this species of counterpoint, and, assigning the practice in the other modes for your work at home, let us proceed to the discussion of double counterpoint at the tenth.

Double Counterpoint at the Tenth

Aloysius. You can gather from what has been said before that double counterpoint as such comprises several species, the differences among which arise from the various transpositions of the parts. The first species, namely double counterpoint at the octave, has been sufficiently treated, I believe. We shall therefore turn to the second species, namely double counterpoint at the tenth. This species owes its name to the fact that it admits the transposition of either of two parts to the upper or lower tenth, without any change in the melodic line, if the use of certain consonances and dissonances is avoided. From the following table of numbers it may be seen which intervals are not to be used.

1	2	3	4	5	6	7	8	9	10
10	9	8	7	6	5	4	3	2	1

You will realize that two thirds or two tenths must not be used successively in direct motion, for by inversion the latter would result in two unisons, the former in two octaves. Similarly, the use of two sixths is forbidden, since their inversion at the tenth would produce two fifths. Furthermore, the tied fourth should be avoided in the upper part, for its inversion would effect a seventh—the use of which is not accepted, as has been explained before.* Finally, the limits of the tenth must not be exceeded. See the example, written upon the cantus firmus we have used before.

Ex. 84

Following is the transposition to the tenth with the cantus firmus remaining in the same place.

Ex. 85

The same result can be achieved by raising the cantus firmus a third and transposing the counterpoint to the lower octave, for the obvious reason that two whole-tone steps added to the octave amount to a tenth.

Ex. 86

This counterpoint may be sung in three parts if the cantus firmus is transcribed note by note to the tenth below and the other two parts remain as before.

Ex. 87

* In discussing the resolutions of tied dissonances that may be used in two-part counterpoint, Fux omits the resolution from the seventh to the octave and refers to "the model of the great masters. . . . There is hardly one among them who has used the seventh resolving in this way. . . ." (*Steps to Parnassus: The Study of Counterpoint*, p. 58.)

This can also be done with the first example of this species of counterpoint if the counterpoint is transcribed to the tenth below and the other two parts are left unchanged.

Ex. 88

Josephus. How amazing is this technique of counterpoint, in which transcribing one part makes a third part arise. But could any two-part setting be extended to three parts in this species?

Aloysius. Yes, if one observes carefully the rules of this species and the fact that each downbeat should be approached by either contrary or oblique motion, as in the preceding examples.

I shall give you now two examples written without the use of a cantus firmus so that you will not lack anything that may be needed for this species of counterpoint.

Ex. 89

If you transcribe the soprano part, note by note, to the lower tenth, you will have a three-part setting which is perfect in every respect.

Ex. 90

If you transcribe the soprano part of the following example to the lower octave and to the upper third, you will obtain an excellent three-part setting.

Ex. 91

I believe that this is all you need in order to write this kind of counterpoint, and I recommend that you practice these exercises until you find that you can write them with ease. Tell me if any doubts remain in your mind.

Josephus. It seems that in the first example, written on a cantus firmus, the limits of the mode are exceeded through the inversion at the beginning as well as at the end.

Aloysius. They are, though the example turns to a mode that is not too alien to the original mode. The present examples, however, are given, not for practical use, but only in order to illustrate the inversion. It is by no means necessary to apply the inversion immediately at the beginning and to use it consistently to the end, but it may appear whenever the opportunity arises and the judgment of the composer so decides. As a rule, this will be after the introduction of the principal subject, which should be well suited to the mode, and of a countersubject that can be inverted to the tenth. I shall illustrate this shortly in a fugue that may serve as an example. If, however, the inversion is to be used in the beginning of the composition, the first or third degree of the mode should be used for the opening. In this case, the inverted part will remain within the limits of the mode, as the preceding examples, written without the use of a cantus firmus, show.

Josephus. If this kind of counterpoint were applied to four-part writing, how would the fourth part have to be treated?

Aloysius. The fourth part could move freely, or rest, or enter with the subject either in contrary motion or in some other permissible manner. I shall show you one way in which our earlier example could be extended to four parts:

Ex. 92

Now let us see how this species of counterpoint can be used in practical composition. I shall do this, taking up again the subject in the first mode that we have used for the simple fugues and other examples.

Ex. 93

Josephus. Please do not hold it against me, Venerable Master, if I interrupt you at this point.

Aloysius. By all means go ahead.

Josephus. It seems that this countersubject lends itself to inversion at the octave. Should it therefore not be used for double counterpoint at the octave?

Aloysius. You judge wrong if you think that the subject does not apply here because it can be inverted to the octave. You should know from the last example of double counterpoint at the octave and from the last examples of this species that those two species, namely counterpoint at the octave and counterpoint at the tenth, may very well be combined. Before we go further, I shall show you that the theme in question can also be inverted to the tenth.

Ex. 94

Here you see that the alto accompanies the countersubject in the bass at the distance of a tenth throughout, thus completing a three-part setting. The same effect would result if the countersubject were transposed to the upper octave and read a third lower, according to the characteristic of this species of counterpoint.

Ex. 95

Josephus. I am very grateful to you, Master, for reminding me of what has been said before and for answering my questions with new examples. I should like you to return now to the same fugue and to continue it in the manner in which it was begun.

Ex. 96

Aloysius. Here you have a short fugue which is to be taken rather as an illustration of double counterpoint at the tenth than as an example of elaborate fugal writing. You may follow this model in the other five modes, using the themes of the simple fugues as they appeared in the different modes. Meanwhile, examine all the instances where the inversions appear in this fugue and tell me if there is anything you do not understand.

Josephus. The measures marked by *Nos. 1, 2,* and *3* do not seem to be properly adapted to the nature of double counterpoint at the tenth since the countersubjects are not spaced at the distance of a tenth, as this species of counterpoint requires, but at the distance of a third or a sixth.

Aloysius. This does not alter the fact that those passages are in accordance with the principles of this species of counterpoint, for if they were arranged in the following manner, they would obviously adhere strictly to its rules.

Ex. 97

Since, however, the tenor, at *No. 1,* and the alto at *No. 2,* could not reach the tenth, it was necessary to move those parts down to the third. The passage at *No. 3* is meant to serve better the consideration of a closer connection between the voices, and the same holds for the passage at *No. 6.* What are your questions at *Nos. 4* and *5?*

Josephus. I remember that you said on another occasion that a rest should be followed by an entrance of the theme—a rule that does not seem to be observed in these instances.

Aloysius. It is true that I said the subject should reappear. Yet this may occur either by direct or by inverted entrance. You will realize that the countersubject is at this point used in opposite or inverted motion. This device is not only permissible, but also it adds a considerable amount of variety to the composition.*

As for the rest, I should like to remind you that a great deal depends upon the composer's good judgment in this kind of composition. Aside from what has to be observed for this species of counterpoint, the parts should always be so arranged that they do not

---

* This is the first instance in which Fux uses the term inversion in the melodic sense rather than in the harmonic sense in which it has appeared throughout the discussion of double counterpoint. An extended discussion of melodic inversion follows in the next section.

exceed the limits of the five lines * or that they do not otherwise
deprive the composition of a well-rounded harmonic sound.

Double Counterpoint at the Twelfth

Aloysius. Double counterpoint at the twelfth is a kind of composition so arranged that one of two or more parts may be transposed
to the upper or lower twelfth. The following series of numbers will
make clear which intervals may be used and which should be
avoided.

1	2	3	4	5	6	7	8	9	10	11	12
12	11	10	9	8	7	6	5	4	3	2	1

This table shows that all intervals except the sixth and the seventh
resolving to the sixth may be used and that the twelfth should not
be exceeded. Since this kind of counterpoint can be read variously
in two, three, or even four parts, each possibility should be separately discussed.

First, double counterpoint at the twelfth in two parts: For this
kind of counterpoint nothing need be noted besides what has been
mentioned before, namely that the sixth and the seventh resolving
to the sixth should not be used. Any other kind of progression, in
direct, contrary, or oblique motion, may be used. See the example
written on a cantus firmus.

Ex. 98

* With the restriction to the five lines, Fux suggests the range of the human voice
as norm for the range to be observed in writing, for the old clefs place the limits of
the vocal ranges so that they coincide with those of the staves. Cf. *Steps to Parnassus:
The Study of Counterpoint,* p. 79.

Josephus. Why did you end the upper part on the fifth and not on the octave?

Aloysius. I did this so that when the counterpoint is transposed to the twelfth, it may end more properly according to the mode, although it would not conflict with the nature of double counterpoint if a transposed part were to move outside the mode. Now transpose the counterpoint written in the soprano part to the lower twelfth without changing the position of the cantus firmus. Use a b♭ wherever it may be needed so that all intervals will correspond to those of the original counterpoint.

Ex. 99

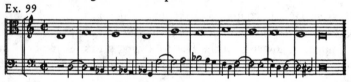

This transposition is correct, although it could also have been achieved by transposing the counterpoint to the lower octave and the cantus firmus to the upper fifth, as in the following example:

Ex. 100

Josephus. This transposition seems to change the setting to an entirely different mode.

Aloysius. Aside from what I have mentioned before, namely that this kind of counterpoint is allowed such liberty, and aside from the fact that the tone a constitutes an interval quite proper to the mode of D, I should like to say that in practical composition for several parts, it will always be possible to form a final cadence suitable to the mode by continuing a melodic line which may provide the ending after the cantus firmus is finished:

Ex. 101

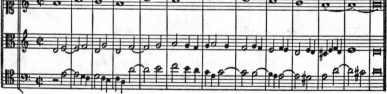

Here follows an example of double counterpoint at the twelfth which may be turned into a three-part setting through the transposition of the counterpoint to the tenth:

Ex. 102

Leaving the cantus firmus in place, transpose the counterpoint to the lower twelfth and then again to the upper tenth, and a three-part setting will result:

Ex. 103

Josephus. What should be observed in this species of counterpoint so that a two-part setting may be extended to three parts?

Aloysius. In addition to observing the other rules for this kind of counterpoint, one must write a fifth at the beginning and the end, so that the part which is transposed to the twelfth may stay within the limits of the mode. All progressions should occur by contrary or oblique motion, and dissonant ties should be avoided. In this way it is possible to obtain a three-part setting.

Josephus. Some of the progressions in these examples seem to sound harsh.

Aloysius. That is true. Yet this is almost invariably so in the case of modes containing the minor third. The transposition of the parts and the inflexibility of the cantus firmus are bound, through the relation of *mi* against *fa*, to result in less graceful melodic writing, which nevertheless may be tolerated because of both the principle of cantus firmus and the modal system. It is different in free composition wherein there is no restraint of the cantus firmus:

Ex. 104 In two parts

By transposing the parts, one can turn this example into a three-part setting in the manner shown in the previous example.

Ex. 105 In three parts

I should like to remind you that when first discussing this species of counterpoint, we said it would necessarily exclude the use of the sixth. This restriction refers to the sixth used independently, not tied. The tied sixth can indeed be used, as in the following example.

Ex. 106

Transposition to the lower twelfth

Now that the three species of double counterpoint have been treated separately, I shall show you in a special example how they may be combined in settings of either two, three, or four parts, in each case producing a new harmonic sound. First, an example of double counterpoint at the twelfth in two parts:

Ex 107 In two parts

An example with the soprano part transposed to the lower twelfth:

Ex. 108 In two parts

An example with the soprano part transposed to the lower tenth:

Ex. 109 In three parts

If the part that is transposed to the lower tenth is raised an octave, the three-part setting will result in a somewhat altered harmonic sound.

Ex. 110 In three parts

Ex. 111   Another version in three parts

Ex. 112   Another version in three parts

Ex. 113   Another version in three parts

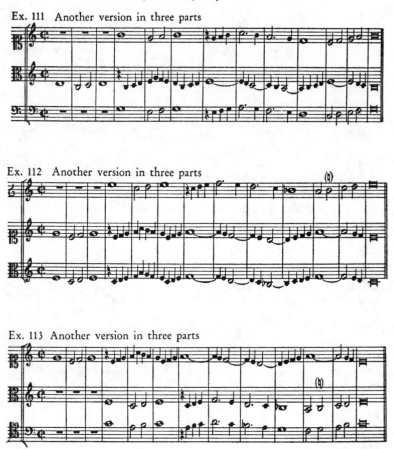

Josephus. Please, Venerable Master, how long will you continue varying this example?

Aloysius. I only want to show you how rich and full of possibilities is the technique of double counterpoint, and what remarkable variety it allows. This multiformity becomes possible if the counterpoint at the twelfth is formed almost entirely by fifths and octaves, preferably introduced in contrary motion, and thirds, introduced by oblique motion. Thus a counterpoint at the octave as well as a counterpoint at the tenth can be derived from the counterpoint at the twelfth, admitting an even greater variety.

Ex, 114 An example of double counterpoint
at the octave in two parts

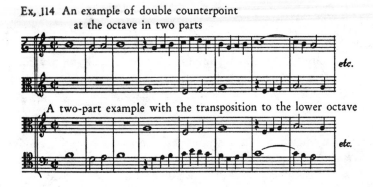

A two-part example with the transposition to the lower octave

Finally, if you let the soprano and the tenor enter together in tenths
and the transposed soprano and bass enter together in tenths, you
will obtain a perfect four-part setting.

Ex. 115 In four parts

Ex. 116 Another version in four parts

You see then, Josephus, that this kind of counterpoint is especially important because it makes it possible to derive three- or four-part settings from two parts, providing they are properly arranged. If you are impressed by this technique, bear in mind how rewarding is the effort spent on its study.

Josephus. I shall try my utmost to master this amazing art. Its usefulness and variety, and above all a great love for this study, spur me on.

Aloysius. Such interest, Josephus, can be the only real incentive to take up and master this work. As I have told you before, your work would become tedious and meaningless if it were based on the ambition for fame or wealth.

Here I must not fail to mention the possibility of applying melodic inversion to any setting that is free of dissonant ties.* This manner of inversion appears in two forms, namely simple and strict. Simple or free inversion arises when the note progressions are merely turned in the opposite direction so that what was ascending before is now descending, without any regard for the position of half-tone steps. See the example on the subject we have used before.

Ex. 117 Original version   Simply inverted version

Strict inversion arises if the progression of notes is so inverted that the relation of *mi* to *fa* † is always retained. The following succession of notes will show you how this is to be arranged.

Ex. 118

If you compare the notes of the ascending scale on the left with those of the descending scale on the right, you will find that the d remains d by inversion, e is inverted to c, f to b, and g to a, as may be seen from the example written on the same subject we used before.‡

---

* Dissonant syncopations cannot be subject to inversion because they "should always resolve descending" (*Steps to Parnassus: The Study of Counterpoint*, p. 56).
† The half-tone relation.
‡ The Dorian scale serves as guide for strict inversion because it is the only diatonic scale which shows an unchanged sequence of whole- and half-tone steps in ascending or descending direction. Cf. Marpurg's explanation for the strict inversion of major and minor scales, pp. 146 ff., below.

Ex. 119 Original version   Strictly inverted version

In order that this strict inversion to the opposite direction may become more clear to you, I shall invert the third of the three-part settings given above—thus dealing no further with simple inversion, since that technique is less difficult and less important.

Ex. 120   Three-part example in strict inversion

Josephus. This inversion is truly amazing. Could any setting without exception be inverted in this manner?

Aloysius. Only those that contain no dissonant ties, as I mentioned before. Since, however, the transposition and inversion turn out well at times and less well at others, according to the nature of the theme and the mode, a great deal of care and judgment is needed in using them; for one might easily damage the anticipated agreeable sound of a composition in the intention to show special artifice and skill. This might apply to some extent in the following fugue which is to be taken as an illustration of double counterpoint at the twelfth rather than as an example of perfect writing.

Ex. 121

I do not believe that further explanation is needed as to how the transposition of the parts and the interchange of themes are arranged in this fugue. I am sure that you know this from all that has been said and from the numerous examples that have been given.

This is what I felt should be discussed about double counterpoint; surely it is not necessary to stress and recommend to you again its great advantages. For what possibility other than the use of double counterpoint would there be of working with several subjects which may be freely interchanged? Without this complex treatment of the subjects, however, a composition—especially a sacred work which is written *a cappella*—will be entirely bare and void of distinction.

Josephus. I have been disappointed in the hope that you would show me how to combine and interchange the original and inverted versions of a theme.

Aloysius. I should have done this indeed if the nature of the subject had admitted it and if the entire composition had gained by this device. It is more likely to be possible if one can choose a theme with these facts in mind so that it can easily be used in inversion, as I shall show you presently with an example. First, however, I shall have to explain how a fugue or imitation can be combined with a cantus firmus and carried through its entire course:

Ex. 122

Josephus. Great Heavens! I am stunned by the amazing skill with which this example is composed. When I consider the extent of this art, I almost lose my courage in striving for a similar accomplishment. How, if I may ask, did you manage to write such a large number of entrances of the first theme through the entire course of the cantus firmus?

Aloysius. Your amazement is not unjustified, Josephus. We are dealing with a task that is difficult, though not as difficult as it may seem to you at the moment. If you keep in mind what has been said so far and if you go over all our lessons again, it will not be hard for you to achieve something similar. It will be necessary, however, to examine carefully all measures of the cantus firmus before deciding on the subject with which it is to be combined, for you must determine whether or not these measures—or the majority of them—will admit the use of the subject either in original or inverted form. Besides, the rules of melodic writing and of good part writing should be observed.

There is even the possibility of choosing a subject more or less directly from the notes of the cantus firmus themselves, with some of the note values changed or syncopated:

Ex. 123

In this or a similar manner, a theme can be used together with a cantus firmus, according to the nature of this cantus firmus, and with due previous consideration as to what portions of the cantus firmus are best suited for thematic entrances.

So far I have kept you under the restriction of either a cantus firmus or a confining theme and within the limits of the diatonic system. I have bidden you take a rough and unpleasant road. Yet in no other way could you have achieved a perfect command of this art. The time has now come to let you leave the thankless demands of these species and enter a more pleasant field of study in which you will feel more richly rewarded.

You may now be guided by your own thoughts and decisions. Choose any subject of your invention, follow your own ideas, and proceed into the mixed system, which is not confined by such narrow limits as the diatonic system. Furthermore, you may use, at your own discretion, time signatures of all kinds—triple, quadruple, and those less generally used, smaller note values, irregular themes, and transposed modes.*

Josephus. I am delighted to be finally released from restrictions and free to discover what I can do with my own imagination. Before I go ahead, however, I should like to ask you to show me, as you promised a short while ago, how the original version of a theme may be combined with its strict inversion.

Aloysius. You remind me just in time. Not only do I want to follow your wish, but also I shall show you how to invert a subject beyond the limits of the diatonic system, and how to combine three different subjects in a composition.

First of all, let me say that for forming a strict inversion in the mixed system it is sufficient if the relation of *mi* to *fa,* and similarly the relation of *fa* to *mi,* is retained, without following the procedure that was mentioned above for the diatonic system:

Ex. 124

According to the rule given above for strict inversion in the diatonic system, the present theme would have to be inverted in this manner:

Ex. 125

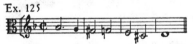

Yet the following manner of inversion is actually much better suited to the mode of this subject.

Ex. 126

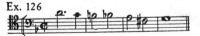

The beginning and end of this inversion stay within the limits of the mode. Following this principle, I shall give you the outline of a fugue:

---

* Fux explains later that by irregular themes he means those requiring various changes in a tonal answer. He adds a brief section presenting a choice of such themes in his chapter on modes. It is not included here, since it is covered in Marpurg's more extensive discussion of the tonal answer, which includes Fux's examples.

Ex. 127

If you alternate the original and inverted versions of the subject in this manner, you will achieve a good setting through the variety that is so essential for a pleasing sound. Notice furthermore the special device of using some smaller note values which makes it possible for the original and inverted versions of the theme to appear together. At times a composer will use only the original version until almost the middle of the piece, and not until then introduce the inverted theme. This is always left to individual judgment and decision.

Josephus. It seems that this fugue is not written in double counterpoint.

Aloysius. Indeed not, for I felt that we had treated that matter fully and sufficiently. What I wanted in this case was to illustrate how a theme might be combined with its inversion. The technique of double counterpoint, on the other hand, is the only means by which it is possible to enhance a composition through the use of several themes distinguished one from another both in character and in movement, as may be seen in the following example.

Ex. 128   Fugue with three subjects

This shows you how to arrange a fugue with three themes, the second of which is written in double counterpoint at the octave, and the third, in double counterpoint at the twelfth. It should be first observed that the subjects are so characterized in note values that through their movements they are easily distinguished. Second, wherever a subject is to appear at the twelfth, care should be exercised that the other parts do not form the interval of a sixth, for this would render the transposition to the twelfth impossible. Third, you will notice that a subject is not always used in its entirety and full length, either because of the entrance of another subject or in the interest of a well-balanced sound.

A composition of this sort with three subjects, however, almost requires a fifth part. This addition would make it possible to achieve greater variety, for there would be less necessity of having all voices constantly occupied, and it would afford each voice more time to rest.

Josephus. Then you will not say anything about writing for more than four voices?

Aloysius. I had indeed intended to include a chapter dealing with composition for more than four parts. Since I am interrupted by ill health, however, and confined to my bed, I can only continue later and write a special study on this subject, if Almighty God chooses to give me further life and renewed strength. With the help of this study you may then learn everything you will still need to know, even without your teacher's instruction. Yet, understand that to him who masters four parts, the path to composition with more than four voices is cleared; for as the number of voices increases, the rules may be less rigidly observed.

Farewell, and pray to God for me.

II

Friedrich Wilhelm Marpurg

Marpurg as Interpreter of Bach

Friedrich Wilhelm Marpurg's *Abhandlung von der Fuge* appeared at an auspicious moment in the history of music. It was prompted by the publication of Bach's *Art of Fugue*, which became available less than a year after Bach's death. When a second edition appeared in 1752, it contained an extensive introductory note by Marpurg, who had "agreed to furnish the esteemed heirs of the late Kapellmeister Bach with a preface to accompany the work." [1] It was hoped that the recommendation of the young theorist, who had just begun a promising career as a writer on music, might foster a more favorable reception than the work had found initially. The second edition, as we know, met with no more success than the first, and after a few years Bach's son Carl Philipp Emanuel decided to sell the plates "upon the first acceptable offer."

The manner in which Marpurg assumed his role as spokesman for the *Art of Fugue* gives him a singular place among the few contemporaries of Bach who recognized the importance of his work. In his preface Marpurg set forth a strong defense of contrapuntal writing—a defense exceedingly difficult to undertake at a time when fugue was considered "the child of ancient aberration." He admonished the composers of his day that only the art of counterpoint could

---

[1] The title *Die Kunst der Fuge* does not appear in Bach's manuscript. It was supplied at the time of publication of the first edition. (Quotations from Marpurg's preface are taken from the edition by Roy Harris and M. D. Herter Norton.)

save music from the "spreading rubbish of effeminate song" and "restore in some measure . . . the honor of Harmony"; and he added a point particularly suited to strengthen his argument: "To me, this work has given the occasion to examine more closely the nature of the fugue and . . . the decision to lay before the world for its consideration, at the earliest moment, my observations on the subject."

The first volume of Marpurg's treatise appeared a year later, with a dedication to Telemann, Bach's friend, and godfather to Carl Philipp Emanuel. The most highly celebrated master of the period, Telemann had proved in his works that the tradition of the old contrapuntal art could be adapted most successfully to modern tastes. Marpurg's second volume followed in 1754. In his dedication to Wilhelm Friedemann and Carl Philipp Emanuel Bach, he summarized the discussion begun in his preface to the *Art of Fugue* and his indebtedness to Bach's work: "I take the liberty of laying before Your Honors the principles of an art which owes its improvement particularly to the excellent efforts of your famous father. . . ."

In taking Bach's work as a point of departure, Marpurg introduces a decisive turn in the theory of fugue. Although his example was followed by a host of eminent theorists, his writing commands an authority that none of his successors could match. Not only was he the first to formulate a number of important principles about Bach's fugal style, but he had had the opportunity of discussing matters of fugal technique with Bach himself.

The authoritative level of Marpurg's instruction is not consistently maintained, for his discussion of fugal writing is often guided by "the rules which in the meanwhile had been drawn up governing its construction," rather than by those derived from Bach. We have one document, however, which traces precepts given in Marpurg's work directly to Bach's remarks. In a letter to Mattheson, Marpurg mentions two particular points of fugal procedure in which his own opinion was "considerably confirmed" through a conversation with Bach.[2] He relates from this conversation Bach's strong criticism of some contemporary works, criticism of one example in which the composer "stuck continuously to his principal subject, without any change," and of another example in which the composer "had not shown enough fire to reanimate the theme by interludes." We can recognize this discussion with Bach in Marpurg's rules: "The melodic

[2] See H. T. David and A. Mendel, *The Bach Reader*, p. 257.

line of a theme should be so arranged that it will admit a number of changes in its accompaniment"; and, "If no episode precedes the cadence, one may introduce an episode rather than a thematic entrance on the cadence in order to increase the listener's anticipation of the new thematic entrance." [3] How delightfully refreshing it is, however, to find (in the same letter) Bach's own wording, which simply refers to the first example as "dry and wooden" and to the second as "pedantic."

Doubtless these are not the only instances in which Marpurg's writing was directly guided by Bach's words. Another rule which suggests a quotation from Bach is the one explaining the thorough examination to which a fugal theme ought to be subjected at the outset,[4] for it recalls a passage which C. P. E. Bach wrote about his father to J. N. Forkel: "When he listened to a rich and many-voiced fugue, he could soon say, after the first entries of the subjects, what contrapuntal devices it would be possible to apply, and which of them the composer by rights ought to apply, and on such occasions, when I was standing next to him, and he had voiced his surmises to me, he would joyfully nudge me when his expectations were fulfilled." [5]

To Marpurg, however, the matter of gathering this valuable information was only a preparation which aided him in his main purpose of drawing up a theory that would help to interpret the works of the "greatest fugue-maker of our time." The present translation contains Marpurg's discussion of the "characteristic elements" of fugal technique. This, the core of his theory, represents the first modern frame of reference for the principles and terminology of fugue.

His writing is, by circumstances and necessity, encyclopedic rather than didactic. Its true significance, however, lies in its origin. It is surprising to find Marpurg—fifty years before Forkel's biography of Bach—telling his contemporaries: "To be an excellent musician and not to appreciate the virtues of the late Bach is a contradiction." But even more important is the fact that Marpurg departs from the convictions of musical writers in the era of Enlightenment to the extent of devoting his efforts to that aspect of music which "had come to sound barbaric to the tender ears" of his time.

[3] See pp. 163, 179, below.
[4] See p. 191, below.
[5] See *The Bach Reader*, p. 277. C. P. E. Bach's letters were the most important source for Forkel's biography of Bach.

From *Abhandlung von der Fuge*

Imitation and Fugue in General

· 1 ·

The restatement of a subject by use of the same tones in the same part is called repetition.

Ex. 129

The restatement of a subject by use of different tones in the same part is called transposition.

Ex. 130

The restatement of a subject through repetition or transposition in different parts is called imitation.

These three terms are often confused. Their essential differences, however, will become clear from the above explanations and the examples accompanying them.

· 2 ·

All voices in which imitation may occur are arranged in four main registers, regardless of the number of voices a composition may have. These four registers are bass, tenor, alto, and soprano. If a composition has more than four voices, the additional voices will be designated by use of numbers, according to the register to which their range is suited: In a composition for several high voices, the highest will be the first soprano, and others, the second soprano, third soprano, and so on. The same applies to the other registers. All voices of the same register use the same clef. The different voices are also at times distinguished by choirs, such as the soprano of the first choir, the soprano of the second choir.

· 3 ·

The alternating use of one subject in various parts may occur not only at the unison but also at all other intervals. Hence there are eight general species of imitation:

1) Imitation at the unison—*imitatio homophona* or *in unisono*.

Ex. 131

2) Imitation at the upper or lower second—*imitatio in secunda superiori* or *inferiori*.

Ex. 132

3) Imitation at the upper or lower third—*imitatio in hyperditono* or *in hypoditono*.

Ex. 133

We might anticipate here that the prefix *epi-* may be used interchangeably with the prefix *hyper-* in this and the following cases. Thus *hypoditonus* means the lower third, whereas *hyperditonus* or *epiditonus* means the upper third.

4) Imitation at the upper or lower fourth—*in hyperdiatessaron* or *in hypodiatessaron*.

Ex. 134

5) Imitation at the upper or lower fifth—*in hyperdiapente* or *in hypodiapente*.

Ex. 135

6) Imitation at the upper or lower sixth—*in hexachordo superiori* or *inferiori.*

Ex. 136

7) Imitation at the upper or lower seventh—*in heptachordo superiori* or *inferiori.*

Ex. 137

8) Imitation at the upper or lower octave—*in hyperdiapason* or *in hypodiapason.*

Ex. 138 *   J. D. Leuthard

* Johann Daniel Leuthard was born in 1706. He served as violinist and composer at the courts of Weimar and Rudolstadt and published several keyboard works.

NOTES

1) If the intervals of the second, third, fourth, are transposed an octave up or down, imitation at the ninth, tenth, eleventh, will result.

2) It is easily seen that imitation at the upper second and at the lower seventh, and imitation at the lower second and at the upper seventh, are, for practical purposes, the same. This holds also for imitation at the lower third and at the upper sixth, imitation at the upper fourth and at the lower fifth, and imitation at the lower fourth and at the upper fifth, and so forth.

· 4 ·

Whatever interval is used, imitation will occur either in similar or dissimilar motion. These terms are subject to different meanings, which should be explained. The study of counterpoint deals, in the elementary phases of composition, with three kinds of harmonic motion by which the succession of consonances and dissonances in two simultaneously moving parts is determined. These three kinds of motion are known as:

1) Direct or similar motion—*motus rectus*, in which the voices ascend or descend together by step or skip.
2) Indirect or dissimilar motion, usually called contrary motion— *motus contrarius*, in which the voices go against or away from each other.
3) Oblique motion—*motus obliquus*, in which one voice moves while the other remains stationary.

At present, however, we are not referring to similar or dissimilar motion of these kinds. The kind of motion considered here concerns two or more voices which are moving one after the other, and thus might be called melodic motion. In this sense, an imitation in similar motion—*imitatio aequalis motus*—is that kind of imitation in which one voice answers the other, using the same direction of interval progressions; an imitation in dissimilar or inverted motion—*imitatio inaequalis motus*—is that kind of imitation in which the ascending intervals in the preceding part become descending in the following part, or vice versa. There are two kinds of inverted imitation: strict and free. Free inversion occurs when the following part imitates the

intervals of the preceding part in inversion but does not retain the
arrangement of whole- and half-tone steps.

Ex. 139

Ex. 140

Strict inversion occurs when the whole- and half-tone steps in the
first part are followed in precisely the same order in the second part.

Ex. 141

Ex. 142

Such strict inversion is called *al contrario riverso* in Italian and and *contrarium stricte reversum* in Latin. Free inversion is simply called *al rovescio, alla riversa, contrarium simplex, motu contrario.* The interval at which an imitation in strict inversion should occur may be found in the following ways:

a) In major keys, an ascending scale on the first degree and a descending scale on the third degree should be placed against each other, for instance in C Major:

c	d	e	f	g	a	b	c
e	d	c	b	a	g	f	e

Thus, if in an imitation written in C Major the first part begins on g or f, the second part should follow on a or b.

b) In minor keys, an ascending scale on the first degree and a descending scale on the seventh degree are placed against each other, for instance in A Minor:

a	b	c	d	e	f	g	a
g	f	e	d	c	b	a	g

If in an imitation written in the key of A Minor, therefore, the first part begins on e or c, the second part should follow on c or e.

The scales of strict inversion quoted under (a) and (b) are arranged only for C Major and A Minor. Those for the other major and minor keys can easily be transposed and found according to the models given.

· 5 ·

Imitation does not always occur so that the part which follows repeats the melodic line of the opening part from beginning to end. It may use the melodic line from end to beginning, that is, in reverse direction. Such imitation is called retrograde imitation—*imitatio retrograda* or *cancrizans* or *per motum retrogradum.*

If this technique is combined with that of inversion, reverse imitation in inversion or inverted retrograde imitation occurs—*imitatio cancrizans motu contrario.*

Ex. 144

These two kinds of imitation are used for the most part in the fugue and the canon. Thus there are four kinds of melodic motion in imitation: (a) direct motion, (b) inverted motion, (c) retrograde motion, and (d) inverted retrograde motion.

· 6 ·

In some instances of imitation, the second part will follow the first part, using changed note values. If this occurs with increased note values, for example with notes twice the original value, so that eighth notes become quarters and quarters become half notes, it is called imitation in augmentation—*imitatio per augmentationem.*

If it occurs with decreased note values, for example with notes half their original value, so that half notes become quarters and quarters become eighth notes, it is called imitation in diminution—*imitatio per diminutionem.*

Ex. 145

Ex. 146

These two kinds of imitation, too, belong properly to the fugue and the canon. If the imitation occurs between three or four voices and each voice follows the preceding voice in proportionately increased or decreased note values, this is called imitation in double or triple augmentation or diminution—*imitatio per augmentationem* or *diminutionem duplicem, triplicem,* etc.

Ex. 147

Ex. 148

· 7 ·

Any imitation, regardless of its motion or changes in note values, may be interrupted by rests so that the melodic line of the answering part is intermittent. This is called interrupted imitation—*imitatio interrupta.*

Ex. 149 *   Johann Theile

* Johann Theile (1646–1724), a pupil of Heinrich Schütz, wrote the works for the opening of the first German opera house at Hamburg in 1678. His collections of polyphonic exercises and his influence as a teacher earned him the title of "father of German contrapuntists."

· 8 ·

If one of two parts written in imitation begins on a strong beat and the other on a weak beat, or vice versa, this is called imitation in contrary rhythm—*imitatio per arsin et thesin* or *in contrario tempore.*

Ex. 150

Ex. 151

Ex. 152

Ex. 153

· 9 ·

If the imitation is such that the voices may be interchanged, that is, the upper part may become the lower part, and vice versa, this is called imitation in double counterpoint or invertible imitation—*imitatio invertibilis*.

Ex. 154

A number of the examples given above can be so inverted, as the reader may discover. The technique of arranging such invertible imitation is treated in the study of double counterpoint.

· 10 ·

All the kinds of imitation which have been discussed are either periodic or canonic.

a) Periodic imitation—*imitatio periodica* or *partialis*—is that form of imitation in which the part which follows uses only a short portion of the opening part. This principle is followed in all examples quoted so far.

b) Canonic imitation—*imitatio canonica* or *totalis*—is that form of imitation in which the part which follows uses the melodic line of the opening part, note for note throughout.

Ex. 155 Rondeau   J. C. Pepusch

A composition of this kind is called a canonic fugue—*fuga canonica, totalis, universalis, mera, integra; fuga in conseguenza;* or simply a *canon.*

· 11 ·

Periodic imitation in all its kinds and species may be used in two ways:

a) Incidental periodic imitation, which, according to the judgment of the composer, may occur here and there in various instrumental and vocal compositions, such as solo sonatas, duets, trios, quartets, concertos, symphonies, cantatas, and arias.

b) Formal periodic imitation, which restricts the imitative use of a basic subject by certain rules to certain places. Such a composition, which is based on a definite theme imitatively developed in various voices under certain rules in a continuous, uninterrupted manner, is called a periodic fugue—*fuga periodica, partialis,* or *fracta.*

· 12 ·

Thus there are two major categories of fugues, namely canonic and periodic. This treatise encompasses both categories. We shall follow common usage, however, and call the canonic fugue simply canon and the periodic fugue, simply fugue.

NOTES

1) The term fugue, which Mattheson properly explains as a piece in which the voices answer each other, has been derived by some musical scholars from *fugare*, to chase—since one part chases the other, so to speak—and by others, from *fugere*, to flee—since one part flees from the other.

2) As a rule, a musical work is divided into either two or more sections. In the case of the fugue, such division does not apply, for the fugue should be continuous from beginning to end. Gigues written in the manner of a fugue are no exception to this rule. They consist of two sections, it is true. Yet, each section shows its own fugal treatment, one usually dealing with the original version of the theme and the other, with the inverted version. Actually, there are two fugues in such a case. The gigues by Graupner * and Kuhnau, to mention just these, prove this fact. In many other cases, gigues might be considered irregular fugues. These points concerning the gigue should therefore be included in our general explanations of the fugue.

· 13 ·

Since a fugue can be written with two, three, four, or more parts, we have to distinguish between two-part fugues, three-part fugues, four-part fugues, and fugues for more than four parts.

· 14 ·

In all fugues five characteristic elements are to be distinguished:
1) The first or opening statement, or the theme: *phonagogos* in

---

* Christoph Graupner (1683–1760) was a pupil of Johann Kuhnau and chosen as his successor in 1722. Only after Graupner and several other candidates had declined was the position offered to Bach. Several of Graupner's works are published in *DdT*, XXX and XLI–XLII.

Greek; *dux, thema, subjectum, vox antecedens* in Latin; *sujet* in French. All of these terms refer to the basic melodic line with which the fugue opens.

2) The answer or second statement: *comes, vox consequens* in Latin; *risposta* or *conseguenza* in Italian; *réponse* in French. These terms refer to the repetition of the opening melodic line as it appears in another voice transposed to a higher or lower register.

3) The exposition: *repercussio* in Latin. This term applies to the arrangement by which the opening statement and the answer are alternately heard in different registers. It is often wrongly used to designate the answer.

4) The counterpart or counterparts. These terms are used for the free melodic writing in the parts which are placed against the fugal theme.

5) The episodes. This term refers to the portions which serve as connection between the different expositions while the theme is not used.

· 15 ·

A fugue, the characteristic elements of which are properly arranged according to the rules, is called a regular fugue—*fuga propria* or *regularis*. A fugue in which these elements are not so arranged but rather are arbitrarily handled is called an irregular fugue—*fuga impropria* or *irregularis*. There are different kinds of irregular fugues, distinguished according to the various ways in which one consideration or another may be followed. No special instructions are needed in this respect, since it is easier to depart from the rules than to follow them. Irregular fugues have often appeared under the title caprice in the keyboard literature. On the other hand, regular fugues were often given the name caprice by Frescobaldi, Froberger, d'Anglebert,* and other masters of their time. In such a case, the term was applied to fugues written on a theme using short note values, so that the entire composition showed rather quick movement. During this period, a composition entitled fugue was allowed slow and delib-

* Jean Henri d'Anglebert (1635–1691), a pupil of Jacques Champion de Chambonnières, harpsichordist and composer at the court of Louis XIV.

erate rhythmic movement only.* One final point, taken from the *Kritische Musicus* of Kapellmeister Scheibe † should be mentioned in this connection: "Irregular fugues of a more recent style do not always begin with only one part using the theme but often with all voices introducing it simultaneously in octaves. Similarly, the first entrance of a theme in one part may be accompanied with other appropriately arranged subjects in some or all of the remaining parts."

· 16 ·

A regular fugue is either strict or free, according to the treatment of the theme.

a) A strict fugue—*fuga obbligata*—is a fugue which deals throughout its course with almost nothing but the theme. The theme will reappear immediately after the first exposition, if not in its entirety at least in its various components. From the theme, or from the counterpart which is set against the answer which repeats the theme, are derived all other accompanying melodic lines and all episodes by either abbreviation, augmentation, diminution, change of rhythm, or the like. All these forms of the original thematic material are then logically combined in harmonic treatment. If such a strict fugue is carried out at length, and if it contains a number of contrapuntal artifices, such as various kinds of imitation, double counterpoint, canonic writing, and modulations, it may be given the Italian name *ricercare* or *ricercata*—a fugue showing utmost skill, a master fugue. Such are most of the fugues of J. S. Bach.

b) A free fugue—*fuga libera, soluta, sciolta*—is a fugue which does not deal with the theme throughout. The theme or its various components do not appear at all times, though rather often; and whenever the theme is relinquished, the techniques of imitation and transposition are applied to a short, well-chosen secondary subject which is related in character to the theme or its counterpart, but not necessarily derived directly from them. Such are most of the fugues by Handel.

---

* Marpurg refers to the rise of the instrumental fugue which accounted for the introduction of new terms, though it did not restrict the use of the old term *fuga*.

† Johann Adolf Scheibe (1708–1776), a pupil of Bach, and one of the important musical writers of the eighteenth century.

NOTE

If all or several voices form a short canonic section on the theme in the course or at the end of a regular fugue, this is called *fuga reditta*—a restated fugue.*

The manner by which a theme is immediately answered, so that the different thematic statements are overlapping, is called close imitation or stretto. This kind of imitation may be applied to the theme in either complete or shortened form, and it may occur in either similar or contrary motion, with either identical or changed note values.

· 17 ·

Instead of using merely one theme, a composer will often use several themes in one composition. Thus there is a distinction between simple and multiple fugues. Simple fugues are based on a single theme; multiple fugues are as a rule summarily called double fugues, and we shall follow this terminology henceforth.

NOTES

1) The opening subject of a double fugue is usually designated as the theme; the others are called countersubjects, or secondary themes—*contrathema, contrasubjectum,* in Latin.

2) In a double fugue, the different themes have to be developed simultaneously. Thus they are placed one against the other either in the high, low, or middle register, depending on the number of voices. This simultaneous development is not possible without the use of double counterpoint, just as in a simple fugue it is not possible to place the opening and answering statements in different voices without a thorough knowledge of this technique.

· 18 ·

According to the various kinds of imitation, six classes of fugues may be distinguished:

* Cf. Berardi's discussion of the term, pp. 45 f., above.

The first class of fugues contains those whose names are determined by the interval at which the answer follows the opening statement. Thus there are fugues at the unison, second, third, fourth, fifth, sixth, seventh, and octave.

It should be noted that in all these cases the intervals are reckoned upward. A fugue at the second, therefore, means invariably a fugue at the upper second.

The second class of fugues contains those which are named according to the kind of melodic motion in which the answer follows the opening statement. In this class are:

a) fugues in similar motion—*fuga recta* or *aequalis motus;*
b) fugues in dissimilar or inverted motion, usually called counter-fugues—*fuga contraria* or *per motum contrarium;*
c) fugues in retrograde and inverted retrograde motion—*fuga retrograda* and *fuga retrograda per motum contrarium.*

The third class of fugues contains those which receive their name through the change of note values with which the answer follows the opening statement. In this class are:

a) fugues by augmentation—*fuga per augmentationem;*
b) fugues by diminution—*fuga per diminutionem.*

The fourth class contains fugues by imitation in contrary rhythm—*fuga per arsin et thesin.*

The fifth class contains fugues with interrupted imitation—*fuga per imitationem interruptam.*

The sixth class contains those fugues in which all the mentioned devices may be combined—*fuga mixta.*

· 19 ·

One species is chosen from the first class of fugues—that which is most natural and most properly suited to the technique of fugal writing. This species, the fugue combining answers at the fourth, fifth, and octave, or simply the fugue at the fifth, is called ordinary fugue. The other species from this class of fugues, namely the fugues at the second, third, sixth, and seventh, are considered extraordinary fugues and are used only in the course of, and as an adornment of, the ordinary fugue at the fifth, in order to provide a variety of expositions. If a regular fugue is to be written at the second, third, sixth, or seventh, all normal rules for the ordinary fugue apply, except for those dealing with the answer, since an extraordinary fugue is not difficult to manage in this respect. This book, however, is concerned only with the ordinary fugue, and further discussion of extraordinary fugues will be deferred to later supplements.

NOTES

1) If we refer to the fugue at the fifth as a fugue combining answers at the fourth, fifth, and octave, this is for the following reason: The answer is meant to follow the opening statement at the upper fifth. This arrangement, however, is not always possible, and some—though not all—tones of the opening statement are often transposed only a fourth higher in the answer. Thus the fugue at the fifth is mixed with the fugue at the fourth. Yet, while asserting that in the fugue at the fifth the answer should follow the opening statement at the upper fifth, we realize from the inversion of intervals that the upper fifth is the same tone as the lower fourth. It makes no difference, therefore, whether the tones of the answer are a fifth higher or a fourth lower than those of the opening statement. The same holds for an answer at the fourth; it does not matter whether its tones are a fourth higher or a fifth lower than those of the opening statement. Now the question remains why we refer to the fugue at the fifth also as a fugue combining answers at the fifth and octave. The reason is that according to the rules for the fugal answer, the opening statement may be repeated at the octave without a previous transposition to the fifth. Furthermore, there are themes the nature of which requires that the opening statement as well as the answer remain based on the same key-tone. Thus the answer at the octave is included among those which this kind of fugue combines.

2) The fact that the fugue at the fifth is the most natural fugue is easily recognized from the choice of the two principal tones of a major or minor key: the first degree and fifth degree, which constitute in their triads the most important harmonies of any key. We shall see that the harmonic structure of the theme and answer refers essentially to these two triads and to the tonalities they represent.

· 20 ·

Insofar as the second class of fugues is concerned, one species is again used above all, namely the fugue in similar motion, although there are quite a few exampes of the counterfugue. Fugues in retrograde and inverted retrograde motion, however, are only occasionally interpolated, for the sake of variety, in the course of a fugue belonging to one of the two other species, just as the inverted theme is occasionally used in the ordinary fugue in similar motion.

· 21 ·

A similar situation exists with the fugues by augmentation and diminution. They are normally used as parts of other fugues. There are some instances, however, in which fugues are expressly written in these techniques.

· 22 ·

Fugues by imitation in contrary rhythm belong properly to the canon. An exchange of strong and weak beats occurs in the entrances of an ordinary fugue only when the theme is to be used in a stretto passage or a canonic passage. There are no regular examples of an ordinary periodic fugue written in this manner.

· 23 ·

Similarly, the interrupted imitation serves only to provide a variety of answers within a conventional fugue.

Finally, all changes to which the answer may be subjected as to its motion, note values, points of entrances, and so on, pertain properly to the strict fugue, and particularly to the strict double fugue. With due discernment, however, one can apply them also to simple fugues and free fugues, as is shown by a good many examples.

· 24 ·

The mixed class includes all those fugues in which the answer follows the opening statement in changed motion as well as in changed note values, or on different beats of the measure, to mention only a few possibilities. One may imagine any number of similar combinations.

· 25 ·

According to the note progressions within a theme the following terms are occasionally used for fugues:

1) *fuga composita* or *recta*—if the notes of the theme follow one another stepwise;
2) *fuga incomposita*—if the notes of the theme progress by skip;
3) *fuga authentica*—if the notes of the theme ascend;
4) *fuga plagalis*—if the notes of the theme descend.

From the matters which have been discussed, the reasons for the order of the following chapters will be clear.

The Theme or Opening Statement

· 1 ·

Not all themes are readily adapted to a fugue. Some themes suggest a fugue for flute and violin rather than a fugue for voices or a fugue for organ or other keyboard instruments. Some themes can be better developed in a two-part fugue than in a three- or four-part fugue. In inventing a theme, therefore, one will have to take into account the particular characteristics of the chosen medium and the number of voices. Whatever the medium and the number of voices, however, two points should be especially observed: (1) the length, and (2) the melodic line of the theme.

· 2 ·

It is true, the length of a theme may be determined by choice. Yet, the intended tempo ought to be considered. The slower the tempo, the fewer should be the measures of which the theme is comprised; the livelier the tempo, the more measures the theme may be allotted. A long series of plain, unaccompanied tones in a slow tempo becomes unbearable for the ear.

The shorter a theme, the more often it may be repeated. The more often a theme is repeated, the better the fugue. A short theme is easily understood and remembered and offers the listener a number of advantages. He can recognize the extent of the theme more easily; he can better understand the various answers in all their transpositions; and he can follow more intelligently the course of the entire fugue. By the same token, the composer, if improvising on the theme, will avoid the danger of losing sight of it and of following a multitude of confused and irrelevant ideas before finding it again. In either case, improvising or writing, he will be able to work with the theme more comfortably and clearly. And how important is this last point— clarity! In short, just as the excellence of a fugue is not commensurate with its magnitude, the quality of a theme is not dependent on its length. Nevertheless, it is not possible to state just how many measures a theme should have. Such ruling would impair the consideration of variety which is the soul of all music. This much, however, is certain: A theme is sufficiently long whenever it expresses a clear thought. This does not always require half a dozen measures. If circumstances permit, it may be achieved within a single measure.

· 3 ·

Insofar as the melody is concerned, various lively figures and runs may occur in the so-called caprices, but they have no place in the fugue proper. All large, unnatural skips, arpeggios, and the like, should be excluded both from the fugue as a whole and from the theme in particular, inasmuch as the theme is the basic melodic line from which all others are derived. At all events this consideration should apply to vocal and keyboard fugues. "The melodic, natural element—simple, noble, and singable—leads to the best fugues. Nothing is more neglected in a pretentious and forced theme than the melodic line," says Mattheson. To be sure, a melodic line of some sort exists in any theme, but it is not always satisfactory. If a theme consists of too many lively, rapid note progressions, and the fugue is written for organ with the use of the pedals, it is obvious that nothing but a confused and unintelligible rumbling will result.

· 4 ·

The melodic line of a theme should be contained within the interval of an octave so that there may be sufficient space for its repetition in all parts in which the answer will occur, and so that, in a vocal fugue, it may stay within the singer's range if the theme appears by modulation in different keys. This rule needs to be less strictly observed in instrumental fugues wherein themes may cover the interval of a tenth or even that of a twelfth. It is always best, however, to follow the rule strictly. There are excellent fugues in which the themes do not exceed the interval of a third or fourth.

· 5 ·

The melodic line of a theme should further be so arranged that it will admit a number of changes in its accompaniment. In this respect it will be useful to imagine the course of the bass and that of the other parts while working on the theme. This method offers the advantage that the composer, while writing the theme, will also perceive whether or not this theme can be easily developed. Not all melodic lines admit a strong and graceful harmonic accompaniment.* One must search for such melodic lines carefully. We are not speaking here of a forced harmonic accompaniment which can be fitted to the most uninteresting and awkward melodic, or rather monodic, line. The beautiful and natural will always win the prize.

· 6 ·

Just as the melodic line should not end on an unsuitable tone, it should not end with a perfect cadence, for this has no place before the conclusion of the fugue. If the composer's invention suggests a formal cadence which seems difficult to avoid, the answer should be introduced immediately on the cadence, or the cadence should be hidden, so to speak, through the use of a melodic artifice, such as adding several notes while those that form the cadence are quickly stopped. Examples will be quoted in the chapter dealing with the answer.

* Marpurg still implies a contrapuntal rather than chordal texture by the term "harmonic."

· 7 ·

Finally, there is no preference as to the point in the measure at which the opening statement begins. But it should naturally close on a strong beat. An exception to this rule is found only in vocal fugues, in which the need for it may arise because of a feminine ending in the text.

The Answer

· 1 ·

The tones of which the theme and the answer of ordinary fugues are comprised belong to the scales based on the tonic and the dominant. Of the two basic scales which are required, one furnishes the tones for the opening and the other, the tones for the answering statement. To find out which tones of these two scales correspond to each other in a fugal answer, the following device may serve as a guide: the basic scale of the key is superimposed on the scale of the dominant so that the first degree of one scale and the fourth and fifth degrees of the other scale align both in the middle and at the end of the scales. If we take, for instance the key of C Major, the tones of the scale on c are placed first and those of the scale on g, the dominant, are placed underneath them in diatonic order.

Scale on the first degree	c	d	e	fg	a	b	c
Scale on the fifth degree	g	a	b	c	d	e	fg

We find g placed against c, a against d, c against f and g, and so on. This table can be applied to all other major keys. Its function might be more clearly expressed for all cases by substituting numbers for letter notation.

Scale on the first degree	1	2	3	45	6	7	8
Scale on the fifth degree	5	6	7	8	2	3	45

From these tables we may gather the following general rules:

1) The second degree is answered by the sixth degree, and vice versa.
2) The third degree is answered by the seventh degree, and vice versa.
3) The fourth and fifth degrees are answered by the first degree, and vice versa.

It is also possible, however, for the sixth and the third degrees, and the fifth and the second degrees, and so on, to answer each other, as will be seen later. For this reason we shall formulate certain specific criteria by which it will be possible to judge the correctness of the answer and by which it will be possible, whenever there are different solutions, to decide which of them is the best.

· 2 ·

The answer, as we have said, is merely a transposition by which the opening statement is repeated in similar manner. In order to achieve this similarity, the notes of the second statement should correspond to those of the first in placement and value. (In exceptional cases, the first note may be changed in duration; it may be shortened or lengthened by half its value, if there seems to be a need for a sudden or unusual entrance—as will be seen in later examples.) There should be no change from the major to the minor mode. Both statements should show the same rhythmic formation and the same rests. Above all, the similarity of the two statements depends upon the fact that the intervals of the opening statement reappear in precisely the same form in the answer; for example, that wherever a third, fourth, or fifth was used in the opening statement, the same intervals are used in the answer, and that a major third in the opening statement will be followed by a major third in the answer, and so on. In short, the melodic line of the answer should be entirely like the melodic line of the opening statement. This is the first principle on which the arrangement of the answer is based.

· 3 ·

Certain changes, however, have to be admitted since the octave scale consists of two unequal half-scales. Progressing diatonically through the half-scales based on the first and fifth degrees, respectively, one will always find more or fewer tones in one than in the other. The C Major scale, for instance, contains the tones c d e f g (ascending) or g f e d c (descending) in one half-scale and the tones g a b c (ascending) or c b a g (descending) in the other half-scale. In order to observe this scale arrangement of the key in fugal writing and in order to even out the intervals in both statements, it is necessary to subject the melodic line to slight changes so that the original key will not be exceeded and abandoned in favor of a different key. This is called the adjustment of the melodic line.* It is the second principle on which the arrangement of the answer is based.

Whatever the first tone of the theme, its melodic line either will retain the character of the original key throughout, or it will lead to the key of the dominant toward its end. In the first case, in which the character of the original key is retained, the answer—after its proper entrance—will simply follow the theme note by note in exact transposition to the dominant key. In the second case, in which the dominant key is approached toward the end of the theme, the melodic line will have to be adjusted in the answer and led back to the original key through the change of some intervals, so that a modulation to a remote key † is avoided. In effecting this adjustment, one should, as a rule, consider what will follow rather than what came before, so that no interval will be wrongly chosen. The adjustment may occur in two ways: (a) by skipping a tone—this takes place in the larger one of the half-scales; or (b) by duplicating or repeating a tone—this takes place in the smaller one of the half-scales. The first procedure might be called widening the melodic line; the second, narrowing the melodic line. Through these adjustments, a unison might be changed to a second, a second to a third, a third to a fourth, a fourth to a fifth, a fifth to a sixth, a sixth to a seventh, a seventh to an octave, and vice versa.

· 4 ·

To the two basic principles we shall add the following rules which determine the nature of the fugue at the fifth.

* The tonal answer.
† The dominant of the dominant.

1) Rules concerning the first note of the opening statement:
   a) If the opening statement begins on the octave or first degree of the key, the answer should follow on the fifth degree of the key.
   b) If the opening statement begins on the fifth degree of the key, the answer should follow on the first degree of the key.

These are the tones on which fugal themes will normally start.

2) Rules concerning the last note of the opening statement:
   a) If the opening statement ends on the first degree, the answer should end on the fifth degree of the key.
   b) If the opening statement ends on the fifth degree, the answer should end on the first degree of the key.
   c) If the opening statement ends on the third degree of the original key, the answer should end on the third degree of the key of the dominant.
   d) If the opening statement ends on the third degree of the dominant key, the answer should end on the third degree of the original key.

These are the tones on which a fugal theme will normally and most easily end. If, in an unusual case, it ends on a different tone, such as the second, fourth, or sixth of the original key, the answer will end on the second, fourth, or sixth of the dominant key unless this is made impossible by the context. If so, the two principal rules should be consulted so that there will be no mistake in choosing the transposition to the upper fifth or to the upper fourth for the intervals of the answer.

NOTES

1) What has been said concerning the fact that the first and fifth degrees of a key should correspond on the first and last tones of the two statements of the theme, holds also for the other notes of the statements, whenever a skip from the fifth to the first degree, or from the first to the fifth degree occurs. There may be exceptions to this rule for reasons which make it necessary to have the first degree answered by the fourth degree or the fifth degree answered by the second degree.

2) The first statement does not necessarily end where the second

statement begins. In order to determine the length of the theme, one must find out how far it extends in its second statement. This is the easiest way to ascertain on which note the theme ends.

· 5 ·

With these rules and principles stated, let us see how they apply in practical examples and where and for what reasons exceptions may occur. Wherever necessary, we shall add further explanations to the basic rules.

The theme ends on the sixteenth note e in the second measure—the third degree of the main key. The tonality has remained unchanged. The rules state: (a) if the opening statement enters at the octave of the original key with the answer following at the fifth, the answer should form an exact transposition of the opening statement to the dominant; (b) if the theme retains the character of the original key, the answer should form an exact transposition of the opening statement to the dominant; and (c) if the opening statement ends on the third degree of the original key, the answer ends on the third degree of the dominant. All these points are followed in the construction of the answer. The tonic c is answered with the dominant g, and all the following tones are imitated with strict observance of the position of whole- and half-tone steps throughout the theme.

The skip from the octave of the main key to the lower fifth was prohibited according to the rules of the old masters because it rendered the establishment of the key uncertain. Yet, from these two authoritative examples one may gather that themes of this sort can produce an excellent effect—"all of which shows," as Mattheson says, "that none of these rules is without exception." * Did not prepossession and false sense of tradition often determine the old precepts?

Ex. 159   J. D. Leuthard

In this example the second statement begins on the third degree of the dominant. Contrary to the rule by which first and fifth degrees must correspond to each other in ending the two statements of the theme, the fifth degree c in the fourth measure is answered with the second degree g in the seventh measure. This exception holds whenever the melodic line can be interpreted in terms of the main key or whenever it returns after a brief departure of this kind through a transitional passage to the main key. If this had not been the case, the answer would have had to be arranged in the following manner:

Ex. 160

In the following example the third degree of the key is answered with the leading tone. This is done because the theme ends on the

---

* The entire paragraph is taken over from J. Mattheson, *Der vollkommene Kapell-meister*, ch. 20.

fifth degree, and the interval which is thus formed with it makes it easier to return to the first degree.

Ex. 161   J. P. Rameau

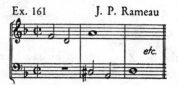

In the next example the third degree of the main key is answered with the second degree of the dominant, although it could have been answered with the tone c♯, as in the preceding example.

Ex. 162

In order to find the answer of a chromatic theme, one must change the theme first to a diatonic version by omitting the accidentals. Then an answer made up of similar diatonic progressions can be found according to the procedure described above. After this has been done, the accidentals may be restored in the opening statement and imitated in the answer. As an example, we might take the following chromatic theme in A Minor:

Ex. 163

Here we have two half-tone steps which do not properly belong to the scale of A Minor, namely c–c♯ and d–d♯. If we omit the two chromatic changes, the following melodic line based on diatonic progressions would remain:

Ex. 164

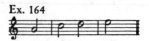

According to our modern tonal system, this would be answered as follows:

Ex. 165

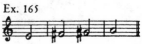

According to the old Aeolian manner, it would be answered with the natural tones:

Ex. 166

Now we should place the two basic melodic lines one against the other:

Ex. 167

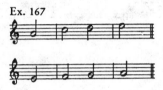

Since the first chromatic change in the theme occurs on c, and the second chromatic change on d, they are imitated on those tones which correspond in the answer to the tones c and d in the theme. These are f and g. Consequently the two thematic statements would be placed one against the other in the following manner:

Ex. 168

This procedure may be applied to all chromatic themes, both ascending and descending, whatever their tonality.*

Another point might be gathered from this example. If the second note c which forms a third with the first note a in the theme were to be transposed to the lower octave, it would form a sixth against the a. Through a similar transposition of the second note f in the answer, the sixth a–c would be answered with the seventh f–g, just as in the following example by Handel the seventh e–f is answered with the sixth a–c.

* Although Marpurg uses the "natural tones" of the Aeolian mode in this example, he is thinking primarily in terms of major and minor scales when he suggests reducing chromatic melodies to basic diatonic progressions (cf. Example 174).

Ex. 169   G. F. Handel

In the following example it should be noted that the third a–c is changed in the answer to the fourth d–g.

Ex. 170   J. H. d'Anglebert

The reason for this lies in the second note d of the answer which properly corresponds to the dominant a in the theme. If an e had been used instead of the d, all melodic progressions of the answer would have been similar to those of the theme, yet the strictness of the rules would have suffered.

It may seem that instead of the third note g in the answer, the note f could have been taken, so that the melodic line would have been arranged in the following manner:

Ex. 171

In this case the dominant a, with which the theme ends, would have been answered with the tonic d, according to the rule. This, however, would have placed the entire melodic line in the key of the fourth degree, G Minor. The close which the theme reaches on the dominant a is an imperfect close, derived from the Phrygian mode, which suggests the main key D, rather than the key of A Minor. Since the answer is to be placed in the key of A Minor, the corresponding close could not have been effected on any other note than e, which suggests the key of A Minor, even though this is not underlined in the counterpart. Nevertheless the key of A Minor is inherent in the melodic line of the answer, and it is easily confirmed if we imagine the harmony e–g♯–b, which would normally occur on the note e with which the answer ends at the beginning of the fourth measure. This exception to the rule of strict correspondence between tonic and dominant on the ending notes of the two statements is observed in all similar cases.

Ex. 172   J. S. Bach

Since, in this case, the theme begins with the tonic and returns to, and ends with, the tonic after various chromatic changes, the answer had only to be transposed to the dominant note by note.

Ex. 173   J. S. Bach

This example shows again a transposition, note by note, to the key of the dominant, except that the g in the second measure is answered with c instead of d. The basic diatonic structure of this chromatic theme is as follows:

Ex. 174

opening statement   etc.

answer   etc.

Ex. 175   Girolamo Frescobaldi

etc.

etc.

In order to obtain a chromatic progression corresponding to bb–b♮, the second a–bb in the first statement had to be answered with the third d–f in the second statement. Everything else is transposed by corresponding intervals.

Ex. 176   J. S. Bach

etc.

Here the opening of the answer is subjected to the same change as in the preceding example. It should be noted, however, that the first two tones of the answer, d and f, have been connected through the passing tone e, in order to achieve a better melodic flow. Everything else is transposed note by note, according to the key of the answer. The end of the theme is actually reached at the opening of the eighth measure on the tonic d. Yet a transitional passage is added, which leads to the seventh degree c and, properly answered in the second statement, to the fouth degree g.

Ex. 177   J. J. Fux

In this example both the key and the melodic line are strictly answered in the second statement, except for the fact that the first note is here shortened by half its value so that the rhythmic motion is maintained.

Ex. 178   J. J. Fux

Choosing the answer to this theme, Fux prefers the second version, since the melodic line is here subjected to less change and since it contains both chromatic progressions of the theme, whereas only one of them appeared in the first version. With themes of this kind, in which, either by diatonic or chromatic progression, the key-tone of the dominant is reached without the use or suggestion of a perfect cadence, this tone may be answered, contrary to the rule given above, with the second degree of the tonic rather than the tonic itself, as we have seen in earlier examples.

The Exposition and the Development of a Fugal Theme

· 1 ·

It is possible to place a fugal theme first in either the soprano, alto, tenor, or bass, just as in many fugues—especially in those based on the old modes—it is possible to use the theme first either in its basic form or in the form of the answer.* There would be too little variety, however, if the theme were immediately repeated in the same range or on the same tone as used in the first entrance. For this reason some rules should be adopted concerning the order of thematic entrances in different voices. These rules apply to all fugues, whatever the number of voices or themes and whatever the melodic motion, the point of entrance, or the note values of the answer. They apply more specifically to the first exposition in all ordinary fugues, that is to that portion in which the theme is first carried through all voices, and they must not be abandoned until later in the fugue. It should be noted that in common time the two strong beats as well as the two weak beats may be exchanged in thematic entrances. There is no strict rule as to their sequence; a theme beginning on the first beat may be answered on the third beat, if circumstances demand. This principle can easily be extended to entrances on all strong and weak beats.

· 2 ·

In two-part fugues for unequal voices, such as soprano and bass,† the voices should always use the theme alternately. This arrangement,

---

* On the tonic or dominant.

† The choice of soprano and bass for a composition in two parts shows that Marpurg, unlike Fux and Martini, thinks primarily in terms of instrumental writing. Fux states that "one should always use neighboring voices" (*Steps to Parnassus: The Study of Counterpoint*, p. 36). The same difference in concept is implied in Marpurg's rule that a theme should normally not exceed the range of an octave (cf. p. 163, above), whereas Martini applies the rule of the octave limit to the distance of the two voices in a two-part fugue. The combination of two distant registers suggests not only a larger range for each voice than would be vocally practicable but also the premise of tone colors which are no longer subject to Fux's rule that "the closer the parts the more perfect the sound" (Fux, p. 112). As always, this transition from vocal to instrumental thinking is guided by the keyboard and its practice rather than by other instruments (see Marpurg's remark at the end of the paragraph).

however, may be changed with the episode after the first or second exposition. At these points the theme may reappear in the same voice in which it was used shortly before—though preferably at another interval, that is, in another tonality.

Two unequal voices are often combined in two-part fugues for organ or other keyboard instruments. J. S. Bach has written many such fugues under the title *Inventions*. In fugues for two flutes, two violins, the two voices are to be considered equal.

· 3 ·

In three-part fugues, the third part may enter at the octave of either the first or the second entrance, after the second voice has answered the first voice by transposition. Yet, in the interest of variety, it seems better if the third voice follows at the octave of the first entrance,* unless circumstances demand the other solution (see Example 156). The third voice may enter either at the regular time, or after a short episode, or it may enter even before the second part has finished the theme.

· 4 ·

In four-part fugues, the voices are grouped in two pairs, each pair consisting of an inner voice and an outer voice, such as soprano and tenor or alto and bass, which correspond to each other in their entrances. Those two voices which correspond to each other repeat the theme always at a similar interval; or, more precisely, one pair of voices uses the opening statement and the other pair uses the answer. Thus the opening statement in a fugue for four voices will be used in the first and third entrances, and the answer, in the second and fourth entrances. To cite an example: If the soprano begins with the opening statement, the alto will take the answer, the tenor will take the opening statement again, and the bass, the answer.

· 5 ·

The placing of several themes is handled just like the placing of the statements derived from one theme. Consequently, the double

* Cf. Fux's discussion of Fugues in Three Parts, p. 91, above.

fugue is subject to the same rules concerning the exposition as the simple fugue. In whatever parts the various themes begin, they will always proceed so that the tenor will refer in its answer to the soprano, and the bass in its answer to the alto. Thus there will be no difficulty in stating and developing the themes in the voices of a double fugue, whatever the number of themes.

· 6 ·

In fugues for more than four voices wherein two voices are used in the same register—such as two sopranos or two altos—even-numbered voices correspond to even-numbered voices and odd-numbered voices correspond to odd-numbered voices, just as in the four-part fugue; so that the first, third, and fifth voices correspond to each other, and the second, fourth, and sixth voices correspond to each other.

· 7 ·

Ordinarily, entrances occur with an exchange of opening statement and answer, and consequently at different intervals, as described above. In extraordinary cases, however, they may occur through imitation at the octave, so that either the opening statement or the answer is used twice in succession, though in different voices. Counting the ordinary possibilities together with the extraordinary possibilities, there are twenty-four combinations, since each of four voices can serve as opening voice for six different possibilities. (See the table below.)

TABLE OF ENTRANCE COMBINATIONS FOR FOUR-PART FUGUES

A) Beginning with the soprano
1) Soprano, alto, tenor, bass
2) Soprano, alto, bass, tenor
3) Soprano, bass, alto, tenor
4) Soprano, bass, tenor, alto
5) Soprano, tenor, alto, bass
6) Soprano, tenor, bass, alto

B) Beginning with the alto
1) Alto, tenor, bass, soprano
2) Alto, tenor, soprano, bass
3) Alto, soprano, bass, tenor
4) Alto, soprano, tenor, bass
5) Alto, bass, tenor, soprano
6) Alto, bass, soprano, tenor

C) Beginning with the tenor
    1) Tenor, alto, soprano, bass
    2) Tenor, alto, bass, soprano
    3) Tenor, bass, soprano, alto
    4) Tenor, bass, alto, soprano
    5) Tenor, soprano, bass, alto
    6) Tenor, soprano, alto, bass

D) Beginning with the bass
    1) Bass, tenor, alto, soprano
    2) Bass, tenor, soprano, alto
    3) Bass, soprano, alto, tenor
    4) Bass, soprano, tenor, alto
    5) Bass, alto, tenor, soprano
    6) Bass, alto, soprano, tenor

The choice among these possibilities is determined by circumstances and by the preference of the composer. For the first exposition of a fugue, however, the order of voice entrances which is quoted in Section 4 and generally accepted should be the rule. Finally, care should be exercised not to let the theme appear constantly just in the outer voices; it should also appear in the middle voices, both with full and sparse harmonic settings.

*

*   *

The first exposition of a theme is usually the least difficult. The real task arises with the other expositions. Yet these, too, can be more easily arranged if the following rules and notes summarizing the most important points are observed:

I) General rules for the development of simple fugues for two, three, or four voices. This category includes all fugues which are based on only one subject, regardless of whether the answer occurs by augmentation or diminution, by direct or contrary motion, etc.

    1) After the theme has appeared in all voices, the contrapuntal fabric may be continued for several measures according to the rules governing the episodes and then led into a cadence; or else, especially if the melodic line of the theme suggests it, the cadence may be formed immediately after the first exposition. The cadence may occur in the original key or in the dominant, whichever the harmonic context seems to require.

    2) While the cadence is formed, either the opening statement or the answer should enter in a voice in which the theme did not appear immediately before. If no episode precedes the cadence, one may introduce an episode rather than a thematic entrance on the cadence in order to increase the listener's anticipation of the new thematic entrance. In this case the theme, either in its opening or

answering version, may reappear on a suitable harmony in any voice in which it was not used immediately before.

3) If the nature of the theme admits answers at different points or if the fugue is not to assume great length, the new entrance of the theme may be answered earlier than the distance between the entrances of the first exposition would suggest. The answer may enter at the octave of the tonic or at the octave of the dominant, according to the point at which the answering voice enters.

4) The second exposition, which is thus begun, may be continued with entrances in some or all of the voices (depending upon the number of voices) and with various episodes, while rests are placed in that voice which is to introduce the theme in the third exposition. The episodes should be arranged so that in each case they make possible a cadence in a related key. The rule prescribes that ordinary modulations should precede the extraordinary ones.* This sequence should be followed by the student until he has acquired enough facility to depart from the rules and to execute any modulations with logic and ease.

5) Now the theme appears at a tone, and probably also in a key, totally different from those of its first entrance. If a change from a major to a minor key has occurred, the answer should be made in another minor key which is related to the original key. If a change from a minor to a major key has occurred, the answer should be made in a related major key.

6) The theme should continually reappear in as many related keys as possible both in complete and shortened statements. The thematic entrances should be accompanied with various suitable harmonic changes. Finally, the original key should be approached again with a carefully arranged modulation, using the complete or abbreviated theme in different forms of periodic and canonic imitation. The fugue should be ended with a final cadence which may possibly be extended or emphasized by a so-called pedal point.

The following analysis of a four-part fugue will help to clarify all that has been said:

---

* Marpurg considers ordinary modulations those to the fifth, sixth, and third degrees in both major and minor keys; extraordinary modulations, those to the fourth and second degrees in major, and to the fourth and seventh degrees in minor keys. This distinction saves the subdominant and related tonalities for the end of the fugue where they help to re-establish the balance of tonalities and to reaffirm the original key.

It may be noted first that the intention of the author * was to introduce modulations through episodes and counterparts rather than through transposition of the theme, since the entrances of the theme are confined to the octave of the main key and the octave of the dominant. This used to be the rule in the old contrapuntal style, and we still find it observed in *a cappella* works written today. In the section dealing with double fugues we shall have ample opportunity to study examples in which the theme appears by modulation in different keys.

The first exposition of the theme spans the first nine bars. Since the tenor begins with the theme, it is restated in the same manner in the soprano, whereas the alto presents the answer, which is imitated at the end of this exposition by the bass. The entrances are presented without episodes, the third entrance occurring on a tied second—a dissonance—and the fourth entrance, which is the final statement of the exposition, occurring on a consonant chord. All entrances are harmonically so well placed that it seems they could not have occurred either earlier or later. We might gather from this example the rule that thematic entrances should not be delayed whenever the texture of the composition permits their close succession; in the opposite case free passages should be interpolated in order to reach the points best suited for entrances.

* See note p. 192.

It may be added that the first statement ends with a melodic line suggesting a cadence, and that for this reason the alto enters immediately. The other voices enter either on the closing note of the preceding statement, as in this case, or directly after it. In order to make some of the entrances possible, the ending of the preceding thematic statement is slightly changed, or the counterparts are so arranged that the contrapuntal fabric can continue uninterrupted.

The second exposition starts with the last beat of the ninth bar and extends to the twentieth bar. The theme is presented again in all parts, but this time in a different manner. Those parts which stated the theme in its original form now state it in the form of the answer, and those which stated it in the form of the answer now state it in its original form. The sequence of entrances, however, is the same as that in the first exposition. The tenor, following the first exposition immediately, without any intervening episode, states the first entrance, this time presenting the answer. Since the progression with which the tenor ends this thematic statement suggests a cadence in the main key, the last note is directly followed by a short melodic continuation, derived from the theme but used in contrary motion. This ending and its imitation in the bass, by which the rhythmic motion is maintained, are marked in the score. After this brief interpolation, the alto, which had paused for a moment, takes up the theme a twelfth above the tone of the bass entrance. At the end of this thematic statement the harmonic fabric again tends toward a final cadence. This effect, however, is canceled by a short intervening passage presented in the three lower voices in imitation, and again marked in the score. Just before the sixteenth bar, the soprano takes up the theme in form of the answering statement, and in the seventeenth bar the bass takes up the theme in its original form, thus concluding the second exposition.

The third exposition begins in the twentieth bar and continues to the twenty-seventh bar. The theme is again stated four times, in still a new manner. Whereas the entrances up to this point occur on different intervals, so that statements of theme and answer alternate, the statements are now presented on the same interval twice in succession. Tenor and soprano state the theme in imitation at the octave, the soprano entrance occurring somewhat earlier, in somewhat closer imitation than had been used before. This is done in order to restore the harmonic motion, which would otherwise subside, due to a cadence in C formed by the other parts. Bass and alto follow with the answer; and with a cadence in B♭ the third exposition comes to a close.

The fourth exposition extends from the twenty-seventh bar to the thirty-fourth bar. Here the theme is treated in stretto entrances occurring at unequal intervals. The tenor begins with the theme. The alto presents the answer in close imitation. Tenor and bass follow in similar close imitation. Note the double counterpoint at the octave by which these last two entrances are set against the two preceding entrances. After this the contrapuntal texture is continued with the use of a small passage derived from the theme, and a cadence in D is reached in the thirty-fourth bar.

The fifth exposition begins with the last beat of the thirty-fourth bar and continues to the thirty-seventh bar. The theme is here presented by two parts moving in parallel thirds and answered similarly by the other parts in close imitation. Alto and bass begin, and soprano and tenor follow directly. After a short episode this exposition is brought to a close.

The sixth exposition begins with the last beat of the thirty-seventh bar and ends in the forty-fourth bar. The thematic entrances are here crowded together as in the preceding exposition. The two upper entrances are set in double counterpoint at the octave against the two upper entrances of the preceding exposition.* The remaining measures form an episode through the use of a melodic line which is related to the theme.

The seventh and last exposition extends from the last beat of the forty-fourth bar to the end of the work. Soprano and tenor present the theme in abbreviated form. Alto and bass follow in close imitation, completing their thematic statements and being answered in another close imitation by soprano and tenor. These two parts enter in parallel thirds, so that both answers occur simultaneously. Finally the fugue is concluded with an extended cadence.

---

* Marpurg may be referring to the accompaniment of the two soprano entrances which are surrounded by the other entrances. The exchange of registers, however, involves only different voices, not different octaves.

NOTES

1) The manner in which a four-part fugue is developed applies also to three-part fugues. Here one might imagine that the fourth entrance is simply omitted in each exposition. The same holds for two-part fugues, wherein the last two entrances would be omitted. Note, however, that two-part fugues are usually written as double fugues, with a countersubject placed against the theme in double counterpoint at the octave. The two-part fugue, either simple or double, poses considerable difficulty, although it may appear to be easy. This is so partly because of the strict rules to which contrapuntal writing in two parts is subjected, and partly because the statements of the theme and the episodes require a particularly skillful use of imitation and a carefully balanced exchange between the two parts. Thus a well-known master is doubtless right in declaring the flawlessly written two-part fugue a model of the art of composition.* Whereas in fugues in which a larger number of voices are used the beauty of the contrapuntal texture becomes the foremost consideration, in the two-part fugue it is the melodic writing which requires most attention; and it is particularly important to find ever new and interesting melodic progressions so that the composition will not become dull and trivial.

2) It is by no means necessary to keep all voices of a fugue going at all times. One or even two of the voices may rest in order to state the theme again with renewed freshness. Generally, however, one voice should rest only when another enters, although this is not to be taken as a strict rule. It should be noted also that two voices pausing together may begin their rests at the same time or one after another.

3) In the counterfugue the answer to a thematic statement may occur at the fifth, octave, third, or another interval. Thus it may occur by free or strict inversion. Whichever manner is chosen, however, should be consistently used and not abandoned until the thematic statements are presented in stretto passages. The initial pattern of entrances may also be varied, and one statement may occasionally answer the preceding statement in direct motion, as long as the third

* Possibly G. M. Bononcini (*Musico prattico*, p. 57), who is also quoted in J. Mattheson, *Das Beschützte Orchestre*, p. 288.

statement returns again to inversion. The following examples will help to explain the different procedures used in counterfugues:

Ex. 180   Gottlieb Muffat

Here the second statement answers the first statement by free inversion at the fifth. The third statement occurs in the same melodic motion as the second, but the fourth entrance returns again to the opposite motion.

Ex. 181   Dietrich Buxtehude

This example is also written in free inversion. Note in the fifth bar the inverted close imitation between soprano and bass and in the sixth bar the simultaneous entrances of alto and tenor which present the theme in parallel thirds.

Ex. 182   L. Battiferri

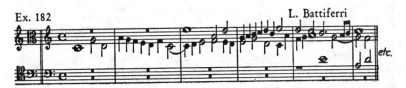

In this case the theme is answered by strict inversion, as can be seen from the succession of identically spaced intervals. The answer occurs at the third. The next entrance presents the theme again in form of the inverted answer, and thus the exchange of melodic motions is interrupted, as in Example 180.

It should be added here that the counterfugue (*fuga contraria*) must not be confused with the inverted or invertible fugue (*fuga inversa*). The term counterfugue designates a fugue in which inversion is applied merely to the answer, although if it is a double fugue, the different themes may in addition be interchanged by double counterpoint.* The term invertible fugue designates a fugue which, with all its counterparts and episodes, is written in such a manner that the whole work, through inversion of all voices, may be read in both contrary motion and double counterpoint.† The following examples of invertible fugues are found in Bach's *Art of Fugue:*

Ex. 183   J. S. Bach

* Cf. the double counterfugue by Bach, which Marpurg quotes as his final example (Example 190).
† The inverted reading thus produces a second, "mirror" fugue through a combination of the principles of melodic and harmonic inversion. The first of the two examples (Example 183) combines not only the two kinds of inversion but both types of fugal writing discussed in this paragraph, since it is an invertible counterfugue.

etc.

In inversion

Ex. 184

Friedrich Wilhelm Marpurg

In inversion

II) General rules for the development of double fugues for two, three, or four voices. This category includes all fugues in which several themes are combined, regardless of whether the answer occurs by augmentation or diminution, by direct or contrary motion, etc. The following points should be observed:

1) The themes should be distinguished one from another both rhythmically and melodically, so that the movement of one against the other will be more easily understood.

2) For the construction of a double fugue it is best to have the number of voices exceed the number of themes by one. Not only does this provision allow the use of more intricate forms of imitation and a more adequate treatment of each theme but also it will make it easier to let one of the voices rest and resume the theme with a fresh entrance. In double fugues with an equal number of voices and themes, on the other hand, all voices will usually be occupied throughout.

3) The themes do not always have to be used in their entirety.

4) The themes should not end together.

5) To prevent the themes of a double fugue from being confused with each other they should be distinguished in the first draft by figures.

6) It is not necessary that theme and countersubject always accompany each other, so that neither appears without the other. It will often be possible to treat one or the other separately before they are combined again.

7) After the initial exposition of the themes, either the principal theme or the countersubject may be resumed first.

8) All the subjects which are to be combined should be tried in double counterpoint before the composition of the fugue is begun, so that all possibilities of interchange are explored. Besides, the subjects should be examined separately as is done in single fugues. Thus it can be determined whether they are adaptable to various forms of imitation, with interchange between two, three, or more voices, or to periodic or canonic stretto passages, and also whether they can be combined with each other. Finally, one should investigate whether these subjects will lend themselves to imitation in augmentation or diminution, to imitation in contrary rhythm, to interrupted imitation, or to imitation in various motions. According to the results of these preliminary studies, the various expositions can be outlined in score.

9) The combination of several themes follows either of two general patterns:

a) One theme is developed at some length, as in a simple fugue, and a cadence suitable for the entrance of the second is formed. This will usually be a cadence in the main key. Then the second theme is developed in various answers and keys. Finally the two themes are unexpectedly introduced in immediate succession and developed in interchanges, transpositions, and different forms of imitation, according to the plan already made. Many double fugues by Battiferri and the younger Muffat are written in this style.* The rules for the composition of fugues with three or more subjects follow those for fugues with two subjects. Each subject may be treated singly before all themes are combined and introduced in immediate succession.

b) All subjects may be introduced together, without separate expositions for any of them.

i) One need not wait until the first subject is completed in the opening voice; the second subject may enter earlier. In this manner are written most of Handel's double fugues.

ii) The second theme may be introduced with the entrance of the second voice, as soon as the first voice has completed the first theme.

iii) The first voice may take up the second theme as soon as it has completed the first theme, while the second voice answers the first theme. This introduction of the second theme should, as a rule, follow after a short rest, so that the difference between the two themes is clearly perceptible. This style is followed in many double fugues by Kuhnau and J. S. Bach.

Concerning the answers of each theme, see the discussion above. What has been said about thematic entrances in a fugue with two subjects can be applied to fugues with more than two subjects by following similar principles. In the case marked (i), the third theme may be introduced before the second voice has completed the second theme, and the fourth theme may be introduced before the third voice has completed the third theme. In the case marked (ii), the third voice introduces a new theme as soon as the second voice has completed the second theme, and the fourth voice introduces another new theme when the third voice has finished its theme. In the case

---

* Luigi Battiferri was composer and chapelmaster at the church of St. Angelo in Vado in the early seventeenth century. Gottlieb Muffat (1690–1770) studied with Fux and became court organist in Vienna. A number of his keyboard works appeared in *DTOe*, III, 3, and XXIX, 2.

marked (iii), the second voice introduces a new theme as soon as it has answered the first theme, and the third voice, after having answered the theme introduced by the second voice, takes up a fourth theme while the fourth voice answers the theme introduced by the third voice. The following examples will help to clarify these rules, and with the explanations accompanying them we shall conclude our discussion of the writing of double fugues.

Ex. 185 G. P. Telemann

This first example shows the beginning of a double fugue for two equal parts. The countersubject enters shortly after the answer to the main subject has been introduced, as was described above in the case marked (iii). The themes are set against each other in double counterpoint at the octave. The episode which follows this first exposition modulates to the key of F♯ Minor. The main subject, which had first appeared in the lower part, now appears in the upper part, and the countersubject is stated immediately afterward in the lower part. Whereas the first exposition closed in the key of B Major, the second exposition closes in the key of F♯ Minor. In both cases, however, the cadence leads directly into an episode, so that the continuous flow of the composition is maintained. The second episode modulates to the key of C♯ Minor, after which the lower part again presents the main subject and the upper part the countersubject. The example shows the treatment of modulation in a fugue and how the theme may be transposed from key to key, but especially how the parts may alternate in presenting the main subject and countersubject.

Ex. 186   G. P. Telemann

This double fugue is also written for two equal parts. The countersubject enters in the manner marked (i) in the text above. The two subjects are written in double counterpoint at the octave, as may be seen at the end of the example where the answers of both themes appear in the key of the dominant.

Ex. 187   J. S. Bach

In this example the entrance of the second subject, which is set against the first subject in double counterpoint at the octave, is handled as in Example 185, except that here the fugue begins with the upper part, whereas before it began with the lower part. After the second subject has entered in the upper part against the answer of the first subject in the lower part, it appears twice in succession in the lower part in different keys. These statements, however, are presented with a new counterpart. The two themes appear again together in the key of G; the upper part states the first theme and the lower part follows with the second theme.

Ex. 188   J. C. Pepusch

This example shows the beginning of a double fugue for two un-equal parts, in which the first theme is developed for some time before the second theme enters. During this development, which extends over the first ten measures, the first theme is alternately placed in both parts. The second theme, which the upper part presents in the middle of the tenth measure, is also developed by itself for some time before it is combined with the first theme. It should be noted that the second theme begins after a cadence in the main key and that the lower part sets out to repeat it at the octave in the eleventh bar but interrupts this statement in order to present the proper answer at the lower fifth in the twelfth bar. The upper part accompanies the theme in thirds and restates it in the thirteenth bar where the harmony has turned to the key of A. At the beginning of the fourteenth bar the lower part states the second theme at the same interval but, without completing it, presents another statement at a new interval. The theme is completed in the fifteenth bar while the upper part introduces the last statement of this exposition at the interval of the preceding entrance. An episode closely related to the theme follows and leads to a full cadence in the key of the dominant.

Now the two themes are finally combined. The first theme appears again in the upper part. Then the upper part states the second theme while the lower part states the first theme. After this the lower part presents the second theme and the upper part the first theme. Thus the two parts are inverted by double counterpoint at the octave, just as in the preceding exposition an inversion in double counterpoint at the octave was applied to the two half phrases of the second theme.

Ex. 189

J. S. Bach

This example presents an entire three-part fugue with two themes which are inverted by double counterpoint at the octave. The countersubject appears in the same part in which the main subject had first appeared. Its entrance is placed at the middle of the answer of the main subject in the upper voice. In the fifth bar, after both subjects have been completed, an episode is introduced which is based on an inverted passage taken from the main subject. It is used first in the lower voice but is imitated immediately in the upper voice. In the next bar the two themes are stated again, this time placed in such a manner that the main subject appears below and the countersubject above.

Another episode follows, beginning in the last half of the seventh bar and continuing through the next two measures. The motif developed in this episode has been marked with an asterisk in the score, and mention should be made of the chromatic progressions which are set against it. With the cadence leading into the tenth bar, the bass returns to the main subject, and on the next quarter—a light beat— the soprano follows in contrary motion. In both parts the theme appears merely in abbreviated form. At the end of this measure, however, the soprano presents the entire theme in direct motion. This entrance is also placed on a light beat. After the completion of this statement in the next measure, the second, chromatic half of the theme is stated once more. The middle part returns at this point to the motif which we had noted before and which again introduces an episode. In the fourteenth bar the middle voice presents the main subject again, and the soprano follows on the light beat a fifth higher in close imitation. At the end of this measure the bass states the countersubject.

This leads into another episode ending with the new statement of the main theme in the seventeenth bar. It is presented in contrary motion by the alto and followed by the bass, which presents the theme in the same motion a quarter later on the light beat. The soprano gives the appearance of joining in this discussion, but does no more than playfully suggest the theme in different motions until a new thematic statement in direct motion is introduced by the bass in the eighteenth bar. This statement, occurring on the last half of this bar, is imitated at the octave on the following light beat by the upper voice. In both cases the theme appears in shortened form.

In the nineteenth bar, the middle voice introduces, after a quarter rest, a short motif which is derived from the main subject and immediately imitated in the other two voices. In the lower voice this imitation is placed on the strong beat, whereas in the upper voice it is placed on the light beat. As indicated in the score, the use of the motif is maintained for a short time in all three voices. It is followed by other thematically related passages and imitations until in the twenty-fifth bar the main subject is resumed, though not completed, by the middle voice. The bass follows on the next beat with the same shortened version of the theme in contrary motion. Finally, however, the theme is stated in its entirety by the soprano, and, after it has been combined once more with the countersubject in the twenty-sixth bar, the fugue is concluded.

The Counterparts

· 1 ·

The function of the counterparts begins as soon as the answer appears, unless the opening statement is accompanied by a counterpart immediately at the beginning of the composition. Such an opening, however, is unusual for a regular fugue, and is ordinarily found only in vocal fugues or in those instrumental fugues which are not written for keyboard instruments. As a rule—and invariably in fugues for organ or other keyboard instruments—the theme begins without any accompanying part. After the theme has been presented, a well-constructed melody should be used in the opening part against the second, transposed statement of the theme which is now appearing in the answering part. If the fugue is written for three parts, the answering part, after presenting the theme, must obviously join the opening part in counterpoint against the third part, which is about to enter. If the fugue is written for four parts, the third part, having completed the theme, joins the first and second parts upon the entrance of the fourth part, and so on.

· 2 ·

The counterpart need not always form a consonance with the entrance of the theme; nor should it necessarily form a dissonance. It is understood that whenever there is an opportunity to introduce the theme, this opportunity should not be forfeited. If it should happen that a thematic entrance can be arranged on a tied dissonance, this is excellent. If this is not possible, the entrance will necessarily form a consonance. These decisions can be made only according to the circumstances under which the thematic entrance occurs.

· 3 ·

It is advisable to follow one or the other basic species of counterpoint in writing the counterpart; the chance of digressing is less than if florid counterpoint is used. Florid or mixed counterpoint might lead to a kind of writing not at all related to the theme and not at all suitable for forming a connection with the theme. It is an important consideration that the different elements of a composition fit so well together that they will provide a beautifully unified effect—a consideration which is of particular importance in a fugue.

Whatever the basic species of counterpoint chosen for the counterpart, it should be used consistently. At times the opening statement will contain portions that can be borrowed for the counterpart so that this can be formed through imitation and transposition of progressions from the theme itself. Such a counterpart is doubtless best suited to the theme. If the composer arranges the theme so that in

the course of the fugue the answer might enter even before the opening statement is completed, and if he explores fully the possibilities
of working with various components of the theme, he will be in the
best position to deal with the theme and thus to succeed in finding
its most suitable counterpart. In fugues with several subjects, which
are combined from the beginning, there is no difficulty in finding satisfactory counterparts. One theme will form the counterpart to the
other. If the themes can be set in thirds one against the other, the
task of finding a counterpart is solved even more easily.

· 4 ·

The larger the number of voices in a fugue, the less florid the
counterparts should be. If one voice is written in a highly ornate
style, the other would necessarily become a mere filling voice. Yet,
in the fugue, all voices should compete on the same level. None
should be given the preference which individual voices receive in
other styles of composition. All voices without exception should
show good melodic writing. The part writing should be strict and
should be characterized by absolute independence of one voice from
another. For this reason, progressions in unison or in octaves, which
are permitted in a free style, have no place in the regular fugue, even
though examples of this sort are found in the writings of the great
masters. We are not speaking here of vocal fugues with instrumental
accompaniment in which the instruments may follow one or the
other voice in unison or in octaves.

· 5 ·

Although the counterparts should not be too elaborate and too
highly embellished, they should not be allowed to become a mere
figured bass exercise. If the late Musikdirektor Kirchhof * of Halle
indicated the counterparts of his well-known fugues in all twenty-
four keys simply by figures, he did this because he wanted to instruct
his students in the various possibilities of thematic entrances and in
the technique of figured bass at the same time. It was not his intention

---

* Gottfried Kirchhof (1685–1746) was, like Handel, a pupil of Friedrich Wilhelm
Zachow and became Zachow's successor as town organist in Halle after Bach had declined the post. He published a number of keyboard works, among them the *A B C
musical*, which is quoted here.

to present these casual creations as models of perfect fugal writing. For those fugue-makers, however, who accomplish nothing more than a simple harmonic support in counterparts, even though actually written out and not indicated by figures, there can be no excuse. In order to avoid such shortcomings, the movement of one voice should always be clearly distinguished from that of the other, either through syncopations or through passing or changing notes, as the circumstances permit.

· 6 ·

In writing the counterparts, one should take care to let the voices move neither too close together nor too far apart. For this purpose it is permissible to let one or several voices rest wherever this can easily be arranged. The rest is best placed in that voice which soon afterwards is to enter with the theme.

The Episodes

· 1 ·

The function of the episodes begins where that of the counterparts ends; or rather, an episode is a continuation of the counterpart and lasts until the fugal theme returns. For this reason it should be related to the theme, as should be the counterpart, and it should be well adapted to the counterpart which is combined with the theme.

· 2 ·

Consequently, the episodes should not contain any such passages as are formed by unusually large intervals, arpeggios or similar figures, extended runs, accompanimental or highly ornate and florid figures, unison or octave progressions, or melodic lines in *arioso* style or in the *style galant*, none of which could easily be developed in all voices by transposition or imitation.

· 3 ·

Where should the composer look for musical ideas from which episodes might be formed? In the theme and in the counterpart with which the theme is combined. If the nature of the theme is such that it does not yield suitable elements, one should invent simple, agreeable melodic progressions for episodes which are well adapted to the character and to the melodic and rhythmic movement of the theme. It is easily seen that it will be necessary to master the various kinds of imitation which were discussed in the first chapter in order to be able to write well-devised episodes.

· 4 ·

The episodes must not be too long or too frequent—especially if the theme itself is long—for either might mean that the theme would not appear often enough.

· 5 ·

The episodes should further be so arranged that they can be easily interrupted by a thematic entrance, unless they end in a cadence at which the theme would re-enter. The decision will depend in each case on the context and the occurrence of intervals which might be well suited to a thematic entrance.

· 6 ·

The episodes need not be formed by all voices. One or two voices may be suspended one after another, or simultaneously, so that the theme may re-enter all the more clearly and emphatically, especially if it appears in an inner voice.

· 7 ·

Finally, all fugues should end with a statement of the theme or a short harmonic turn following the theme. Examples of both solutions are found in the literature. The first is doubtless better. In either case, however, the fugue should end with all voices, just as it should begin with a single voice.

*

*   *

In conclusion, we shall discuss the following vocal fugue. The author's name will be reason enough to consider it a model of its kind.

Ex. 190   J. S. Bach

This fugue is written for the usual combination of four voices. Instrumental parts are added to support the vocal parts: The first violin follows the soprano in unison, the second violin follows the alto, and the viola follows the tenor. An instrumental bass part is added below the vocal bass. At times the two bass parts are joined, at times the instrumental bass forms an independent support. There are three themes, the first written to the words *Kyrie eleison,* the second to the word *eleison,* and the third to the words *Christe eleison.* The three portions, which normally appear as separate sections, are in this case treated as an entity.

The first two themes are answered in contrary motion and interchanged by double counterpoint, so that we are dealing with a double counterfugue. The third theme, which enters somewhat later, is used in combination with either the first or the second theme, or with both of them, in a richly varied contrapuntal texture.

The vocal bass begins with the first theme at (*1*) supported by a harmonic accompaniment of the instrumental bass. On the last note of the theme, at (*2*), the tenor answers a fifth higher in contrary motion, and the bass places the second theme against the tenor at (*3*).

The tenor having completed the first theme, continues with the second theme at (*5*), placing the two themes immediately one after the other, as did the bass at (*1*) and (*3*). This thematic entrance occurs again by inverted motion, whereas the soprano enters with the answer of the first theme in direct motion at (*4*). The inversion by which the entrances at (*4*) and (*5*) are placed against those at (*2*) and (*3*) is founded on double counterpoint at the octave, in that the themes, while not interchanged, appear in contrary motion.* The alto, which is the last part to enter, presents the first theme in inverted motion at (*6*), whereas the soprano immediately takes the answer of the second theme in similar motion at (*7*). Now that all vocal parts have entered, the instrumental bass and the vocal bass are joined.

After the first theme is completed in the alto, the second theme is stated in the same part, as has been done in the preceding entrances. This statement is made with the answer of this theme in contrary motion at (*9*), whereas the tenor appears with the first theme in

* Harmonic as well as melodic inversion of two themes results in the exchange of intervals which is shown in the table of numbers quoted by Fux in his discussion of double counterpoint. When harmonic and melodic inversion are applied simultaneously, this exchange therefore will be canceled, and all intervals will remain the same. When only melodic inverson is used, but the voices remain in the same relative position, the exchange of intervals applies, as in this case.

direct motion at (*8*). Below (*9*) and (*8*), the vocal bass takes the beginning of the second theme at the lower tenth and then pauses for a few measures. The two entrances at (*8*) and (*9*) are written in inverted double counterpoint against those at (*2*) and (*3*)—the parts are interchanged and appear in contrary motion. It should also be noted that the soprano imitates the second subject at the same time in a stretto diminution, just as the bass had done before. These places have been marked in the score above (*9*) and below (*5*).

The first two themes are finally restated at (*10*) and (*11*), and with the new entrance of the vocal bass, the first exposition is concluded in a full setting of all parts.

The second part of the fugue begins with the statement and several canonic imitations of the third theme at (*12*), (*13*), (*14*), and (*15*), the entrances occurring at successive lower fourths. Before these statements are completed, the theme appears again in the soprano and alto parts at (*16*) and (*17*). The reader who is familiar with perpetual canons modulating through different keys will see that it would be possible to place entrances similarly in all twelve keys; in fact, he might do this for the sake of exercise.

Before the thematic statement begun in the soprano at (*16*) is concluded, the alto part interrupts the thematic statement begun at (*17*) and resumes the first theme at (*18*). A shortened version of the second theme is placed against this in the tenor part at (*19*), followed immediately by the first theme, which appears also in shortened form. The soprano and bass parts answer the statement of the second theme in close imitation at the places marked with asterisks. Note the modulations through which the thematic statements appear in a number of different keys. Just as the first part of the fugue was primarily based on the keys of the tonic and dominant, so the second part is primarily based on the tonalities of the third and sixth degrees, namely B Minor and E Minor.

The third theme is now abandoned for a while, and only the first two themes are treated in the bass and tenor entrances at (*22*) and (*23*) and the alto and soprano entrances at (*24*) and (*25*). The shortened statements of these two themes, marked at (*21*) in the soprano and marked with an asterisk directly below it in the alto, serve as a preparation for the statements that follow in the other parts.

It is easily understood that the instrumental bass moves either with the vocal bass or independently and that it supports the other voices whenever the vocal bass rests. It should also be mentioned that full cadences are avoided either through changes of modulation or through extended melodic lines or through thematic entrances. For instance at (*26*), where soprano, alto, and vocal bass parts form a cadence, the continuous flow is maintained both through the progression of the instrumental bass and the introduction of the first theme in the tenor. At (*27*) the second theme is placed against this statement of the first theme in diminution; this entrance is answered by the alto at (*28*) but not imitated by any of the other parts.

The bass resumes the first theme at (*29*), the tenor presents the beginning of the third theme briefly, twice in succession, at (*30*) and (*32*), and the soprano states the beginning of the second theme at (*31*). This entrance is continued with a melodic line taken from the first theme and developed at some length, as was done in the alto following the entrance at (*28*); and thus the second part of the fugue is ended.

The third theme, which had formed the beginning of the second part of the fugue, forms also the beginning of the third part. This theme is stated at (*33*), (*34*), (*35*), and even in the accompanying instrumental bass at (*36*). In its full extent, however, it is heard only in the tenor; in the other parts the melodic line of the theme is changed immediately after each entrance. Before the tenor has completed the statement of the third theme, the soprano takes up the first theme at (*37*). The keys of A Minor and D Minor provide a harmonic basis for this portion of the fugue, as may be seen from these entrances, the entrances at (*38*) and (*39*), and those that follow. As the reader will recall from the discussion of the first part of the fugue, the statement of the first and second themes occurs in constantly changing melodic motion. After the thematic entrance at (*39*), the second theme is abandoned and only the first and third themes are developed together.

A stretto of the first theme appears in the tenor and bass parts at (*40*) and (*41*), while the upper parts present a shortened version of the third theme at (*42*) and (*43*). A similar stretto imitation between tenor and bass occurs at (*44*) and (*45*), while the soprano resumes the first theme at (*46*). The third theme, which is then taken up at (*47*) by the tenor part, is answered by the other parts at (*48*), (*49*), and (*50*), yet presented in its full extent only in the soprano and bass parts. At the same time a pedal point begins in the instrumental bass part. It is placed on the extended dominant of the main key, which the modulation has now reached again and which becomes the harmonic basis for the fourth and last part of the fugue. The pedal point ends with the new thematic entrances in the three upper voices at (*51*), (*52*), and (*53*), against which the first theme is stated once more at (*54*). These entrances of the third theme are spaced at intervals other than those used before. A new pedal point stressing the return to the tonic appears together with further statements of the third theme at (*55*), (*56*), (*57*), and (*58*), placed again at different intervals; and the fugue is finally concluded.

These are the most important points to be discussed concerning the composition of the fugue in general. The matter of placing the text is easily understood. One will profit greatly by using the structure of this fugue as a guide in working out new themes—before following completely free ideas and individual judgment; for the best and most direct way to gain competence in the composition of fugues is to adhere to the examples of the great masters.

III

Johann Georg Albrechtsberger

Albrechtsberger as Teacher of Beethoven

Johann Georg Albrechtsberger's *Gründliche Anweisung zur Komposition* appeared in 1790—two years before Beethoven arrived in Vienna to study with Haydn. It is one of the ironic facts of the history of music that this association of Haydn and Beethoven proved unsuccessful. Beethoven felt that his work was not given enough attention and correction and eventually turned to Haydn's friend and colleague Albrechtsberger for instruction. Thus, very shortly after its publication, Albrechtsberger's *Anweisung* found its historic mission: It was used as the basis for Beethoven's studies.

Beethoven's choice is all the more interesting because it stresses the fact that a particular need for didactic aid arose toward the end of the eighteenth century. There is no question that a feeling of great mutual respect existed between Beethoven and Haydn. Beethoven's dedication of his trios Op. 1 shows his regard for the older friend and master, and it was a particular satisfaction to Haydn to be able to hear the first public performance of these works before he made his second journey to London—the journey which, according to original plans, Beethoven was to have undertaken with him. What Beethoven missed in Haydn's teaching was a methodical treatment of the basic laws of composition understandable in terms of his generation and its widened scope of musical ideas. Haydn used for the lessons with Beethoven his own abstract of Fux's *Gradus*,[1] which could not sufficiently serve this purpose.

Martini had stressed twenty years earlier that the greatest obstacle confronting the young composer was the growing number of different styles of composition. The necessity of dealing with this enlarged musical practice brought about a stronger distinction between the tasks of the composer and those of the teaching theorist than the first half of the century had known.

Albrechtsberger's writing shows that he assumed his role as one of the first modern theorists with understanding and competence. No longer concerned with the establishment of a method or the defense of a system, he based his work on the experience that eighteenth-century theory had gathered, and applied it to the needs of his own era with a sense for the important and for the practical and with many expressions of musical and esthetic judgment which lend a refreshing quality to his style.

Fux, who had occupied the post of chapelmaster at St. Stephan's in Vienna almost a century before Albrechtsberger, was his chief guide. Following the general plan and substance of the *Gradus ad Parnassum* as "his oracle,"[2] he adapted Fux's teaching to major and minor tonalities. He added a chapter on the chorale fugue, the combination of fugue and cantus firmus setting, which Fux mentions only briefly, and a chapter on the canon, which is not treated in Fux's *Gradus*, and in which Albrechtsberger refers to Marpurg rather than Fux. These two chapters are the portions with which Albrechtsberger's writing is here represented.

Beethoven's notes on the course of studies he followed under Albrechtsberger have been preserved. Along with the musical examples we find copious comments, often presenting digressions which arrested Beethoven's attention; for example: "Albrechtsberger told me today that there are some works by the old master Froberger in which the use of the fourth, even that occurring by inversion of the triad, is completely avoided. This was done because the perfect triad, as symbol of the Holy Trinity, was to be maintained with absolute purity." The examples lead from simple cantus firmus settings to

---

[1] "Elementarbuch der verschiedenen Gattungen des Contrapunkts, aus dem grösseren Werke des Kapellmeisters Fux von Joseph Haydn zusammengezogen" (cf. C. F. Pohl, *Joseph Haydn*, I, 176 f.).

[2] *J. G. Albrechtsberger's sämtliche Schriften*, ed. by I. Ritter von Seyfried, p. viii.

fugal studies and finally to a combination of both in the chorale fugue. A particularly interesting discussion between student and teacher is evident from the portions of one of the chorale fugues, which are quoted below.

After giving Beethoven a cantus firmus, Albrechtsberger derives from it a fugal theme and shows how this theme might be set in a stretto passage.

Ex. 191

Ex. 192

Beethoven begins the chorale fugue—probably in Albrechtsberger's presence. He writes an exposition of the theme in three parts, introducing the cantus firmus with the fourth entrance, according to Albrechtsberger's instructions.[3]

Ex. 193

Chorale

After the cantus firmus is completed, Beethoven begins a new exposition which leads to a tenor entrance of the cantus firmus at the tonic.

The first problems in Beethoven's work arise here because of the necessity of reconciling a four-part fugal texture to the cantus firmus setting. Albrechtsberger suggests various changes which gradually

[3] See The Chorale Fugue, p. 221, below.

grow into an independent continuation of the work. But once he feels his points have been illustrated sufficiently, he again turns it over to Beethoven, who completes the fugue. The entire work was finally copied once more by Beethoven, with all of Albrechtsberger's variants.

Albrechtsberger's first changes are concerned with the preparation of the second cantus firmus entrance.

Ex. 194

He points out that the use of a three-part texture should serve to let the voices rest alternately and that the use of rests should serve to accentuate thematic entrances. Thus he extends the rest before the tenor entrance and ends the preceding tenor phrase immediately after the beginning of a thematic phrase prepared by rests in the soprano. Albrechtsberger's criticism is directed chiefly at the alto part, which he subjects to the most extensive changes. Here he removes the rests completely in order to avoid an entrance which, carrying no thematic significance in itself, weakens the most important entrance of the exposition with which it coincides.

The changes in all parts, including the bass, are made with the use of thematic material. This principle is consistently followed in Albrechtsberger's corrections, especially in order to avoid a slackening of the rhythmic motion during the statements of the cantus firmus. At the next entrance of the cantus firmus, Albrechtsberger uses therefore a motif from Beethoven's initial exposition in the soprano and bass parts. He also introduces twice the ascending fourth, which suggests the opening of the theme, in the tenor part.

Ex. 195

At a point where the accompaniment of a later cantus firmus statement leads to the imitation of a new motif, Albrechtsberger substi-
tutes a similar change in the tenor part for the rests in Beethoven's
version, yet lets the tenor part pause long enough to stress the imitation of this new motif with a fresh entrance.

Ex. 196

To this last change Albrechtsberger adds the remark: "It is not good
to place the beginning of a new phrase at the distance of a seventh
or ninth from the end of the preceding phrase."

In another case, Albrechtsberger's corrections lend poignancy to
the harmonic changes suggested in the outer parts, while avoiding a
tritone progression and an entrance without reference to thematic
material in the inner parts.

Ex. 197

Interesting, finally, is the comparison of the two versions in the last exposition, for which Beethoven uses Albrechtsberger's stretto setting of the theme twice in succession.

Ex. 198

Like Beethoven, Albrechtsberger finds it impossible to complete the thematic statement in the alto. But rather than letting the part rest, he changes the end of the theme. He marks this departure carefully ("license"). Having decided on it, however, he uses it to full advantage. Imitating the changed ending in the soprano and suggesting it again in the alto, Albrechtsberger continues these two parts while the stretto is repeated in the tenor and bass entrances. Consequently, this repetition leads the exposition with greater intensity to the cantus firmus entrance. With a brief rest in the soprano part and a rhythmically different placing of the thematic ascending fourth in the alto part, Albrechtsberger gives further emphasis to the last cantus firmus statement before returning to Beethoven's version for the remainder of the work.

The spirit of strict discipline which speaks from these pages stands in strong contrast to the popular image of the composer's unfettered genius. Yet this spirit never left Beethoven's working procedure. We can recognize it in the ever-changing versions of his sketches and in his exhaustive use of thematic material. An essential part of Beethoven's nature emerges from this conscientious account of his studies, which he concludes with the words: *"Omnia ad majorem Dei gloriam*/Patience, diligence, persistence, and sincerity will lead to success."

Albrechtsberger's *Anweisung* appeared in several editions, including English and French translations, and finally in the edition of J. G. *Albrechtsberger's sämtliche Schriften* by Ignaz Ritter von Seyfried, which was used for the present translation.

Seyfried, a pupil of Mozart and Albrechtsberger, became the chief advocate of Albrechtsberger's teaching, and it is mainly through his editions that Albrechtsberger's work has continued to reach the student of counterpoint and fugue. Seyfried's publication of Beethoven's studies with Albrechtsberger (1832), widely acclaimed and trans-

lated into French (by Joseph-François Fétis, 1833) and into English
(by Henry Hugh Pierson, 1853), was eventually superseded by the
critical edition of Gustav Nottebohm (1873), who rightly con-
demned Seyfried's interference with the original text. On the other
hand, Seyfried's editorial role serves to advantage in the publication
of Albrechtsberger's collected writings. Aside from a few minor
changes, he presents Albrechtsberger's wording intact, and he confirms the interesting fact that this text follows almost literally the
"usual, unadorned manner" of Albrechtsberger's verbal instruction.
Seyfried's additions to Albrechtsberger's text are placed at the end
of the work, where they are easily distinguished from the original.[4]
He widened Albrechtsberger's discussion of riddle canons through
a choice of contemporary examples, and he included four canons by
Mozart which are doubtless among the most extraordinary contrapuntal works written at the time. Thus the examples which he added,
in order to keep the edition abreast of the most recent "incredibly
rapid progress in this field of art," help to complete a picture of the
world in which Johann Georg Albrechtsberger taught.

[4] Albrechtsberger's text ends with Example 225 in the present translation. For Seyfried's changes, see also the Notes on the Classic Texts, pp. 318 ff.

From *Gründliche Anweisung zur Komposition*

The Chorale Fugue

In writing a fugue on a chorale melody or cantus firmus * it is best to take a progression of several notes directly from the chorale melody as a theme, using it in successive entrances of the first three voices, as in a regular fugue. The fourth voice is then introduced with the chorale melody itself. If the chorale melody begins on the tonic, another voice might take it later at the upper fifth or lower fourth—the dominant—as the opportunity arises. Whenever a voice takes the chorale melody, however, the other voices should be set against it in imitation. Occasionally it may also be possible to introduce a stretto passage or some other contrapuntal artifice in such a fugue.

Ex. 199

* The German term *Choral*, originally applied to Gregorian Chant and later to the Lutheran hymn, assumed in both cases the meaning of cantus firmus, in which it is here used.

The *N.B.* in the tenor marks an exception by which the answering statement may enter with a half note instead of a whole note.

There are also cases in which the chorale melody is taken by only one voice. The other voices are again imitatively written in florid counterpoint.

Ex. 200   Johann Christoph Bach

The most effective chorale fugues are those in which the chorale is written in whole notes throughout, or at least in notes of larger value than those which are used in the fugal accompaniment furnished by the other voices. Only through the use of such contrasting combination does the principal melodic line emerge clearly, intelligibly, and importantly at all times. In the opposite case, if all voices were written in similar note values, the ear would never be able to detect the entrances of the chorale melody, each of which should stand out against all fugal answers. This type of fugue is used to greatest advantage in sacred works and oratorios, especially if it is first developed in the manner of a regular fugue and during its course the chorale melody is suddenly introduced. Thus the entire composition will receive new life and striking beauty. Models of this kind can be found in the writings of eminent masters of the past and of more recent times.

The Canon

The word canon in its musical meaning designates a kind of fugue in which the strictest imitation is observed throughout. In a canon for either two or more parts the entire melodic line of the opening part must be answered in imitation. Whether the original melodic line suggests the style of an aria or a contrapuntal piece, the answering parts must imitate in notes of precisely the same value and—in canons at the unison or octave—in notes of precisely the same pitch or name. The answering parts must strictly observe all rests (except those which might be marked before the first entrance), imitate all ties and syncopations, all skips and progressions, all whole- and half-tone steps, all appoggiaturas and embellishments, in short, the entire melody in all details.

There are concluded and perpetual or infinite canons. There are canons written in retrograde motion, augmentation, diminution, or inversion, just as in the case of special fugues. There are double canons (for four voices), triple canons (for six voices), and quadruple canons (for eight voices). There are canons at the second, third, fourth, fifth, and at all other intervals. Entrances at different intervals, however, may not be mixed in one and the same canonic voice. Finally, there are canons to which several of the mentioned techniques can be applied.

The regular canons, which are both the easiest and the strictest, are those at the unison and at the octave; for only at those intervals can the answers be made strict even with regard to all whole- and half-tone steps—although such strictness may at times be forced upon answers at the fifth and at the fourth. In canons at the second, third, sixth, seventh, or ninth it is impossible to carry out the strict imitation of whole- and half-tone steps.

In writing a canon for two voices at the unison or octave, neither the technique of double counterpoint nor any special study is needed. One may take any suitable musical idea and write it out in both parts note by note and skip by skip, placing the entrance of the answering part a half or full measure or more after that of the opening part. Furthermore, it makes no difference whether a canon at the unison or at the octave begins with the upper part or with the lower part. It would be incorrect, however, to have a canon at the unison performed by the combination of a soprano and a tenor voice or an alto and a bass voice. It would also be incorrect to have a canon at the octave performed by two equal voices. In either case the effect would be misleading. In canons for three or more voices which are not written at the unison and cover more than one register, this incorrect performance is often caused by the absence of boys' or women's voices. If an open or closed canon is performed, for instance, by four men's voices, a six-four chord will often result instead of the perfect five-three. This effect is bad particularly in the first or in the last measure or on any strong beat which is not tied to the preceding rhythmic unit. In order to have a canon performed correctly, therefore, the clefs or registers must be strictly observed.

Three examples of two-part canons follow:

Ex. 201   Two-part canon at the unison

Vir - gam vir- tu - tis tu -   ae e-mit - tet

keyboard accompaniment

Vir - gam vir- tu - tis tu -

do - mi-nus ex Si - on, ex Si - on, ex Si - on.

ae e-mit - tet do - mi-nus ex Si - on, ex Si - on.

Ex. 202   Two-part canon at the unison   J. P. Kirnberger

Ex. 203   Two-part canon at the lower fifth

The first example is a concluded canon, as is indicated by the *N.B.* above the first soprano. Thus it is not repeated. The second canon is perpetual, as is indicated by the repeat sign at the second measure and at the last measure—in which no cadence is formed. The third canon is also perpetual, although it makes use of the hold or ending mark, which serves to indicate where, after several repeats, each voice should be held or ended.

Actually, a concluded two-part canon may be turned into a perpetual canon, and vice versa, by similar devices. Note the following points:

1) If a canon is to be perpetual, a closing note should be omitted in either part, and repeat marks should be placed at the beginning of the second measure and at the end of the last measure. Both voices, however, will have to be arranged so that each can easily go from the last note of the last measure to the first note of the second measure, as may be seen in the second canon above (Example 202).

2) If the canon is to have an ending, the repeat marks are placed in the same manner, but a final note is added in each voice. The in-

terval formed by the two final notes may be a unison or an octave,
or a third, as in this example:

Ex. 204

These two final notes are, in fact, the first notes of the second
measure. They would in any event have to form the end after the
canon had been repeated several times, even if they were not expressly marked—since all things must come to an end. If the canon
is arranged without repeat marks and if the first part is not to end
before the second part, a special ending has to be added through the
use of a tied second (2 3 | 1) or a tied seventh (7 6 | 8).

Two-part canons at the second, third, fourth, fifth, sixth, seventh,
and ninth, are somewhat more difficult to invent than those at the
unison and octave. In unusual instances it happens that several answers are hidden in the melodic line of which the canon is to be
formed, especially if this melodic line moves by steps rather than
skips. An example of this sort is found in the first canon, with keyboard accompaniment (Example 201). This canon can also be answered at the upper second, at the lower third, at the upper sixth, at
the lower seventh, at the upper and lower octaves, at the lower ninth,
and at the lower tenth, as is shown in the examples. The keyboard
accompaniment, however, would have to be changed; only in the
examples at the octave could it be used in the original form.

Ex. 205   Canon at the second

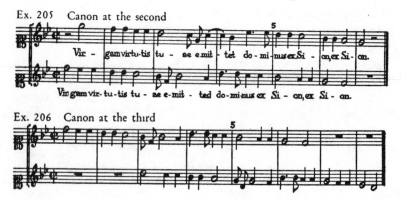

Ex. 206   Canon at the third

Ex. 207   Canon at the sixth

Ex. 208   Canon at the seventh

Ex. 209   Canon at the octave   or:

Ex. 210   Canon at the ninth or at the second

Ex. 211   Canon at the tenth

The canons at the sixth, at the seventh, and at the octave arise through the use of double counterpoint at the octave, whereas the canon at the tenth uses a mere transposition in simple counterpoint which places the second soprano an octave lower in the tenor register. If, similarly, the canon at the ninth is considered a transposed canon at the second, it may in turn be read as a canon at the seventh through the use of double counterpoint.

The writing of a three-part canon at the unison presents little additional difficulty. One may write any three-part setting for equal voices, using identical clefs, and arranging the first measure so that not all voices start at the same time. This is called the first draft—*inventio* in Latin. If such a first draft is properly written according to the rules of strict, free, or mixed counterpoint, it may be turned into an open or closed canon.* The open canon is called *apertus* in Latin, the closed canon *clausus*.

Ex. 212   First draft of a canon for three voices

Antonio Caldara

Ex. 213   Open canon

* The first draft, the open, and the closed canon contain actually the same material. The first draft shows only the harmonic outline, the closed canon only the melodic outline of the work. The open canon combines both in full score with proper entrances, rests, and repetitions. The term first draft (*Entwurf*) is not to be understood in the meaning of a tentative version, and the terms open and closed canon are not to be confused with the terms infinite and concluded canon.

For the purposes of performance, the first and second parts need to be copied only up to the points marked *N.B.*, for by this time they have completed all three sections.

Now the closed version of the same canon:

Ex. 214

In an open canon, the upper part of the first draft—serving as the principal melodic line—is written first in all voices, and immediately after it that part of the first draft which forms the bass cadence,* even if this is the middle part, as in this case. When this part is completed, the third part is added. In order to determine whether all transpositions are properly arranged, and in order to let the lowest part complete all three sections, the first and second sections must be repeated in the upper voice; in the middle voice only the first section need be repeated. Since the upper voice, as well as the two others,

* The skip of a fifth down or fourth up which determines the final cadence.

presents all three sections of the first draft in continuity, the quarter
rest at the beginning of the second section has to be omitted and the
half rest at the beginning of the third section has to be reduced to a
quarter rest.

For the purposes of performance, each voice must be copied separately. The one which begins the canon is inscribed *canto primo;* the
one which answers first, in this case after four measures rest, is inscribed *canto secondo;* and the one which answers second, in this
case after eight measures rest, *canto terzo.* The performers may take
any number of repeats, even though there are no repeat marks, and
they may close with whatever section they choose. For this reason,
the final note of each section could actually receive the closing
sign ⌒.

In a closed canon all three voices are written as one melodic line.
The first section is again connected with the second section, which
forms the bass cadence; and the second section, in turn, is connected
with the third section so that all three performers can use the same
part. One performer begins the canon, and when he reaches the sign
§, which should be placed at the beginning of the second section, the
second performer begins the canon; when the second performer has
reached the same sign, the third performer enters the canon—each of
them singing the complete melodic line. The canon is repeated any
chosen number of times, and it may be concluded at any of the marked
signs with all voices ending simultaneously. One of the performers
should direct the ending, unless the number of repeats is arranged
beforehand.

The composition of a canon for four or more voices follows the
same technique and procedure:

Ex. 215   First draft of a canon for four voices

In the open canon, the first quarter note of the second section is placed immediately after the last quarter note of the first section, while the quarter rest on the downbeat is omitted. Similarly, the eighth rests in the third and fourth sections are omitted in the open canon, and the last notes of the preceding sections substituted in the form of eighth notes. Since one part begins alone, rests should again be placed in the other parts up to the points of their proper entrances:

Ex. 216

For performance purposes each voice is again written out separately. The three upper voices, however, are copied only up to the *N.B.*, for at that point they have completed all four sections. The lowest part is written out in its entirety because it contains no repetition. Such a circular canon may be repeated any number of times, and it may be concluded with any section, as long as each voice finishes at the closing sign ⌢. In the open version of this canon, the fourth voice of the first draft must be exchanged for the third voice because it forms the bass cadence; and the third voice must be exchanged for the fourth voice, for if it were to retain its original place, it would produce the effect of the incorrect six-four chord on three strong beats of its first appearance. The first and second parts of the first draft retain their places as first and second sections. In the closed canon, the same procedure has to be followed for the same reason, except that in this case all sections are written one after the other in the same part:

Ex. 217 Closed canon for four voices at the unison

In writing the first draft, one should observe above all the following points:

1) Each voice in itself should present a well-constructed melodic line.

2) The first two or three voices in themselves should form a perfect two- or three-part setting. For this reason they should be written only with the use of those intervals which are most important for a complete harmonic structure.

3) The addition of the fourth voice, finally, should complete the harmonic structure of a regular four-part setting.

Two further examples of canons at the unison follow:

Ex. 218 Canon for four voices

Tur - nus des - cen - det ad   in - fe - ros.

Ex. 219 Canon for five voices

Tur-nus des-cen-det ad in. -   fe-ros, ad in-fe - ros.

Whenever a canon is written not at the unison but at the upper fifth or octave or at the lower fifth or octave, the entrances of the different voices are indicated in their proper order by clefs preceding the clef of the opening part and the time signature. The points at which the entrances occur may be marked above or below the proper notes by the usual sign or by figures indicating the respective intervals:

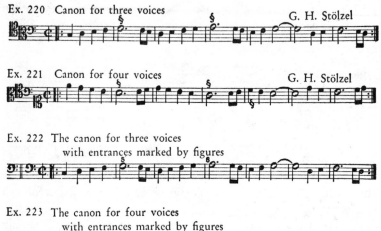

Ex. 220 Canon for three voices   G. H. Stölzel

Ex. 221 Canon for four voices   G. H. Stölzel

Ex. 222 The canon for three voices
         with entrances marked by figures

Ex. 223 The canon for four voices
         with entrances marked by figures

NOTES

1) Canons in which the entrances are indicated by figures may even be written with the use of only one clef. Yet it should be explained to those performers who are not themselves trained in this technique of composition that the figures placed above the notes signify intervals reckoned upwards and those placed below the notes, intervals reckoned downwards. The same consideration holds for the usual sign if no clefs are indicated for the answering parts.*

2) The intervals indicated by figures are always counted from the first note—not from the note above or below which they are placed. Thus the tenor answers the bass at the upper fifth g where 5 appears in the third of the examples quoted above—as it does in the first

* This remark presupposes a choice of intervals specified in the title.

example. After the tenor entrance, the alto answers where *8* is indicated on the tone c, an octave above the bass entrance. In the fourth example, the alto answers at the lower fifth where *5* appears—just as in the second example. At *8*, the tenor answers at the lower octave e. Finally, at *12*, the bass answers at the lower twelfth a. It is understood that the voices which enter later have to be transposed to their proper clefs.

So much about circular canons or, as they are called, rounds. As to the more elaborate canons—which are always open and concluded canons and in which each new subject forms a new canonic section— there can be no denying the fact that they are by no means easily invented and that they absolutely require that kind of skill which is based on constant practice. Many great masters of the old Italian, Flemish, and German schools have left models of this kind by which their names will be remembered for all time.

A four-part example follows:

Ex. 224

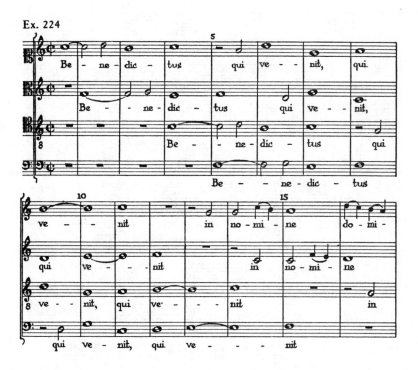

In this case, the sign § is not placed as a help for the performance, since the parts are written out; rather it indicates the end of the formal canon in the different parts. The remaining measures follow as a free addition and serve only to form a more definite ending.

A five-part example follows in which, up to the points marked by the sign §, the technique of double canon is used, in that the two lower parts form one canon and the three upper parts another.

Ex. 225   Canon for five voices   G. P. da Palestrina

One might say that the characteristic charm of canonic writing, of which four further examples by our immortal German master will follow, lies in the fact that a work of art appears before us in the act of its very creation. First a single voice is heard without any harmonic vesture. Gradually a second and then a third voice join, contours grow, and, as they become more rounded, begin to form an animated unity. Finally the musical picture is completed and shows a clear chordal structure, almost unexpected after the seemingly fragmentary portions heard before.

Four Canons by W. A. Mozart

Ex. 226 Canon for four voices

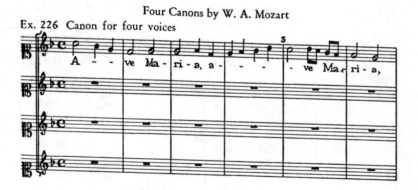

This perpetual canon possesses a lovely tenderness enhanced by the style of its invention and its simple, unadorned part writing. A gentle, quieting expression of melodic unity arises from the immediate return of the opening measure after the entrance of the second part and its modified reappearance as upbeat after the third entrance.

Ex. 227 Canon for four voices

The magnificent part writing in this canon deserves fullest attention. The character of each melodic line is formed by the plaintive text, and each new part is interwoven with the preceding one—all of them linked melismatically and chromatically in contrary motion.

Ex. 228   Canon for four voices

The theme follows strictly the ecclesiastic melody as it is intoned by the priest at the altar. The livelier countersubjects with their tied dissonances form an effective contrast to the solemn rhythmic movement of the principal melody.

Ex. 229 Canon for three voices

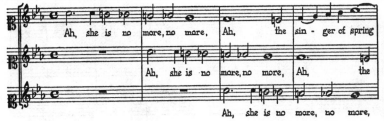

Johann Georg Albrechtsberger

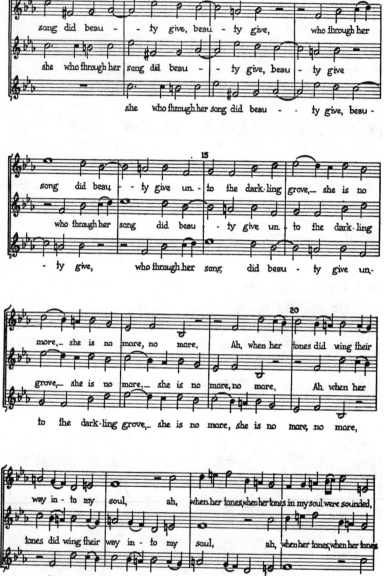

A careful analysis of this canonic masterpiece reveals a structure formed by eleven skillfully joined subjects, each of which seems so perfectly phrased that it can be combined easily with the preceding one as an upper or lower voice in uninterrupted sequence, even though the entrances are spaced only one measure apart; the deeply moving melody is pervaded by an ever-consistent thought, so that the first four notes of the last subject even serve to form the final bass cadence in the third voice.

Without any small local pride, we may claim that even the most celebrated masters of the contrapuntal schools through the centuries have left no examples more admirable than these in this style of composition.*

Finally, here are a few remarks about riddle canons. These contain neither signs nor figures nor letters marking the four voices, and often there is not even a clef indication. In order to solve the riddle of such a closed canon (which would bear no indication except possibly the number of voices for which it is intended), various intervals, such as the upper or lower third, must be tried until the proper answer is found. Often one must experiment with the techniques of inversion, retrograde motion, inverted retrograde motion, or with the use of the three clefs and their transpositions. The three clefs and their transpositions offer altogether nine possibilities.

Ex. 230

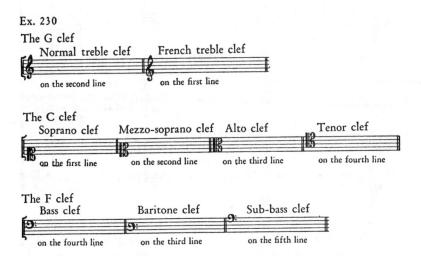

The solution may also be found through the use of whole or half rests or even shorter rests placed in one or several measures, or through augmentation or diminution. Such an example is found in Kirnberger's canon *All of us fail, but each fails in a different way.* Among more recent composers, Friedrich Kuhlau has written rather ingenious riddle canons, several of which are given below.

---

* This remark reflects the fact that German music had not yet won the high general esteem that French and Italian music held at the end of the eighteenth century. "The time was . . . not very remote when Lecerf de la Viéville made careless mention of the Germans 'whose reputation in music is not great'" (Romain Rolland, *A Musical Tour through the Land of the Past,* p. 198).

Ex. 231   Canon for eight voices
by reverse inversion

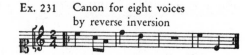

Ex. 232 * Solution

From the combination of all eight voices it is evident that the entire invention is based simply on three chords—a major triad on e, a
minor triad on a, and a diminished chord in six-five inversion on b—
which form a tone complex of no great harmonic interest. Actually,
a satisfactory solution requires that the tone g be altered to g♯ in the
alto, tenor, and bass voices. But such is a riddle! One may rack one's
brains to find the solution, and when the mystery is finally solved,
the gain seems negligible. "Parturiunt montes . . . ," to quote the
famous dictum.† Still, such speculative play may sharpen the inven-

* In the original clefs, the placement of each melodic line within the five-line system
is the same.

† "Parturiunt montes, nascetur ridiculus mus" (Horace, *Ars Poetica*, vs. 139)—the
classical equivalent for "Much ado about nothing."

tiveness, and accomplishments of this sort may serve to fill the composer's album.

Ex. 233 Canon for eight voices

Solution: A second canon can be formed by reading this canon backwards; a third canon by reading it in inversion; a fourth canon will result if the third version is read backwards.

Ex. 234

The imitation here is in retrograde motion. Each measure is answered with its retrograde version in the following voice. The entire setting, however, results in only two harmonies, the tonic D, and the dominant A. A mirror version can be worked out with the minor chords on c and f as ruling harmonies, though with melodic lines which are less satisfactory.

Ex. 235   Canon for eight voices

Ex. 236   Solution

The first note c in the soprano is answered with f in the alto, d in the tenor, and g in the bass. Rests of proper length have to be found in order to space the entrances correctly. In several cases the tone e has to be used in place of eb in the answering parts, according to the tonal changes.

Ex. 237 Canon for four voices

Ex. 238 Solution

The even more complex structure of this last canonic exercise is based on the following points:

1) A full measure rest precedes the entrance of the answering voices.

2) The answering voices are transposed to the bass register in order to allow enough space for the entire setting.

3) The rhythmic units of each measure appear in a different order in the answering voices. The third quarter is placed first, the first quarter second, and the second quarter last. This interchange applies also to ties, rests, and so on. Once this clever device has been found, everything will easily unfold, and the discoverer may flatter himself with the title of musical sage.

* * *

When Joseph Haydn, weakened by old age, found himself unable to congratulate personally his friend Albrechtsberger on his name day, he sent him the well-known musical greeting composed on the text "I am old and weak," which was printed without his knowledge under the title *Canon*. Albrechtsberger, suffering acutely from gout, and himself unable to visit his old friend and colleague on the next feast of St. Joseph, sent him the following memento:

Pieridum Frater!
qui dudum noster Apollo diceris:
hunc Canonem fecit, dedicatque Tibi
vetus et sincerus amicus
Georg. Albrechtsberger
1806
Josepho Haydn *

Ex. 239   Perpetual canon for four voices with entrances
at the lower fifth and at the lower octave.

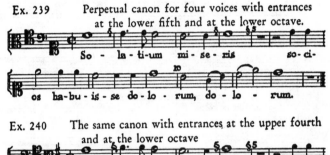

So - la - ti-um   mi - se - ris   so - ci-
os ha-bu-is-se do-lo - rum, do - lo - rum.

Ex. 240   The same canon with entrances at the upper fourth
and at the lower octave

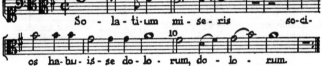

So - la - ti-um   mi - se - ris   so - ci-
os ha-bu-is-se do-lo - rum, do - lo - rum.

Ex. 241   Solution 1

* Dear Brother in Music!
Long called the Apollo of our time:
This canon was written and dedicated to you by
Your old and sincere friend
Georg Albrechtsberger
1806
To Joseph Haydn

The text of the canon reads: "It is a solace to those in distress to have companions in
their suffering."

Ex. 242   Solution 2

IV

Giambattista Martini

Martini as Mentor of a New Age

"Padre Martini, the great counterpoint teacher of the eighteenth century, has left no really didactic work," says Knud Jeppesen in his *Counterpoint*.[1] Jeppesen, in describing the impression which Martini's *Esemplare* is bound to make upon the student trained in the conventional methods of music theory, concludes that this is "no actual textbook of counterpoint." On the other hand, Willi Reich, in his dissertation on Martini's teaching, has convincingly shown that the *Esemplare* gives a true picture of the author's method of instruction—a method "neither divided into chapters and paragraphs . . . nor based on mere precepts."

Martini's work, in its deliberate turn to analysis and its blending of historical and theoretical discussion, reflects indeed the mind and personality of an unusual teacher and the process of an unusual didactic method. It is to be understood as a "graduate course," intended for the student who has completed his apprenticeship in counterpoint and fugue. It is for this reason that Martini's discussion is placed at the end of the present selection of texts. Although his writing precedes that of Albrechtsberger, Martini's work guides the student's view far beyond the teaching of the Viennese master.

Martini's didactic method is directed, above all, at enlarging the student's perspective and strengthening his independence. This view

[1] P. 52.

is supported by such evidence of Martini's personal instruction as we are able to gather. A valuable account has survived in the correspondence between Martini and Johann Christian Bach. In his early twenties, Bach's youngest son went to Bologna to study under Martini, and this sojourn was followed by a lively exchange of letters between student and teacher. The very first matter which J. C. Bach mentions with regard to his work is that of analysis—the study of Palestrina scores which Martini had recommended. Unable to find any copies of Palestrina's works, Bach asks whether he may have scores from Martini's library copied, adding that Count Litta, Bach's employer and patron, would "unfailingly and at once meet the expense." [2]

Although he inquires about specific problems of part writing—such as dissonance resolutions, hidden parallels, and the use of parallel fourths—it is clear that he invariably asks for advice rather than rules, and in some instances he submits an answer to his own question for the Padre's opinion. A particularly striking example is J. C. Bach's comment about fugal entrances placed alternately on the first and third beats in common time: "In connection with a fugue I wrote under your direction, the criticism was lately offered, that the answer must enter on the downbeat if the original subject does so, e.g.:

Ex. 243

I could think of no better answer than to take up my pen and divide the tempo C into 2/4." [3]

We find Martini's influence upon J. C. Bach reflected in some measure in the remarkable master-disciple relationship between J. C. Bach and the young Mozart during Mozart's visit to London in 1764–1765. Only a few years later, however, the Mozart family traveled to Italy, and Wolfgang Amadeus became Martini's direct student.

Among the works which Mozart wrote under Martini's guidance, one is of particular interest because it has been preserved with Mar-

[2] The complete letter is quoted in C. S. Terry, *J. C. Bach*, p. 27.
[3] C. S. Terry, *J. C. Bach*, pp. 30 f.

tini's correction. This is the setting of a Gregorian antiphon which Mozart prepared as test for admission to the Bologna Accademia dei Filarmonici. Two versions of the work exist, one written by Mozart and the other by Martini. A comparison of these two versions shows that Martini, rather than correcting details, carefully chose the best ideas from Mozart's work and used them as thematic material for a complete new example. Martini's version is related to Mozart's in almost every measure, yet it stands as a finished masterpiece against the much less polished though amazing work of the fourteen-year-old Mozart (see Examples 244 and 245).

Martini's most obvious changes are the omission of Mozart's second subject and the use of perfect cadences to confirm the tonality of F in the eleventh measure and the tonality of D at the end. These two changes contain his basic criticism and show where he feels greater economy or greater variety is needed. Indirectly Martini criticizes the infrequent use of Mozart's second subject and the hidden octaves and fifths in which it results. But he admits that the problem lies in the theme itself, in its range and complexity rather than in its placing. He therefore adopts a different second subject. He utilizes a thought from Mozart's third measure and achieves through this choice a more consistent use of both themes.

The imitations of this subject in the sixth, seventh, and eighth measures appear still as accompaniment to melodic lines derived from the first subject. Not until the first perfect cadence has been reached is full emphasis given to the second subject with the statements in the fourteenth, fifteenth, sixteenth, and seventeenth measures. Thus Martini saves the subject for the final return to D, which, written entirely in the slower note values of this subject, forms a natural ritardando before the extended final cadence.

The cadence in the eleventh measure marks both the structural center of the work and the crucial point in Martini's correction, since it leads into a measure which is easily the strongest in Martini's and the weakest in Mozart's version. The difficulty arises from the tone repetitions in the cantus firmus and the impeded harmonic motion which this stationary bass is apt to produce. Martini realizes that if the tonality F is reached one measure earlier than in Mozart's version, the pedal point can be used to full advantage, for once the linear and harmonic accents have coincided, the unchanging harmony suggests natural unfolding rather than indecision.

Giambattista Martini

Mozart's version

Quaeri - te pri - mum re - gnum De - - - - - i et ju -

sti - ti - am e - - jus, et haec o - mni - a ad - ji - ci - -

en - - tur vo - - - bis. Al - le - - lu - ja!

Martini's version

Ex. 245

Quae-ri-te pri-mum reg-num De - - - - - i et ju-sti-ti-am e - - - - - ius, et haec om - - - - ni-a ad-ji-ci - - - en - - tur_____ vo - - - - - bis al - - le - - - lu - - - - - - ja.

This effect is carefully prepared. Two earlier suggestions of cadences in F are weakened, in the fifth measure through the use of
the sixth d, and in the seventh measure through the use of a three-
part texture, whereas the cadence in the eleventh measure is made
stronger than the bass would normally allow through a crossing of
the two lower voices. A similar crossing in the tenth measure leads
the tenor to the tone d, which both melodically and harmonically
contributes to the fresh entrance of the new tonality in the following measure. Although Martini reaches the harmony of F earlier
than Mozart, he delays the strong emphasis on the harmony of D
considerably longer. In fact, the more interesting harmonies, which
Mozart uses (diminished seventh in the eighth bar, and Neapolitan
sixth in the ninth bar), Martini avoids, just as he avoids the use of
Mozart's more complex rhythmic and melodic means. In their places
stand clear tonal planning, consistent thematic development, and perfect part writing.

We know that the impression this instruction left upon Mozart
was deep and lasting. "Padre Martini's counterpoint lessons came as
a revelation: Now he began to understand the power of polyphony.
A whole series of contrapuntal compositions followed his discovery." [4]

Thus Martini's role is that of the mentor who establishes a standard
for the student through example rather than assignment and correction. In this spirit he quotes the writing of his own teachers and of
the masters of the past. The manner in which he introduces the student to the great heritage of his art heralds a new age, a thoroughly
modern and enlightened approach to musical instruction.

Martini published his *Esemplare* in two volumes—the first (1774)
devoted to works based on a cantus firmus which serves in each case
as a continuous "subject," the second (1775) devoted to works in
which the guiding thought is the fugal treatment of one or several
more concise subjects. Whereas Fux ends his work with the discussion of fugal writing in four parts, Martini reviews fugal theory
from the duo to the double choir motet in eight parts. [5] The chapters
are arranged according to the number of voices. Each contains a
group of annotated examples, and one example from each group has
been chosen for the present translation.

[4] P. H. Lang, *Music in Western Civilization*, p. 640.
[5] Cf. Nicola Piccini's comment on Fux's *Gradus:* "the eminent work that the
learned Padre Martini has given a final conclusion—an achievement in which Italy
may justly take pride" (preface to the Italian edition of the *Gradus ad Parnassum*).

From *Esemplare o sia saggio fondamentale prattico di contrappunto fugato*

Now that the most important rules for the composition of all species of fugue have been explained, there remains only the task of giving the young composer a series of models chosen from the writings of the best and most authoritative masters. He will find these models in the fugues for two to eight voices which form this second part of our work. The comments which have been added may help him understand the manner and style in which the great masters have written. May he profit from their example and gain from the study of their technique.

Before taking up the discussion of these learned works, however, I cannot help emphasizing that without serious and devoted work, the young composer will never succeed in living up to the standards set by these eminent composers who have perfected and ennobled the art of music with their skill. Rather, I hope that he will spare no labor or thought so that through acquaintance with the work of such masters he will become an able composer himself. Then I shall have the satisfaction of seeing fulfilled the only purpose which guided me in the work attempted in this volume.

Two-Part Fugue

Giacomo Antonio Perti
Chapelmaster of the collegiate church
San Petronio in Bologna

Ex. 246

I have chosen this first example from among the numerous works of one of my teachers in order to present to the young composer a duo *a cappella* written with strict observance of contrapuntal rules and at the same time with the greatest natural ease. The composer's name has become famous not only in the field of sacred music but also in that of dramatic music, and he was held in the highest esteem by his contemporaries.

Before discussing this duo, it may be useful to clarify the distinction between the term duo and the term duet. The duo is written *a cappella*, without keyboard accompaniment, and contains, for the most part, notes of long values. In the duo, the great masters have been conscientious in following the rules of strict counterpoint and vocal writing. In the duet quicker note values and a more customary time signature are used. Although it may be written in a fugal manner, it admits the exceptions required by whatever style it may be following, and it is performed with keyboard accompaniment.

In this duo, the composer begins the lower part with a subject in the first mode at (*1*), to which the upper part answers at (*2*), a fifth above. The skip of a fourth appearing in the lower part from the octave to the fifth degree, and that of a fifth appearing in the upper part from the fifth to the first degree, show by their combination that we are dealing with a fugue which is true to the mode,* for the answer remains within the limits of the mode.

The two parts are continued in contrapuntal fashion, forming singable individual lines until the lower part which first presented the subject at the octave resumes it at (*3*) at the fifth degree. This is called the inversion of the fugal answer.† Presently the upper voice resumes the subject at the octave. The two parts are carried on in imitative counterpoint until at (*5*) they form a cadence on the third degree. Later the parts repeat the opening and answering statements from the beginning of the duo; and since the nature of the subject does not admit the stretto which normally concludes a fugue, the composer uses another artifice, namely that of inverting and at the same time completing the sequence of fugal answers, as may be seen at (*6*) and (*7*), so that a passage in double counterpoint at the upper and lower octave arises.‡ The end is formed by the theme itself—a device which has been practiced and handed down to us by the great masters and which is in order whenever a theme is so constructed that it can be used in a final cadence.

* Martini's use of the term *fuga del tuono* shows the overlapping of the modal and tonal systems. The *fuga del tuono* became the "tonal fugue," once the concepts of modal theory were relinquished. The terms tonal and modal which are distinguished in present-day terminology are here identical in meaning.

† Martini uses the term "inversion" not only in the harmonic and melodic sense but also in the sense of interchanging the opening statement and answer in consecutive entrances.

‡ Through the two thematic entrances after (5) and the entrances at (6) and (7).

Three-Part Fugue

Ex. 248

Cristoforo Caresana

From Op. 1, Second Book of Duos

Together with the duos which the composer published under the title quoted here, he published a number of three-part *solfeggiamenti*— works based on subjects made up of scale progressions using all intervals from the second to the octave. I have chosen the first of these short works in order to present to the young composer a remarkable example of a fugue for three voices, written with the greatest skill yet with the characteristic ease of solfeggio exercises.

There are two subjects in this fugue. The ascending and descending octave scale which is introduced in the upper voice at (*1*) serves as the first subject. The second subject is presented in the second part at (*2*) and answered at (*3*) in the third part at the lower eleventh, that is, the fifth degree of the scale. By inversion of answers the third part resumes this subject at (*5*), a fourth above, at the octave or eighth degree until the scale of the first part is finished and taken up by the middle part at (*6*). Later, at (*7*), the third part presents the scale, and with the use of this subject and the various uses of the second subject, the composition of the fugue is admirably completed.

The great masters made it a carefully observed rule that whenever a rest appeared in a fugal voice, it had to be followed immediately with an entrance of the theme or at least a part thereof. The asterisk marks the solution used in this case, wherein the composer, unable to resume the second subject after one measure rest, presents a portion of this subject, namely the progression in the third measure, *sol fa mi re*. This principle should be adopted by the young composer and followed as a norm so that in his fugal writing the voices will not enter with arbitrary and irrelevant progressions after a rest and so that his fugues will not become conglomerations of divergent and thematically unrelated elements.

Four-Part Fugue

Angelo Predieri
Ecclesiastic of the third order of St. Francis
From a four-part Dixit for voices and instruments

Ex. 249

The composer of this work, a priest who possessed all the remarkable qualities of a truly outstanding ecclesiastic, has earned my deepest gratitude, for he was my first teacher. Born in January, 1655, at Bologna, he studied with Camillo Cevenini, chapelmaster at the church of San Pietro and member of the Accademia dei Filomusi, and with Agostino Filipucci, chapelmaster at the seminary and church of San Giovanni in Monte and a founding member of the Accademia dei Filarmonici, which extended membership to Predieri in 1671. He was ordained a priest of the third order of St. Francis in 1672 and distinguished himself as a singer, organist, and master of counterpoint. Above all, however, he possessed a rare gift of teaching, coupled with a sensitive understanding of the principles and laws of music. These qualities marked him as one of the first musical educators of his time. Among his students there are many organists who are still active in Bologna as outstanding soloists and accompanists. He died in 1731 at the age of seventy-six.

In this fugue, the composer shows his ability to write in strict, fugal style, yet with great clarity and simplicity. The theme is introduced in the alto at (*1*) and answered in the soprano a fifth higher at (*2*). Since the opening statement extends from the first to the fourth degree, the answer in the soprano extends from the fifth degree to the octave, covering also the interval of a fourth. The beginning of the fugue, consisting of the two progressions covering the interval of a fourth, from d to g and from a to d, is therefore formed by a real rather than a tonal answer.

At (*3*) the alto introduces a countersubject which descends from the first to the fifth degree, and while the bass answers the first subject an octave below at (*4*), the soprano answers the countersubject at (*5*) with a progression descending from the fifth to the first degree. Thus the countersubject forms a tonal answer, and through the combination of answers of the first and second themes there arises a mixture of tonal and real fugue.

At (*6*) the tenor answers the first theme at the lower fourth, and at (7) the bass answers the countersubject at the lower octave. At (*8*) the soprano answers the countersubject by inversion. At (*9*) the tenor answers the countersubject a fourth below, while at (*10*) the soprano resumes the first subject at an interval other than the one used at its first entrance. Thus the soprano begins an inversion of answers of the first subject which is continued with the entrances of the alto at (*11*), the tenor at (*12*), and the bass at (*13*). Similarly, the countersubject is presented by inversion of answers in the entrances of the soprano at (*14*), the alto at (*15*), the tenor at (*16*), and in the somewhat modified imitation of the bass at (*17*).

At (*18*) the soprano resumes the first theme at the lower fourth, g *sol, re, ut.** A similar entrance occurs in the bass at (*19*). Thus both the first and second subjects are transposed by modulation to the fourth degree until the stretto of the first subject begins in the tenor and alto at (*20*) and (*21*), followed by the soprano and bass at (*22*) and (*23*). At (*24*) all four parts form a stretto of the countersubject, presenting it in both the original and inverted versions; and while the bass, for the duration of three measures, holds the tone which effects the final cadence, the other three parts use the countersubject to form a highly intricate artifice.

* See note p. 82.

It should be noted that the composer has developed this fugue with the use of only those harmonies which arise from the basic chords, namely the chords of the first, fifth, and fourth degrees, avoiding those of the third and sixth degrees; for an entrance at one of these would not allow the subject to appear by real or tonal answer but simply by imitation: *

Ex. 250   Entrance on the first degree   Entrance on the third degree

The clarity, simplicity, and regularity with which the subject and countersubject in this fugue are developed are to the particular credit of the author and might guide the young composer in his own style of writing.

Five-Part Fugue

Giovanni Antonio Ricieri
From the Domine for five voices and instruments

Ex. 251

* This remark describes the practices of modulation that were accepted before the period which fully adopted formal structures based on the exchange of relative keys.

Giovanni Antonio Ricieri was born in Vicenza. He took up studies in singing and counterpoint there with Domenico Freschi and later in Ferrara with Giovanni Battista Bassani. Whereas he met with only moderate success as a singer, he distinguished himself as a composer through a highly expressive style and a keen sense for musical structure. He had many students, and I myself have had the good fortune to be one of them. He became a member of the Accademia dei Filarmonici in Bologna as a composer in 1704. In 1722 he was called to Poland by Prince Stanislaw Rzewski and served there as a composer of sacred music, chamber music, and dramatic music. He wrote a number of psalms for the papal choir at St. Peter's in Rome and, after serving in various other capacities, died at Bologna in 1746.

This fugue is based on two subjects which form tonal answers. The first subject is presented by the soprano at (*1*) with a descending skip from the fifth to the first degree. In the answering statement, the alto descends at (*2*) by skip from the first to the fifth degree, thus effecting the tonal answer of the first subject. The countersubject is presented in the entrances of the same soprano part at (*3*) and of the alto at (*4*), which also form a tonal answer. The tenor takes up the statement of the soprano an octave lower at (*5*) and the bass, that of the alto an octave lower at (*6*).

It should be noted that the fifth part *—which in this case is the

---

* *Quinta vox*—the part used in addition to those representing the four main registers.

second soprano entering at (7)—does not always follow the strict rules to which the other fugal parts are subjected. It may vary with respect to its point of entrance, its note values, its tones, or its interval progressions. This practice was established by the great masters because of the difficulties which would arise if all answers involving the fifth part were arranged by the same rules as the other answers. The attempt to observe strictly the rules of the answer might postpone the entrance of the fifth part, so that the fugue would become too long, or it might render the fugue forced and uninteresting. In order to avoid such imperfections, which would occur even more often in fugues for six, seven, eight, or more voices, the great masters used some special devices, such as introducing the fifth part ahead of time, or letting it enter with a modified imitation of the subject or countersubject or even with a non-thematic contrapuntal line, thus postponing the thematic answer until a later, more opportune point. The composer has advanced the entrance of the second soprano in this fugue by four and a half measures so that the combination of all parts would not be delayed too long and so that no major section would be deprived of the five-part harmony in which the fugue is meant to be written. It should be noted, however, that the stepwise ascending melodic line of the fifth part reaches the fourth degree at (4) instead of returning to the opening note of the first subject. This is one of the exceptions admitted by the great masters. Another exception of this kind appears at several places, similar to the one marked with an asterisk, namely that the first note of the counterpart, although it forms the interval of a fourth, is treated like a consonance and not subjected to the strict rules applying to dissonances.*

Between figures (8) and (12) there is a stretto of the first subject which is so excellently arranged that it is pleasing not only to the ear but, in its perfect regularity, even to the eye. After forming cadences at the sixth and third degrees—a practice adopted by a number of masters closer to our own time—the composer resumes the countersubject in a stretto passage and, with another skillful use of the same subject, returns from the third degree to the first degree, as is seen between (13) and (16). Since the first subject opens with the two tones forming the cadence on a, the first degree, the composer can easily resume the stretto of the first subject and lead the en-

---

* This remark refers only to the unsupported fourth which is formed with the lowest part.

trances closer and closer together. Similarly, he uses the counter-subject in close imitation between (*17*) and (*20*), thus concluding a fugue in which he may justly take pride, for it is characterized by both skillful writing and a pleasing sound—a combination which is as rare to find as it is difficult to obtain.

In studying the unusual writing in this fugue, the young composer will doubtless learn a great deal, especially about the technique of five-part writing, which is not easily mastered and executed with clarity. A complete harmony includes the basic tone, third, fifth, and, according to the opinion of most composers, also the octave. In order to obtain a composition actually consisting of five voices, the composer will therefore have to use all his ingenuity by doubling one of the other parts either at the octave or at the double octave.*

Six-Part Fugue

Claudio Monteverdi
From the six-part Mass *In illo tempore*

Ex. 252

* From Martini's suggestion for the arrangement of five-part chords, it is evident that he does not recommend the use of unison doublings (cf. Fux, *Steps to Parnassus: The Study of Counterpoint*, pp. 38 and 79). The same point is stressed in the discussion of Example 252.

In this example the young composer will find excellent proof of the fact that the great masters have always distinguished carefully between the styles of sacred and secular music in their writing. Upon comparing this Agnus Dei with the madrigals of the same composer, he will realize that its style is guided by the principles of contrapuntal writing rather than by the wish to express the text. Since the word-expression achieved through a practically unrestricted use of dissonances and a continuous use of unusual progressions is such that it stirs the senses of the listener rather than his mind, and since, on the other hand, the principal goal of sacred music is to bring forth in the thoughts of the listener a sense of devotion, service, and reverence for the infinite glory of God, the great masters have taken care to use in their sacred compositions a style suited to this purpose and entirely different from that of their secular works. This is done to a remarkable degree by the composer of the present example, which shows both his great musical experience and his ability to adapt his writing to whatever style his compositions demand.

The composer introduces in this Agnus Dei a subject in the second tenor at (*1*), which is answered in the bass at (*2*). Since the tenor uses the skip of a descending fifth from d to g and the bass uses the skip of a descending fourth from g to d, a tonal fugue arises. At (*3*) the tenor takes up the opening statement at the unison, and at (*4*) the second soprano takes up the answer at the upper octave. At (*5*) and (*6*) the alto and the first soprano answer at the third of the fifth degree and at the third of the first degree, respectively, rather than at the first or fifth degrees proper, as the other parts did.

The license of letting these two parts answer differently from the other four parts has been justly adopted by the great masters, for whenever four parts, which in themselves can constitute a full harmony, have served this purpose, the parts which exceed the number of four may answer at any interval which is convenient and which will produce good sound. Nevertheless, later in the fugue, the first soprano takes up the subject at the fifth degree at (*7*), and the alto takes up the subject at the octave at (*8*). Thus even these parts eventually follow the strict rule of the answer at the fifth or octave.

On the words *Qui tollis*, the composer introduces another subject which is answered in several parts according to their register, and this new subject is skillfully combined with the first subject on the repetition of the words *Agnus Dei*, where a highly intricate contrapuntal passage is formed. Its particular merit lies in the close six-part writing which avoids the use of unisons—although this can be done only with great difficulty when a large number of voices are used within a narrow space.

On the last words of the Agnus Dei, namely *Miserere nobis*, a new subject is introduced by the first tenor at (*9*) and answered at the octave by the second soprano at (*10*). This subject is taken up successively by the other four voices and carried in various answers throughout the remaining part of the work. It should be noted that both the opening and answering statements of this subject, at (*9*) and (*10*), begin on the tone a, the second above the tone g on which the Agnus Dei is based. This matter of beginning a subject at an unusual interval is not infrequently found even in the writings of the most outstanding masters. Nevertheless, the great masters were careful to delay such practice in their compositions, since an entrance at an unusual interval, especially at the second or seventh, would be awkward and inappropriate for the beginning of a fugue and would cause the listener difficulty in recognizing the tone on which the composition is based.*

It should also be observed that the composer has applied a special artifice with the last subject, namely letting the parts which enter at (*11*), (*12*), (*13*), and (*14*) appear in note values larger than those used in the first two statements of the subject. All these points prove the excellent craftsmanship of this great composer and his sovereign command and judicious use of different styles.

---

* Martini excepts from this rule unusual entrances which are caused by the dependence upon a cantus firmus.

Seven-Part Fugue

Costanzo Porta

From the collection of fifty-two motets for five, six, seven & eight voices (printed in 1580, when he was chapelmaster in Loretto).

Ex. 253

Costanzo Porta is celebrated for his works both as a composer and as a writer on music and other subjects. "Ansaldus Cotta, in his account of eminent scholars of Cremona of 1653, wrote: 'The name of Costanzo Porta has won unusual distinction both among the citizens of this town and among the members of the order of St. Francis. His musical ability is admired as unsurpassed, just as Rome, the queen, is admired as unsurpassed among all cities of Italy'" (Francesco Arisio in *Cremona Literata*, II, pp. 453, 454). He occupied positions as chapelmaster in Padua, Osimo, Ravenna, and Loretto. He had many students, and his printed works give outstanding proof of the model he set as their master. There are eighteen volumes of his works, published by himself and others, which have won the greatest universal acclaim. He died in 1601 at the height of his fame.

In the sixteenth and seventeenth centuries, a number of artifices of contrapuntal writing, such as special fugues, canons, and inversions, were held in high esteem. They appeared with the school of Jean Ockeghem (or Okenheim), his pupil Josquin des Prez, and Adrian Willaert—a pupil of Josquin des Prez * and the teacher of Costanzo Porta who showed a keen sense for these contrapuntal artifices in his

---

* Willaert studied with the Josquin pupil Jean Mouton.

own writing. Although devices of this kind are directed at the intellect and not, in keeping with the principal object of music, at the sense of hearing, they nevertheless may be of value in training the ingenuity of the composer. Moreover, they may prove the amazing thoroughness and thought with which the art of music was practiced by these masters, who wanted their writing to appeal not only to the ear, with melodic and harmonic means, but also to the mind—the master of our hearing—so that the mind would not become subordinated to the senses.

The artifices used in this example are specially marked by the composer in the parts of the tenor and *cantus* or soprano. With the words *subjectum ordinarium, & contrapositum septem vocum*, he explains that this fugue is written on a single subject which is introduced in the fifth part at (*1*); the other six parts answer this entrance variously—three by inverted and three by direct motion. The words *in se tantum continens quatuor partes, nempe cantum, tenorem, sextam partem, & septiman* indicate that there are four parts which use one melodic line taken from the opening of the fifth part. The soprano begins a canon at (*2*), which at (*3*), four measures later, is taken up an octave lower by the sixth part, as is indicated by the words *consequentia quatuor temporum in diapason remissum juxta posita*. The words which are placed inverted underneath the soprano part, *ab hexachordo post duo tempora consequentia in diapason intensum quatuor temporum contra posita*, signify that the tenor follows the entrance of the soprano after two measures at the sixth degree in contrary motion and that this tenor entrance, in turn, is followed after four measures at the upper octave by the seventh part, at (*5*).

The different meanings of the words *juxta posita* and *contra posita* should be noted. The words *juxta posita* indicate that the answer occurs in similar motion, precisely imitating the opening statement. The words *contra posita* indicate that the second statement answers in contrary motion, or rather in strict inversion, for the position of semitones remains exactly the same. In fact, while the tenor follows the inverted soprano note by note, it reads this part backwards, from right to left—as Hebrew script is read. This is implied by the use of the C clef—which normally serves for the alto—placed before the G clef of the soprano. When the soprano part is inverted, the entire melodic line revolves around the C clef, as is evidenced by the words *ab hexachordo post duo tempora*, etc., printed in inversion against the other words.

Ex. 254

Above the tenor part appear the words *Resolutio ex subjecto Canon: Fuga quatuor temporum ex diapason intensum*, indicating again that the tenor forms a canonic or strict fugue, which is followed four measures later by the seventh part at (*5*).

The composer uses three terms for his composition, namely *fuga*, *canon*, and *consequentia*. The first term, *fuga*, which has been fully explained, applies to the free or periodic fugue as well as the strict fugue. Both are used by the composer in this example. A periodic fugue appears in the first two answers, one formed through the entrance of the alto at (*6*) occurring in contrary motion at the upper octave, and the other formed through the entrance of the bass at (*7*) occurring in direct motion at the lower fifth. A strict fugue appears between the soprano as opening part and the tenor as answering part, the latter imitating the soprano part strictly from beginning to end. The second term, *canon*, applies both to these two parts and to the sixth and seventh parts. The first two parts, namely the soprano and tenor, form a canon by direct motion, and the other two a canon by contrary motion.* Finally, the third term, *consequentia*, which was introduced by Adrian Willaert, the founder of the old Venetian school, has been taken over not only by Costanzo Porta but also by his other students and contemporaries, especially by Zarlino (*Istitu-*

---

* I.e., the melodic lines of the soprano and tenor parts appear in direct motion after the soprano part has been inverted, whereas the sixth and seventh parts remain inverted against each other in the notation in which they are given. On the other hand, since the canon formed by the soprano and tenor parts is repeated by the sixth and seventh parts, the sixth part forms a direct canon with the soprano, and the seventh part forms a direct canon with the tenor.

As Martini points out, free and canonic imitation are combined in the work. Four parts are written in strict canon, and the other three (alto, *quinta vox*, bass) are added as accompanying voices which are free, although they anticipate and often return to the melodic line of the canonic parts. Yet Porta, following the Willaert-Zarlino tradition, uses the terms *fuga* and *consequentia* only to designate strict imitation. The term *canon*, according to its original meaning, serves only for the inscription, and no term is applied to free imitation.

The closing sign is used in the same manner in which it is used in Albrechtsberger's discussion (Example 224), but the canonic voices are here maintained strictly, without the addition of a free ending.

tioni harmoniche, Pt. III, ch. 51, in the first two editions, and ch. 54 in the later editions). The term serves to describe the course of the answering part as "consequent" to the opening part after several measures.

Thus the composer applies in this work the most important rules of fugal writing which were established by the great masters, as well as the principal contrapuntal artifices and the principal terms which are used along with the generic term *fuga,* namely *canon* and *consequentia.*

Eight-Part Fugue

Ex. 255

Filippo Baroni

From the Magnificat contained in his *Psalmodia Vespertina*, 1710

Filippo Baroni, chapelmaster at the cathedral of his native Ancona, published in 1702 a work small in size but great in value which contained a series of canons for two voices showing the most outstanding contrapuntal artifices that were used by the great masters. Aside from this work, he published an equally valuable collection of psalm compositions for full choir of eight voices; from this we have taken the present example, which we recommend to the young composer as a model.

In this example, the bass of the first choir introduces a subject at (*1*) which is answered at the fifth, or rather at the twelfth, by the soprano of the first choir at (*2*) and at the octave by the alto of the first choir at (*3*).

Experience has shown that whenever a composition begins against the measure, that is on a beat other than the first (as in this case, where the subject begins on the second quarter), the singers or players are apt to delay or anticipate their entrances, so that a confused sound results. In order to avoid this danger, the composer has wisely used a short motif of eighth notes in the tenor at the sign (*), so that the tempo is adjusted by the time the bass begins on the second beat of the measure.

At (*4*) the bass of the second choir answers the first statement at the unison. Similarly, at (*5*) the soprano of the second choir answers the entrance of the soprano of the first choir, and at (*6*) the alto of the second choir answers the entrance of the alto of the first choir at the unison.

It should be noted that each exposition, while carried through only three parts in both first and second choirs, contains one additional entrance using a theme other than the first. It is likely that the composer chose a treatment of this kind for several reasons. The first may have been to limit the fugue to a normal length; the second, that many repetitions of the theme might tire the listener, since the theme is very short. Thus the composer introduced a brief countersubject at the places marked (**), which is taken up by one part after another in order to avoid the monotony which the appearance of the first subject alone might cause. Excepted, however, are the two bass parts; they must maintain the principal theme, for upon them rests the entire structure of the eight-part writing. Since men of consummate skill do not work without alertness but make wise use of any detail according to the circumstances, this master has realized the possibility of resuming the short motif introduced at the beginning by the tenor at the sign (*) and of using it as an additional subject in the course of the fugue, stating it in various parts of the first and second choirs. Thus the fugue is actually written with the use of three subjects, which are well distributed and produce a poignant and pleasing effect.

Finally, it should be observed that after the middle of this fugue the composer has reduced in both choirs the number of measures over which the expositions of the themes extend, narrowing the answers of the first subject to the space of two measures and eventually to a single measure, in which this subject is combined with the other two. This is one of the ways in which the great masters completed the treatment of a theme which does not admit the use of a stretto passage.

*
* *

And thus I shall end this second part, concluding with it the entire work. The excellence of the quoted examples will have to compensate for whatever my own modest efforts in the added text have not been able to achieve. I have no doubt that this choice of works will be of the greatest help to the young composer in his task of learning to use the noblest artifices and finest subtleties of the art of musical composition—the lofty heritage bequeathed by the great masters. This was the only object I had in mind in embarking on whatever work I have done. If this aim is attained to any extent commensurate with my wishes, I shall indeed be happy and content in the knowledge of having served the reader.

Notes on the Classic Texts

Certain sections of the four texts have been omitted in order to avoid digressions or duplication. Duplication was not avoided, however, in places where a comparison of ideas or different approaches to the same thought seemed of particular value. The most important cross references are given with the texts; the reader is invited to trace further comparisons with the help of the index.

I. Johann Josef Fux, *Gradus ad Parnassum*

(Page numbers refer to the original edition of 1725.)

The translation covers *Exercitium* IV and *Exercitium* V, *Lectio* 1 to *Lectio* 7, of the second book of the *Gradus ad Parnassum* (pp. 140 to 217). The opening two sentences are taken from the conclusion of Fux's discussion of counterpoint (pp. 139 f.). A brief explanation of the use of suspensions in free writing, which precedes the chapter on imitation, is not included in this translation. The following sentence, which precedes the remarks introducing Example 124, has also been omitted: "In addition, I shall explain how far you might deviate from the accepted use and general rules of counterpoint in a free style through changes of melodic patterns" (p. 212). It refers to a section entitled *De Figura Variationis & Anticipationis* (the use of unprepared and unresolved dissonances) which follows the study of fugue in Fux's text (pp. 217 to 220). The final paragraph appears several chapters after Fux's study of fugue, at the end of his text (p. 279).

II. Friedrich Wilhelm Marpurg, *Abhandlung von der Fuge*

(Page numbers refer to the edition of 1806, in which the two volumes of the original edition are bound together as Part (*Teil*) I and Part II.)

The translation presents portions from the first six chapters of Part I and from the seventh chapter of Part II.

Imitation and Fugue in General: Notes for Section 8 (pp. 5 f.), containing an explanation of strong and weak beats in different time signatures, have been omitted. Section 11 is followed by a number of additional examples for imitation in three parts and in four parts (pp. 7 to 10; Tables IV to IX), which are not included in this translation. The series of three-part examples ends with Marpurg's explanation of the stretto technique (p. 157 in this translation). Section 19 contains a reference to extraordinary fugues, quoted in Marpurg's discussion of double counterpoint, and a reference to Marpurg's discussion of themes written in the church modes (pp. 14 f.); neither is included in this translation.

The Answer: The first two rules given in Section 4 (pp. 22 f.) are followed by a reference to a later discussion of examples for themes beginning at unusual intervals (the second, third, fourth, sixth, or seventh), which is not included in this translation. Omitted also is a reference to the entry "ending" (*Schluss*) in the index of the original text given before the notes for Section 4 and inviting the reader to check examples for themes ending at an unusual interval.

Section 5 contains the following two additional sentences: "All that has been said about the characteristics of the answer refers only to simple fugues or to the first themes in double fugues; the second statements of countersubjects or secondary themes are less subject to definite rules, as will be seen in the chapter dealing with the exposition. For the sake of greater clarity we shall present the examples for this chapter in several separate sections (*Abschnitte*)." The *Abschnitte* are arranged under the following eleven headings:

1) Themes which begin at the octave of the main key and remain in the main key
2) Themes which begin at the fifth degree and remain in the main key
3) Themes which turn to the key of the dominant
4) Themes which begin at the third degree of the main key
5) Themes which begin at the fourth degree of the main key
6) Themes which begin at the sixth degree of the main key
7) Themes which begin at the second degree of the main key
8) Themes which begin at the seventh degree of the main key

9) Themes written in the church modes
10) Chromatic themes
11) Various irregularly answered themes (*Vermischte Fugen-sätze*)

The discussion of these eleven sections covers pp. 24 to 60 and includes the examples given in Tables X to XXXVIII. The following examples were chosen for the present translation:

Table X, no. 1   (Example 156)
Table XII, no. 1   (Example 157)
Table XII, no. 2   (Example 158)
Table XV, no. 4   (Example 159)
Table XV, nos. 11, 12   (Examples 161, 162)
Table XXIII, no. 7   (Example 169)

(This example is used twice in Marpurg's discussion. In the first instance, which is here translated, the reader is referred to the later context including Table XXIII where the example is given.)

Table XXII, no. 1   (Example 170)
Table XXII, no. 3   (Example 172)
Table XXII, no. 5   (Example 173)
Table XXV, no. 2   (Example 175)
Table XXV, no. 3   (Example 176)
Table XXV, no. 5   (Example 177)
Table XXV, nos. 6, 7   (Example 178)

Abschnitt 10 (Tables XXII to XXV) is divided into four paragraphs. The text translated here is contained in paragraph 4. The end of the discussion of Example 170 includes a reference to Marpurg's discussion of the church modes, which is omitted in this translation.

The Exposition and the Development of a Fugal Theme: The end of Section 4 (p. 62) contains a reference to an earlier example, not included in this edition. The second sentence of Section 7 (p. 63) contains a reference to earlier examples, not included in this edition.

Section 8 (p. 63), which is omitted in this translation, contains a brief introduction to the three following separate sections (*Abschnitte*) dealing with the study of modulation (pp. 64 to 67) and of cadences (pp. 67 to 72) and with the manner in which cadences and modulation are applied to fugal development (pp. 73 to 93). For the present translation only portions of the third *Abschnitt* were chosen from pp. 73, 77 to 81, 83 to 85, and text accompanying the following examples:

Tables XXXIV and XXXV	(Example 179)
Table XXXVI, no. 1	(Example 180)
Table XXXVI, no. 3	(Example 181)
Table XXVI, no. 4	(Example 182)
Table XXXVII, no. 1	(Example 185)
Table XXXVII, no. 2	(Example 186)
Table XXXVII, no. 3	(Example 187)
Table XXXVIII, no. 1	(Example 188)
Tables XLII, XLIII	(Example 189)

At the end of his discussion of simple fugues, Marpurg gives a reference to the chapter dealing with melodically inverted double counterpoint in the second volume of his work, which is not included in this translation. The examples which he quotes (Examples 183 and 184) appear in the original text in Vol. II, Table XI, no. 3, to Table XIII, no. 1.

The Counterparts: At the end of Section 2 Marpurg adds: "In order to save ourselves the trouble of quoting new examples, we refer the reader to the examples given in our discussion of the answer and the development of a fugal theme" (p. 94). Sections 3 and 5 contain similar references to the preceding chapter (pp. 94 f.). The text of the conclusion is taken from Vol. II, chapter 7, Section 18 (pp. 86 to 89). The example (Example 190) appears in Tables XLVI to L.

III. Johann Georg Albrechtsberger, *Gründliche Anweisung zur Komposition*

(Page numbers refer to Vol. III of the edition of 1837 in Ignaz Ritter von Seyfried's *J. G. Albrechtsbergers sämtliche Schriften.*)

The chapter on the chorale fugue appears on pp. 1 to 11, the chapter on the canon appears on pp. 85 to 135.

Example 193 is followed by a reference to Fux's chorale fugue on the text *Ave Maria* (*Gradus ad Parnassum,* pp. 256 to 261) and by an unidentified setting of the text *Ave maris stella,* which are omitted in this edition. The chorale fugue by Johann Christoph Bach was added by Seyfried (see below, Notes on the Musical Examples).

The opening paragraph of the chapter on the canon contains references to earlier chapters of Albrechtsberger's work and to the second volume of Marpurg's *Abhandlung,* which have been omitted in this translation.

Example 218 is preceded by another three-part example (p. 100), which is omitted in this edition. Example 229 is followed by an example of free imitative writing from Athanasius Kircher's *Musurgia universalis* (pp. 109 to 111), which has also been omitted in this edition. In the original text of Albrechtsberger's *Gründliche Anweisung* this example is followed by the few remarks concerning riddle canons which Seyfried places after Example 169. The discussion of Mozart's canons, the riddle canons by Kuhlau, and Albrechtsberger's own riddle canon dedicated to Haydn (pp. 111 to 135) was added by Seyfried.

IV. Giambattista Martini, *Esemplare o sia saggio fondamentale prattico di contrappunto fugato*

(Page numbers refer to the original edition.)

Two-part fugue: pp. 3, 4. The opening two paragraphs appear on p. xxxxvi. The biographical sentence about Perti is somewhat reduced in this translation. Martini mentions a number of prominent patrons who were admirers of the composer, among them the Emperors Leopold I and Charles VI.

Three-part fugue: pp. 31 to 33.

Four-part fugue: pp. 135 to 141.

Five-part fugue: pp. 156 to 163. In Martini's text a symbol in addition to (*) is mentioned by which the entrances forming the interval of the fourth are marked. The symbol, however, is not consistently used in the musical text of the original.

Six-part fugue: pp. 242 to 250.

Seven-part fugue: pp. 265 to 275. Martini's mention of strict melodic inversion is followed by a reference to the first volume of his work in which an explanation of this technique corresponding to that by Bononcini and Fux is given. The last paragraph is preceded in the original text by a discussion of the term *tempus* as related to the value of the breve and a detailed explanation of the note values in mensural notation.

Eight-part fugue: pp. 303 to 310. The final paragraph appears on p. 316.

Notes on the Musical Examples

Example	
26–128	without mention. Bar lines have been added in some
(*cont'd*)	cases to make the use of 4/4 consistent. The first fugal theme is taken from the Dorian cantus firmus which is used for Fux's counterpoint examples. The complete cantus firmus appears in Examples 77 and 122. The principle of using one basic melody for a wide range of contrapuntal elaboration is the same as that discussed by Zacconi.
129	It is interesting that Marpurg's initial example is a variant of a theme by Bach (*Musical Offering*, Trio Sonata).
144	The entrance of the bass reads in the original:

156	*Well-Tempered Clavier*, I, No. 1.
157	*Ibid.*, II, No. 5.
158	Fugues for organ or harpsichord, Op. 3, No. 4. *Werke*, Vol. II (Leipzig, 1859), p. 168.
169	*Ibid.*, No. 5 (II, 171). Handel used this fugue again in *Israel in Egypt* (Chorus No. 4).
172	*Well-Tempered Clavier*, I, No. 5.
173	*Musical Offering.*
176	*Chromatic Fantasy and Fugue.*
177 and 178	*Gradus ad Parnassum*, orig. ed., p. 235.
179	Reduced from four staves.
182	Reduced from four staves; Marpurg's example is concluded with the last full measure.
183	*Contrapunctus* XVI.
184	*Contrapunctus* XVIII; in the original edition, which Marpurg follows, the order of *rectus* and *inversus* is in both cases reversed.
185	*Sonates sans basse*, Hamburg, 1727, No. 6. New eds. by Rudolf Budde, Wolfenbüttel, 1926, and by Fritz Rikko, New York, 1944.
186	*Ibid.*, No. 4.
187	*Well-Tempered Clavier*, I, No. 10.
189	See note for Example 172.

Example

190   *Missa Brevis* No. 4. Bach's *Werke*, VIII, 155.
(Originally Cantata No. 179.)

191 to 198 The complete work is quoted in Gustav Nottebohm,
Beethovens Studien, pp. 112 ff.

200   Johann Christoph Bach's chorale fugue was substituted by Seyfried for another example in Albrechtsberger's text. The fugue is part of the motet *Ich lasse
dich nicht*, which was long considered a work by
J. S. Bach (cf. Bach's *Werke*, XXXIX, pp. xxix f.).
The text is based on Genesis 32:26. The chorale is
modeled after the third stanza of Hans Sachs's song
Warum betrübst du dich, mein Herz. A few details,
in which Seyfried's edition departs from the original,
have been changed to conform to the text of the
Bach Gesellschaft edition.

225   *Missa ad fugam*. Albrechtsberger's placing of the text
differs in various points from the edition in Palestrina's
complete works (*Opera omnia*, II, 57).

226   K. 554.

227   K. 555.

228   K. 553.

229   K. 229 (3rd ed. by Alfred Einstein = 382^a). The
German text *Sie, sie ist dahin* after Hölty appears in
the Breitkopf and Härtel edition of 1804, but not in
the autograph.

243   After C. S. Terry, *J. C. Bach*, p. 31.

244 and 245 K. 86 (Einstein = 73^v).

Bibliographical Abbreviations

Couss. Script. Coussemaker, Edmond de, *Scriptorum de musica medii aevi nova series*, 4 vols., 1864–1876, 1908. Facs. ed., Milan, 1931.

DDT *Denkmäler deutscher Tonkunst*, 65 vols., 1892–1931.

DTOe *Denkmäler der Tonkunst in Oesterreich*, 87 vols., 1894–1951.

Gerb. Script. Gerbert, Martin, *Scriptores ecclesiastici de musica sacra potissimum*, 3 vols., 1784. Facs. ed., Milan, 1931.

PGM *Publikationen älterer praktischer und theoretischer Musikwerke*, published as *Publikationen der Gesellschaft für Musikforschung*, 27 vols., Leipzig, 1873–1905.

PIM *Publikationen der Internationalen Musikgesellschaft*, Leipzig, 1901–1914, Beihefte, Series I, 1–10; Series II, 1–13.

SIM *Sammelbände der Internationalen Musikgesellschaft*, Leipzig, 1900–1914.

VfM *Vierteljahrsschrift für Musikwissenschaft*, Leipzig, 1884–1894.

Bibliography

Adam von Fulda, *Musica*, 1490. Ed. in *Gerb. Script.*, III.

Albrechtsberger, Johann Georg, *Gründliche Anweisung zur Komposition*, Leipzig, 1790. Rev. ed. in J. G. *Albrechtsbergers sämtliche Schriften* by Ignaz Ritter von Seyfried, 3 vols., Vienna, 1837.

André, Johann Anton, *Lehrbuch der Tonsetzkunst*, 4 vols., Offenbach, 1832–1842.

Aron, Pietro, *Libri tres de institutione harmonica*, Bonn, 1516.

—— *Il Toscanello in musica*, Venice, 1523.

Artusi, Giovanni Maria, *L'Arte del contrappunto*, Venice, 1586–1589.

Bach, Carl Philipp Emanuel, *Essay on the True Art of Playing Keyboard Instruments* (Berlin, 1753, 1762), tr. and ed. by William J. Mitchell, New York, 1949.

Bach, Johann Sebastian, *The Art of the Fugue* (c. 1751), ed. by Roy Harris and M. D. Herter Norton, New York, 1936.

—— *The Bach Reader*. *See* David, Hans T., and Arthur Mendel.

Beldemandis, Prosdocimus de, *Tractatus de contrapuncto*, 1412. Ed. in *Couss. Script.*, III.

Bellermann, Heinrich, *Der Contrapunkt*, Berlin, 1862.

Berardi, Angelo, *Documenti armonici*, Bologna, 1681.

—— *Raggionamenti musicali*, Bologna, 1687.

Bernhard, Christoph, *Tractatus compositionis augmentatus*, c. 1650. Ed. in Joseph Maria Müller-Blattau, *Die Kompositionslehre Heinrich Schützens in der Fassung seines Schülers Christoph Bernhard*, Leipzig, 1926.

Bononcini, Giovanni Maria, *Il Musico prattico*, Bologna, 1673.

Bontempi, Giovanni Andrea, *Historia musica*, Perugia, 1695.

Brossard, Sébastien de, *Dictionnaire de musique*, Paris, 1703.

Buchner, Johannes, *Fundamentbuch, c.* 1525. Ed. by K. Paesler in *VfM*, Leipzig, Vol. V, 1889, pp. 1–192.

Bukofzer, Manfred, *Music in the Baroque Era*, New York, 1947.

Busi, Leonida, *Il Padre G. B. Martini*, Bologna, 1891.

Calvisius, Seth, *Melopoeia sive melodiae condendae ratio*, Leipzig, 1592.

Cannon, Beekman C., *Johann Mattheson, Spectator in Music*, New Haven, 1947.

Caus, Salomon de, *Institution harmonique*, Frankfurt, 1615.

Cerone, Pietro, *El Melopeo y maestro*, Naples, 1613.

Cherubini, Luigi, *Cours de contrepoint et de fugue* (actually by J. F. Halévy), Paris, *c.* 1837.

—— *A Course of Counterpoint and Fugue*, tr. by J. A. Hamilton, 2 vols., London, 1837.

Coperario, Giovanni, *Rules for Composing, c.* 1610. Facs. ed. by Manfred Bukofzer, Los Angeles, 1952.

Cotton, John, *De Musica, c.* 1100. Ed. in *Gerb. Script.*, II.

Coussemaker, Edmond de, *Scriptorum de musica medii aevi nova series*, 4 vols., Paris, 1864–1876, 1908. Facs. ed., Milan, 1931. [*Couss. Script.*]

David, Hans T., and Arthur Mendel, *The Bach Reader*, New York, 1945.

Diruta, Girolamo, *Il Transilvano*, Venice: Pt. I, 1597; Pt. II, 1609.

Dittersdorf, Karl Ditters von, *Lebensbeschreibung*, ed. by K. Spazier, Leipzig, 1801.

Eckstein, Friedrich, *Das Finale von W. A. Mozarts Jupiter-Symphonie*, Vienna, 1923.

Fétis, Joseph-François, *Traité de la fugue et du contrepoint*, Paris, 1824.

Forkel, Johann Nikolaus, *Über Johann Sebastian Bachs Leben, Kunst und Kunstwerke*, Leipzig, 1802.

Fux, Johann Josef, *Gradus ad Parnassum*, Vienna, 1725.

—— *Gradus ad Parnassum; oder, Anführung zur regelmässigen musikalischen Composition*, tr. by Lorenz Christoph Mizler, Leipzig, 1742.

—— *Salita al Parnasso*, tr. by Alessandro Manfredi, Carpi, 1761.

—— *Traité de composition musicale*, tr. by Pietro Denis, Paris, 1773.

—— *Practical Rules for Learning Composition* (without name of translator), London, 1791.

Fux, Johann Josef, *Die Lehre vom Kontrapunkt*, tr. by Alfred Mann, Celle, 1938; 2d ed., 1951.

—— *Steps to Parnassus: The Study of Counterpoint*, tr. by Alfred Mann, New York, 1943.

—— *The Study of the Fugue*, tr. by Alfred Mann, in *The Musical Quarterly*, New York, Vols. XXXVI–XXXVII, October 1950–July 1951.

Gafori, Franchino, *Practica musica*, Venice, 1496.

Galilei, Vincenzo, *Dialogo della musica antica e della moderna*, Florence, 1581.

Gédalge, André, *Traité de la fugue*, Paris, 1901.

Gehrmann, Heinrich, "Johann Gottfried Walther als Theoretiker," in *VfM*, Leipzig, Vol. VII, 1891, pp. 468–578.

Geminiani, Francesco, *Art of Playing on the Violin*, London, 1751. New ed. by David D. Boyden, Los Angeles, 1952.

Gerbert, Martin, *Scriptores ecclesiastici de musica sacra potissimum*, 3 vols., St. Blasien, 1784. Facs. ed., Milan, 1931. [*Gerb. Script.*]

Ghislanzoni, Alberto, "La Genesi storica della fuga," in *Rivista Musicale Italiana*, Milan, Vols. XLVIII–LIII, 1946–1951.

Glarean, Heinrich, *Dodekachordon*, Basel, 1547. Ed. by P. Bohn in *PGM*, Leipzig, 1888–1890.

Grocheo, Johannes de, *Theoria*, c. 1300. Ed. by Johannes Wolf in *SIM*, Leipzig, Vol. I, 1899.

Guilelmus Monachus, *De Preceptia artis musice*, c. 1480. Ed. in *Couss. Script.*, III.

Halévy, J. F. *See* Cherubini.

Haller, Michael, *Kompositionslehre für den polyphonen Kirchengesang*, Regensburg, 1891.

Hawkins, John, *General History of the Science and Practice of Music*, 5 vols., London, 1776.

Hohn, Wilhelm, *Der Kontrapunkt Palestrinas und seiner Zeitgenossen*, Berlin, 1918.

Jacobus of Liége, *Speculum musicae*, c. 1330. Ed. in *Couss. Script.*, II.

Jadassohn, Salomon, *Lehre vom Canon und von der Fuge*, Leipzig, 1884.

Jeppesen, Knud, *Counterpoint* (Copenhagen, 1931), tr. by Glen Haydon, New York, 1938.

Kinkeldey, Otto, *Orgel und Klavier in der Musik des 16. Jahrhunderts*, Leipzig, 1910.

Kircher, Athanasius, *Musurgia universalis*, Rome, 1650.

Kirnberger, Johann Philipp, *Die Kunst des reinen Satzes,* Berlin, 1774.

Kitson, Charles Herbert, *Studies in Fugue,* London, 1922.

Kleber, Leonhard. *See* Loewenfeld, Hans.

Köchel, Ludwig Ritter von, *Johann Josef Fux,* Vienna, 1872.

Kurth, Ernst, *Grundlagen des linearen Kontrapunkts,* Berlin, 1911.

Lang, Paul Henry, *Music in Western Civilization,* New York, 1941.

Levarie, Siegmund, "Fugue and Form," paper presented before the American Musicological Society, Midwest Chapter, 1941.

Lobe, Johann Christian, *Lehrbuch der musikalischen Komposition,* 4 vols., Leipzig, 1850–1867.

Loewenfeld, Hans, *Leonhard Kleber und sein Orgeltabulaturbuch,* Berlin, 1897.

Marpurg, Friedrich Wilhelm, *Abhandlung von der Fuge,* Berlin, 1753–1754; 2d ed., 1806.

—— *Traité de la fugue,* tr. by the author, Berlin, 1756; rev. ed. by Simon Sechter, Vienna, *c.* 1850.

Martini, Giambattista, *Esemplare o sia saggio fondamentale prattico di contrappunto,* Vol. II, Bologna, 1775.

—— *Storia della musica,* Bologna, 1757, 1770, 1781.

Marx, Adolf Bernhard, *Lehre von der musikalischen Komposition,* 4 vols., Leipzig, 1837–1847.

Mattheson, Johann, *Das Beschützte Orchestre,* Hamburg, 1717.

—— *Das Neueröffnete Orchestre,* Hamburg, 1713.

—— *Der volkommene Kapellmeister,* Hamburg, 1739.

Mendel, A. *See* David, Hans T., and Arthur Mendel.

Mersenne, Marin, *Harmonie universelle,* Paris, 1636.

Morley, Thomas, *A Plain and Easy Introduction to Practical Music,* 1597. New ed. by R. Alec Harman, London, 1952.

Morris, Reginald O., *Contrapuntal Technique in the Sixteenth Century,* Oxford, 1922.

Müller-Blattau, Joseph Maria, *Grundzüge einer Geschichte der Fuge,* 1923; 2d ed., Kassel, 1931.

Muris, Johannes de, *Libellus cantus mensurabilis, c.* 1320. Ed. in *Couss. Script.,* III.

Nivers, Guillaume Gabriel, *Traité de la composition,* Paris, 1667.

North, Roger, *The Musical Grammarian, c.* 1728. Ed. by H. Andrews, Oxford, 1925.

Nottebohm, Gustav, *Beethovens Studien,* Leipzig, 1873.

Nucius, Johannes, *Musices poeticae sive de compositione cantus praeceptiones utilissimae,* Breslau, 1613.

Odington, Walter, *De Speculatione musice*, *c.* 1300. Ed. in *Couss. Script.*, I.

Oldroyd, George, *The Technique and Spirit of the Fugue*, Oxford, 1948.

Paolucci, Giuseppe, *Arte prattica di contrappunto*, Venice, 1765–1772.

Paumann, Konrad, *Fundamentum organisandi*, 1452. Facs. ed. by K. Ameln, Kassel, 1925.

Picerli, Silvero, *Specchio di musica*, Naples, 1630–1631.

Playford, John, *Introduction to the Skill of Music*, 12th ed., London, 1694.

Pohl, Carl Ferdinand, *Joseph Haydn*, 3 vols., Berlin, 1875–1882.

Ponzio, Pietro, *Raggionamenti di musica*, Parma, 1588.

Porter, Quincy, *Study of Fugal Writing*, Boston, 1951.

Praetorius, Michael, *Syntagma musicum:* Vol. II, Wolfenbüttel, 1619; facs. ed. by W. Gurlitt, Kassel, 1929. Vol. III, Wolfenbüttel, 1619; ed. by E. Bernoulli, Leipzig, 1916.

Prout, Ebenezer, *Fugue*, London, 1891.

Purcell, Henry, *Of Fuge, or Pointing*, 1694. Ed. by Barclay Squire, "Purcell as Theorist," in *SIM*, Leipzig, Vol. VI, 1904–1905, pp. 521–567.

Rameau, Jean Philippe, *Traité d'harmonie*, Paris, 1722.

Ramos de Pareja, Bartolomeo, *Musica practica*, 1482. Ed. by Johannes Wolf in *PIM*, Leipzig, Beihefte, Folge I, Heft 2, 1901.

Reich, Willi, "Padre Martini als Theoretiker und Lehrer," diss., Vienna, 1934.

Reicha, Anton, *Traité de haute composition*, Paris, 1824–1826.

Reinken, Jan Adams, *Kompositionslehre*, 1670. Ed. by H. Gehrmann in Vol. X of Jan Pieterszoon Sweelinck's *Werken*, Leipzig, 1891.

Richter, Ernst Friedrich, *Lehrbuch der Fuge*, Leipzig, 1859.

Riemann, Hugo, *Geschichte der Musiktheorie*, Leipzig, 1898.

—— *Grosse Kompositionslehre*, Leipzig, 1902.

—— *Handbuch der Musikgeschichte*, Leipzig, 1907.

—— *Katechismus der Fuge*, Leipzig, 1890–1891.

—— *Lehrbuch des Kontrapunkts*, Leipzig, 1888.

Riepel, Joseph. *See* Twittenhoff, Wilhelm.

Ritter, A. G., *Zur Geschichte des Orgelspiels*, Leipzig, 1884.

Rolland, Romain, *A Musical Tour Through the Land of the Past*, tr. by Bernard Miall, London, 1922.

Sabbatini, Luigi Antonio, *Trattato sopra le fughe musicali*, Venice, 1802.

Sachs, Curt, *The Commonwealth of Art*, New York, 1944.

―― *The Rise of Music in the Ancient World*, New York, 1943.

Santa María, Tomás de, *Arte de tañer fantasía*, Valladolid, 1565. Part of the second volume has been edited in a German translation by E. Harich-Schneider, Leipzig, 1937.

Schenker, Heinrich, *Neue musikalische Theorien und Phantasien*, Vol. II, Vienna, 1910.

Schmid, Bernhard, the younger, *Tabulaturbuch von allerhand auserlesenen schönen Preludiis*, Strasbourg, 1607.

Schütz, Heinrich, *Geistliche Chormusik*, Dresden, 1648. New ed. by Wilhelm Kamlah, Kassel, 1935.

Shedlock, John South, "The Evolution of Fugue," in *Proceedings of the Musical Association*, London, Vol. XXIV, 1898.

Spitta, Philipp, *J. S. Bach*, Leipzig, 1843–1880. Tr. by Clara Bell and J. A. Fuller Maitland, London, 1884–1885.

Sweelinck, Jan Pieterszoon, *Werken von Jan Pieterszn. Sweelinck*, ed. by M. Seiffert, *et al.*, 12 vols., 1895–1903.

Terry, Charles Sanford, *Bach, the Historical Approach*, Oxford, 1930.

―― *John Christian Bach*, London, 1929.

Tigrini, Orazio, *Il Compendio della musica*, Venice, 1588.

Tinctoris, Johannes, *Diffinitorium musicae*, c. 1475. Ed. in *Couss. Script.*, IV.

―― *Liber de arte contrapuncti*, 1477. Ed. in *Couss. Script.*, IV.

Tunstede, Simon, *Principalia musices*, 1351. Ed. in *Couss. Script.*, IV.

Twittenhoff, Wilhelm, *Die musikalischen Schriften Joseph Riepels*, Halle, 1935.

Vicentino, Nicola, *L'Antica Musica ridotta alla moderna prattica*, Rome, 1555.

Vogler, Georg Joseph, *Choral-System*, Copenhagen, 1800.

―― *System für den Fugenbau*, Offenbach, 1811.

Walther, Johann Gottfried, *Musikalisches Lexikon*, Leipzig, 1732.

―― See Gehrmann, Heinrich.

Weinlig, Theodor, *Anleitung zur Fuge*, Leipzig, 1845.

Zacconi, Lodovico, *Prattica di musica*, Venice: Pt. I, 1596; Pt. II, 1622.

Zarlino, Gioseffo, *Istitutioni harmoniche*, Venice, 1558, 1562, 1573.

Index

ALFRED MANN, Professor Emeritus, Rutgers University, is currently Professor of Musicology at the Eastman School of Music. Born in Hamburg and trained in Berlin and Milan, and at the Curtis Institute of Music, Philadelphia, he took his Ph.D. from Columbia University in 1955. He has contributed volumes to the complete editions of the works of Handel, Mozart, Schubert, and Fux and published German and English translations of Fux's basic counterpoint text from the *Gradus ad Parnassum* (*The Study of Counterpoint*). As a specialist in the choral music of the Baroque, he succeeded the late Arthur Mendel as conductor of New York's Cantata Singers and has served as conductor of the Bach Choir of Bethlehem, with guest conducting and recording engagements in Europe and this country. Since 1962 he has been editor of the *American Choral Review*.

A CATALOG OF SELECTED

DOVER BOOKS

IN ALL FIELDS OF INTEREST

A CATALOG OF SELECTED DOVER
BOOKS IN ALL FIELDS OF INTEREST

DRAWINGS OF REMBRANDT, edited by Seymour Slive. Updated Lippmann, Hofstede de Groot edition, with definitive scholarly apparatus. All portraits, biblical sketches, landscapes, nudes. Oriental figures, classical studies, together with selection of work by followers. 550 illustrations. Total of 630pp. 9⅛ × 12¼.
21485-0, 21486-9 Pa., Two-vol. set $25.00

GHOST AND HORROR STORIES OF AMBROSE BIERCE, Ambrose Bierce. 24 tales vividly imagined, strangely prophetic, and decades ahead of their time in technical skill: "The Damned Thing," "An Inhabitant of Carcosa," "The Eyes of the Panther," "Moxon's Master," and 20 more. 199pp. 5⅜ × 8½. 20767-6 Pa. $3.95

ETHICAL WRITINGS OF MAIMONIDES, Maimonides. Most significant ethical works of great medieval sage, newly translated for utmost precision, readability. Laws Concerning Character Traits, Eight Chapters, more. 192pp. 5⅜ × 8½.
24522-5 Pa. $4.50

THE EXPLORATION OF THE COLORADO RIVER AND ITS CANYONS, J. W. Powell. Full text of Powell's 1,000-mile expedition down the fabled Colorado in 1869. Superb account of terrain, geology, vegetation, Indians, famine, mutiny, treacherous rapids, mighty canyons, during exploration of last unknown part of continental U.S. 400pp. 5⅜ × 8½. 20094-9 Pa. $6.95

HISTORY OF PHILOSOPHY, Julián Marías. Clearest one-volume history on the market. Every major philosopher and dozens of others, to Existentialism and later. 505pp. 5⅜ × 8½. 21739-6 Pa. $8.50

ALL ABOUT LIGHTNING, Martin A. Uman. Highly readable non-technical survey of nature and causes of lightning, thunderstorms, ball lightning, St. Elmo's Fire, much more. Illustrated. 192pp. 5⅜ × 8½. 25237-X Pa. $5.95

SAILING ALONE AROUND THE WORLD, Captain Joshua Slocum. First man to sail around the world, alone, in small boat. One of great feats of seamanship told in delightful manner. 67 illustrations. 294pp. 5⅜ × 8½. 20326-3 Pa. $4.50

LETTERS AND NOTES ON THE MANNERS, CUSTOMS AND CONDITIONS OF THE NORTH AMERICAN INDIANS, George Catlin. Classic account of life among Plains Indians: ceremonies, hunt, warfare, etc. 312 plates. 572pp. of text. 6⅛ × 9¼. 22118-0, 22119-9 Pa. Two-vol. set $15.90

ALASKA: The Harriman Expedition, 1899, John Burroughs, John Muir, et al. Informative, engrossing accounts of two-month, 9,000-mile expedition. Native peoples, wildlife, forests, geography, salmon industry, glaciers, more. Profusely illustrated. 240 black-and-white line drawings. 124 black-and-white photographs. 3 maps. Index. 576pp. 5⅜ × 8½. 25109-8 Pa. $11.95

THE BOOK OF BEASTS: Being a Translation from a Latin Bestiary of the Twelfth Century, T. H. White. Wonderful catalog real and fanciful beasts: manticore, griffin, phoenix, amphivius, jaculus, many more. White's witty erudite commentary on scientific, historical aspects. Fascinating glimpse of medieval mind. Illustrated. 296pp. 5⅜ × 8¼. (Available in U.S. only) 24609-4 Pa. $5.95

FRANK LLOYD WRIGHT: ARCHITECTURE AND NATURE With 160 Illustrations, Donald Hoffmann. Profusely illustrated study of influence of nature—especially prairie—on Wright's designs for Fallingwater, Robie House, Guggenheim Museum, other masterpieces. 96pp. 9¼ × 10¾. 25098-9 Pa. $7.95

FRANK LLOYD WRIGHT'S FALLINGWATER, Donald Hoffmann. Wright's famous waterfall house: planning and construction of organic idea. History of site, owners, Wright's personal involvement. Photographs of various stages of building. Preface by Edgar Kaufmann, Jr. 100 illustrations. 112pp. 9¼ × 10.
23671-4 Pa. $7.95

YEARS WITH FRANK LLOYD WRIGHT: Apprentice to Genius, Edgar Tafel. Insightful memoir by a former apprentice presents a revealing portrait of Wright the man, the inspired teacher, the greatest American architect. 372 black-and-white illustrations. Preface. Index. vi + 228pp. 8¼ × 11. 24801-1 Pa. $9.95

THE STORY OF KING ARTHUR AND HIS KNIGHTS, Howard Pyle. Enchanting version of King Arthur fable has delighted generations with imaginative narratives of exciting adventures and unforgettable illustrations by the author. 41 illustrations. xviii + 313pp. 6⅛ × 9¼. 21445-1 Pa. $5.95

THE GODS OF THE EGYPTIANS, E. A. Wallis Budge. Thorough coverage of numerous gods of ancient Egypt by foremost Egyptologist. Information on evolution of cults, rites and gods; the cult of Osiris; the Book of the Dead and its rites; the sacred animals and birds; Heaven and Hell; and more. 956pp. 6⅛ × 9¼.
22055-9, 22056-7 Pa., Two-vol. set $20.00

A THEOLOGICO-POLITICAL TREATISE, Benedict Spinoza. Also contains unfinished *Political Treatise*. Great classic on religious liberty, theory of government on common consent. R. Elwes translation. Total of 421pp. 5⅜ × 8½.
20249-6 Pa. $6.95

INCIDENTS OF TRAVEL IN CENTRAL AMERICA, CHIAPAS, AND YUCATAN, John L. Stephens. Almost single-handed discovery of Maya culture; exploration of ruined cities, monuments, temples; customs of Indians. 115 drawings. 892pp. 5⅜ × 8½. 22404-X, 22405-8 Pa., Two-vol. set $15.90

LOS CAPRICHOS, Francisco Goya. 80 plates of wild, grotesque monsters and caricatures. Prado manuscript included. 183pp. 6⅝ × 9⅜. 22384-1 Pa. $4.95

AUTOBIOGRAPHY: The Story of My Experiments with Truth, Mohandas K. Gandhi. Not hagiography, but Gandhi in his own words. Boyhood, legal studies, purification, the growth of the Satyagraha (nonviolent protest) movement. Critical, inspiring work of the man who freed India. 480pp. 5⅜ × 8½. (Available in U.S. only)
24593-4 Pa. $6.95

ILLUSTRATED DICTIONARY OF HISTORIC ARCHITECTURE, edited by Cyril M. Harris. Extraordinary compendium of clear, concise definitions for over 5,000 important architectural terms complemented by over 2,000 line drawings. Covers full spectrum of architecture from ancient ruins to 20th-century Modernism. Preface. 592pp. 7½ × 9⅝. 24444-X Pa. $14.95

THE NIGHT BEFORE CHRISTMAS, Clement Moore. Full text, and woodcuts from original 1848 book. Also critical, historical material. 19 illustrations. 40pp. 4⅝ × 6. 22797-9 Pa. $2.25

THE LESSON OF JAPANESE ARCHITECTURE: 165 Photographs, Jiro Harada. Memorable gallery of 165 photographs taken in the 1930's of exquisite Japanese homes of the well-to-do and historic buildings. 13 line diagrams. 192pp. 8⅜ × 11¼. 24778-3 Pa. $8.95

THE AUTOBIOGRAPHY OF CHARLES DARWIN AND SELECTED LET-TERS, edited by Francis Darwin. The fascinating life of eccentric genius composed of an intimate memoir by Darwin (intended for his children); commentary by his son, Francis; hundreds of fragments from notebooks, journals, papers; and letters to and from Lyell, Hooker, Huxley, Wallace and Henslow. xi + 365pp. 5⅜ × 8. 20479-0 Pa. $5.95

WONDERS OF THE SKY: Observing Rainbows, Comets, Eclipses, the Stars and Other Phenomena, Fred Schaaf. Charming, easy-to-read poetic guide to all manner of celestial events visible to the naked eye. Mock suns, glories, Belt of Venus, more. Illustrated. 299pp. 5¼ × 8¼. 24402-4 Pa. $7.95

BURNHAM'S CELESTIAL HANDBOOK, Robert Burnham, Jr. Thorough guide to the stars beyond our solar system. Exhaustive treatment. Alphabetical by constellation: Andromeda to Cetus in Vol. 1; Chamaeleon to Orion in Vol. 2; and Pavo to Vulpecula in Vol. 3. Hundreds of illustrations. Index in Vol. 3. 2,000pp. 6⅛ × 9¼. 23567-X, 23568-8, 23673-0 Pa., Three-vol. set $36.85

STAR NAMES: Their Lore and Meaning, Richard Hinckley Allen. Fascinating history of names various cultures have given to constellations and literary and folkloristic uses that have been made of stars. Indexes to subjects. Arabic and Greek names. Biblical references. Bibliography. 563pp. 5⅜ × 8½. 21079-0 Pa. $7.95

THIRTY YEARS THAT SHOOK PHYSICS: The Story of Quantum Theory, George Gamow. Lucid, accessible introduction to influential theory of energy and matter. Careful explanations of Dirac's anti-particles, Bohr's model of the atom, much more. 12 plates. Numerous drawings. 240pp. 5⅜ × 8½. 24895-X Pa. $4.95

CHINESE DOMESTIC FURNITURE IN PHOTOGRAPHS AND MEASURED DRAWINGS, Gustav Ecke. A rare volume, now affordably priced for antique collectors, furniture buffs and art historians. Detailed review of styles ranging from early Shang to late Ming. Unabridged republication. 161 black-and-white drawings, photos. Total of 224pp. 8⅞ × 11¼. (Available in U.S. only) 25171-3 Pa. $12.95

VINCENT VAN GOGH: A Biography, Julius Meier-Graefe. Dynamic, penetrating study of artist's life, relationship with brother, Theo, painting techniques, travels, more. Readable, engrossing. 160pp. 5⅜ × 8½. (Available in U.S. only) 25253-1 Pa. $3.95

HOW TO WRITE, Gertrude Stein. Gertrude Stein claimed anyone could understand her unconventional writing—here are clues to help. Fascinating improvisations, language experiments, explanations illuminate Stein's craft and the art of writing. Total of 414pp. 4⅝ × 6⅜. 23144-5 Pa. $5.95

ADVENTURES AT SEA IN THE GREAT AGE OF SAIL: Five Firsthand Narratives, edited by Elliot Snow. Rare true accounts of exploration, whaling, shipwreck, fierce natives, trade, shipboard life, more. 33 illustrations. Introduction. 353pp. 5⅜ × 8½. 25177-2 Pa. $7.95

THE HERBAL OR GENERAL HISTORY OF PLANTS, John Gerard. Classic descriptions of about 2,850 plants—with over 2,700 illustrations—includes Latin and English names, physical descriptions, varieties, time and place of growth, more. 2,706 illustrations. xlv + 1,678pp. 8½ × 12¼. 23147-X Cloth. $75.00

DOROTHY AND THE WIZARD IN OZ, L. Frank Baum. Dorothy and the Wizard visit the center of the Earth, where people are vegetables, glass houses grow and Oz characters reappear. Classic sequel to *Wizard of Oz*. 256pp. 5⅜ × 8. 24714-7 Pa. $4.95

SONGS OF EXPERIENCE: Facsimile Reproduction with 26 Plates in Full Color, William Blake. This facsimile of Blake's original "Illuminated Book" reproduces 26 full-color plates from a rare 1826 edition. Includes "The Tyger," "London," "Holy Thursday," and other immortal poems. 26 color plates. Printed text of poems. 48pp. 5¼ × 7. 24636-1 Pa. $3.50

SONGS OF INNOCENCE, William Blake. The first and most popular of Blake's famous "Illuminated Books," in a facsimile edition reproducing all 31 brightly colored plates. Additional printed text of each poem. 64pp. 5¼ × 7. 22764-2 Pa. $3.50

PRECIOUS STONES, Max Bauer. Classic, thorough study of diamonds, rubies, emeralds, garnets, etc.: physical character, occurrence, properties, use, similar topics. 20 plates, 8 in color. 94 figures. 659pp. 6⅛ × 9¼. 21910-0, 21911-9 Pa., Two-vol. set $14.90

ENCYCLOPEDIA OF VICTORIAN NEEDLEWORK, S. F. A. Caulfeild and Blanche Saward. Full, precise descriptions of stitches, techniques for dozens of needlecrafts—most exhaustive reference of its kind. Over 800 figures. Total of 679pp. 8⅛ × 11. Two volumes. Vol. 1 22800-2 Pa. $10.95
Vol. 2 22801-0 Pa. $10.95

THE MARVELOUS LAND OF OZ, L. Frank Baum. Second Oz book, the Scarecrow and Tin Woodman are back with hero named Tip, Oz magic. 136 illustrations. 287pp. 5⅜ × 8½. 20692-0 Pa. $5.95

WILD FOWL DECOYS, Joel Barber. Basic book on the subject, by foremost authority and collector. Reveals history of decoy making and rigging, place in American culture, different kinds of decoys, how to make them, and how to use them. 140 plates. 156pp. 7⅞ × 10¾. 20011-6 Pa. $7.95

HISTORY OF LACE, Mrs. Bury Palliser. Definitive, profusely illustrated chronicle of lace from earliest times to late 19th century. Laces of Italy, Greece, England, France, Belgium, etc. Landmark of needlework scholarship. 266 illustrations. 672pp. 6⅛ × 9¼. 24742-2 Pa. $14.95

ILLUSTRATED GUIDE TO SHAKER FURNITURE, Robert Meader. All furniture and appurtenances, with much on unknown local styles. 235 photos. 146pp. 9 × 12. 22819-3 Pa. $7.95

WHALE SHIPS AND WHALING: A Pictorial Survey, George Francis Dow. Over 200 vintage engravings, drawings, photographs of barks, brigs, cutters, other vessels. Also harpoons, lances, whaling guns, many other artifacts. Comprehensive text by foremost authority. 207 black-and-white illustrations. 288pp. 6 × 9. 24808-9 Pa. $8.95

THE BERTRAMS, Anthony Trollope. Powerful portrayal of blind self-will and thwarted ambition includes one of Trollope's most heartrending love stories. 497pp. 5⅜ × 8½. 25119-5 Pa. $8.95

ADVENTURES WITH A HAND LENS, Richard Headstrom. Clearly written guide to observing and studying flowers and grasses, fish scales, moth and insect wings, egg cases, buds, feathers, seeds, leaf scars, moss, molds, ferns, common crystals, etc.—all with an ordinary, inexpensive magnifying glass. 209 exact line drawings aid in your discoveries. 220pp. 5⅜ × 8½. 23330-8 Pa. $3.95

RODIN ON ART AND ARTISTS, Auguste Rodin. Great sculptor's candid, wide-ranging comments on meaning of art; great artists; relation of sculpture to poetry, painting, music; philosophy of life, more. 76 superb black-and-white illustrations of Rodin's sculpture, drawings and prints. 119pp. 8⅜ × 11¼. 24487-3 Pa. $6.95

FIFTY CLASSIC FRENCH FILMS, 1912-1982: A Pictorial Record, Anthony Slide. Memorable stills from Grand Illusion, Beauty and the Beast, Hiroshima, Mon Amour, many more. Credits, plot synopses, reviews, etc. 160pp. 8¼ × 11. 25256-6 Pa. $11.95

THE PRINCIPLES OF PSYCHOLOGY, William James. Famous long course complete, unabridged. Stream of thought, time perception, memory, experimental methods; great work decades ahead of its time. 94 figures. 1,391pp. 5⅜ × 8½. 20381-6, 20382-4 Pa., Two-vol. set $19.90

BODIES IN A BOOKSHOP, R. T. Campbell. Challenging mystery of blackmail and murder with ingenious plot and superbly drawn characters. In the best tradition of British suspense fiction. 192pp. 5⅜ × 8½. 24720-1 Pa. $3.95

CALLAS: PORTRAIT OF A PRIMA DONNA, George Jellinek. Renowned commentator on the musical scene chronicles incredible career and life of the most controversial, fascinating, influential operatic personality of our time. 64 black-and-white photographs. 416pp. 5⅜ × 8¼. 25047-4 Pa. $7.95

GEOMETRY, RELATIVITY AND THE FOURTH DIMENSION, Rudolph Rucker. Exposition of fourth dimension, concepts of relativity as Flatland characters continue adventures. Popular, easily followed yet accurate, profound. 141 illustrations. 133pp. 5⅜ × 8½. 23400-2 Pa. $3.50

HOUSEHOLD STORIES BY THE BROTHERS GRIMM, with pictures by Walter Crane. 53 classic stories—Rumpelstiltskin, Rapunzel, Hansel and Gretel, the Fisherman and his Wife, Snow White, Tom Thumb, Sleeping Beauty, Cinderella, and so much more—lavishly illustrated with original 19th century drawings. 114 illustrations. x + 269pp. 5⅜ × 8½. 21080-4 Pa. $4.50

SUNDIALS, Albert Waugh. Far and away the best, most thorough coverage of ideas, mathematics concerned, types, construction, adjusting anywhere. Over 100 illustrations. 230pp. 5⅜ × 8½.   22947-5 Pa. $4.00

PICTURE HISTORY OF THE NORMANDIE: With 190 Illustrations, Frank O. Braynard. Full story of legendary French ocean liner: Art Deco interiors, design innovations, furnishings, celebrities, maiden voyage, tragic fire, much more. Extensive text. 144pp. 8⅞ × 11¾.   25257-4 Pa. $9.95

THE FIRST AMERICAN COOKBOOK: A Facsimile of "American Cookery," 1796, Amelia Simmons. Facsimile of the first American-written cookbook published in the United States contains authentic recipes for colonial favorites—pumpkin pudding, winter squash pudding, spruce beer, Indian slapjacks, and more. Introductory Essay and Glossary of colonial cooking terms. 80pp. 5⅜ × 8½.
24710-4 Pa. $3.50

101 PUZZLES IN THOUGHT AND LOGIC, C. R. Wylie, Jr. Solve murders and robberies, find out which fishermen are liars, how a blind man could possibly identify a color—purely by your own reasoning! 107pp. 5⅜ × 8½. 20367-0 Pa. $2.00

THE BOOK OF WORLD-FAMOUS MUSIC—CLASSICAL, POPULAR AND FOLK, James J. Fuld. Revised and enlarged republication of landmark work in musico-bibliography. Full information about nearly 1,000 songs and compositions including first lines of music and lyrics. New supplement. Index. 800pp. 5⅜ × 8¼.
24857-7 Pa. $14.95

ANTHROPOLOGY AND MODERN LIFE, Franz Boas. Great anthropologist's classic treatise on race and culture. Introduction by Ruth Bunzel. Only inexpensive paperback edition. 255pp. 5⅜ × 8½.   25245-0 Pa. $5.95

THE TALE OF PETER RABBIT, Beatrix Potter. The inimitable Peter's terrifying adventure in Mr. McGregor's garden, with all 27 wonderful, full-color Potter illustrations. 55pp. 4¼ × 5½. (Available in U.S. only)   22827-4 Pa. $1.75

THREE PROPHETIC SCIENCE FICTION NOVELS, H. G. Wells. *When the Sleeper Wakes, A Story of the Days to Come* and *The Time Machine* (full version). 335pp. 5⅜ × 8½. (Available in U.S. only)   20605-X Pa. $5.95

APICIUS COOKERY AND DINING IN IMPERIAL ROME, edited and translated by Joseph Dommers Vehling. Oldest known cookbook in existence offers readers a clear picture of what foods Romans ate, how they prepared them, etc. 49 illustrations. 301pp. 6¼ × 9¼.   23563-7 Pa. $6.00

SHAKESPEARE LEXICON AND QUOTATION DICTIONARY, Alexander Schmidt. Full definitions, locations, shades of meaning of every word in plays and poems. More than 50,000 exact quotations. 1,485pp. 6½ × 9¼.
22726-X, 22727-8 Pa., Two-vol. set $27.90

THE WORLD'S GREAT SPEECHES, edited by Lewis Copeland and Lawrence W. Lamm. Vast collection of 278 speeches from Greeks to 1970. Powerful and effective models; unique look at history. 842pp. 5⅜ × 8½.   20468-5 Pa. $10.95

THE BLUE FAIRY BOOK, Andrew Lang. The first, most famous collection, with many familiar tales: Little Red Riding Hood, Aladdin and the Wonderful Lamp, Puss in Boots, Sleeping Beauty, Hansel and Gretel, Rumpelstiltskin; 37 in all. 138 illustrations. 390pp. 5⅜ × 8½. 21437-0 Pa. $5.95

THE STORY OF THE CHAMPIONS OF THE ROUND TABLE, Howard Pyle. Sir Launcelot, Sir Tristram and Sir Percival in spirited adventures of love and triumph retold in Pyle's inimitable style. 50 drawings, 31 full-page. xviii + 329pp. 6½ × 9¼. 21883-X Pa. $6.95

AUDUBON AND HIS JOURNALS, Maria Audubon. Unmatched two-volume portrait of the great artist, naturalist and author contains his journals, an excellent biography by his granddaughter, expert annotations by the noted ornithologist, Dr. Elliott Coues, and 37 superb illustrations. Total of 1,200pp. 5⅜ × 8.

Vol. I 25143-8 Pa. $8.95
Vol. II 25144-6 Pa. $8.95

GREAT DINOSAUR HUNTERS AND THEIR DISCOVERIES, Edwin H. Colbert. Fascinating, lavishly illustrated chronicle of dinosaur research, 1820's to 1960. Achievements of Cope, Marsh, Brown, Buckland, Mantell, Huxley, many others. 384pp. 5¼ × 8¼. 24701-5 Pa. $6.95

THE TASTEMAKERS, Russell Lynes. Informal, illustrated social history of American taste 1850's–1950's. First popularized categories Highbrow, Lowbrow, Middlebrow. 129 illustrations. New (1979) afterword. 384pp. 6 × 9.
23993-4 Pa. $6.95

DOUBLE CROSS PURPOSES, Ronald A. Knox. A treasure hunt in the Scottish Highlands, an old map, unidentified corpse, surprise discoveries keep reader guessing in this cleverly intricate tale of financial skullduggery. 2 black-and-white maps. 320pp. 5⅜ × 8½. (Available in U.S. only) 25032-6 Pa. $5.95

AUTHENTIC VICTORIAN DECORATION AND ORNAMENTATION IN FULL COLOR: 46 Plates from "Studies in Design," Christopher Dresser. Superb full-color lithographs reproduced from rare original portfolio of a major Victorian designer. 48pp. 9¼ × 12¼. 25083-0 Pa. $7.95

PRIMITIVE ART, Franz Boas. Remains the best text ever prepared on subject, thoroughly discussing Indian, African, Asian, Australian, and, especially, Northern American primitive art. Over 950 illustrations show ceramics, masks, totem poles, weapons, textiles, paintings, much more. 376pp. 5⅜ × 8. 20025-6 Pa. $6.95

SIDELIGHTS ON RELATIVITY, Albert Einstein. Unabridged republication of two lectures delivered by the great physicist in 1920–21. *Ether and Relativity* and *Geometry and Experience.* Elegant ideas in non-mathematical form, accessible to intelligent layman. vi + 56pp. 5⅜ × 8½. 24511-X Pa. $2.95

THE WIT AND HUMOR OF OSCAR WILDE, edited by Alvin Redman. More than 1,000 ripostes, paradoxes, wisecracks: Work is the curse of the drinking classes, I can resist everything except temptation, etc. 258pp. 5⅜ × 8½. 20602-5 Pa. $3.95

ADVENTURES WITH A MICROSCOPE, Richard Headstrom. 59 adventures with clothing fibers, protozoa, ferns and lichens, roots and leaves, much more. 142 illustrations. 232pp. 5⅜ × 8½. 23471-1 Pa. $3.95

PLANTS OF THE BIBLE, Harold N. Moldenke and Alma L. Moldenke. Standard reference to all 230 plants mentioned in Scriptures. Latin name, biblical reference, uses, modern identity, much more. Unsurpassed encyclopedic resource for scholars, botanists, nature lovers, students of Bible. Bibliography. Indexes. 123 black-and-white illustrations. 384pp. 6 × 9. 25069-5 Pa. $8.95

FAMOUS AMERICAN WOMEN: A Biographical Dictionary from Colonial Times to the Present, Robert McHenry, ed. From Pocahontas to Rosa Parks, 1,035 distinguished American women documented in separate biographical entries. Accurate, up-to-date data, numerous categories, spans 400 years. Indices. 493pp. 6½ × 9¼. 24523-3 Pa. $9.95

THE FABULOUS INTERIORS OF THE GREAT OCEAN LINERS IN HISTORIC PHOTOGRAPHS, William H. Miller, Jr. Some 200 superb photographs capture exquisite interiors of world's great "floating palaces"—1890's to 1980's: *Titanic, Ile de France, Queen Elizabeth, United States, Europa,* more. Approx. 200 black-and-white photographs. Captions. Text. Introduction. 160pp. 8⅞ × 11¾. 24756-2 Pa. $9.95

THE GREAT LUXURY LINERS, 1927–1954: A Photographic Record, William H. Miller, Jr. Nostalgic tribute to heyday of ocean liners. 186 photos of Ile de France, Normandie, Leviathan, Queen Elizabeth, United States, many others. Interior and exterior views. Introduction. Captions. 160pp. 9 × 12. 24056-8 Pa. $9.95

A NATURAL HISTORY OF THE DUCKS, John Charles Phillips. Great landmark of ornithology offers complete detailed coverage of nearly 200 species and subspecies of ducks: gadwall, sheldrake, merganser, pintail, many more. 74 full-color plates, 102 black-and-white. Bibliography. Total of 1,920pp. 8⅝ × 11¼. 25141-1, 25142-X Cloth. Two-vol. set $100.00

THE SEAWEED HANDBOOK: An Illustrated Guide to Seaweeds from North Carolina to Canada, Thomas F. Lee. Concise reference covers 78 species. Scientific and common names, habitat, distribution, more. Finding keys for easy identification. 224pp. 5⅜ × 8½. 25215-9 Pa. $5.95

THE TEN BOOKS OF ARCHITECTURE: The 1755 Leoni Edition, Leon Battista Alberti. Rare classic helped introduce the glories of ancient architecture to the Renaissance. 68 black-and-white plates. 336pp. 8⅜ × 11¼. 25239-6 Pa. $14.95

MISS MACKENZIE, Anthony Trollope. Minor masterpieces by Victorian master unmasks many truths about life in 19th-century England. First inexpensive edition in years. 392pp. 5⅜ × 8½. 25201-9 Pa. $7.95

THE RIME OF THE ANCIENT MARINER, Gustave Doré, Samuel Taylor Coleridge. Dramatic engravings considered by many to be his greatest work. The terrifying space of the open sea, the storms and whirlpools of an unknown ocean, the ice of Antarctica, more—all rendered in a powerful, chilling manner. Full text. 38 plates. 77pp. 9¼ × 12. 22305-1 Pa. $4.95

THE EXPEDITIONS OF ZEBULON MONTGOMERY PIKE, Zebulon Montgomery Pike. Fascinating first-hand accounts (1805–6) of exploration of Mississippi River, Indian wars, capture by Spanish dragoons, much more. 1,088pp. 5⅜ × 8½. 25254-X, 25255-8 Pa. Two-vol. set $23.90

A CONCISE HISTORY OF PHOTOGRAPHY: Third Revised Edition, Helmut Gernsheim. Best one-volume history—camera obscura, photochemistry, daguerreotypes, evolution of cameras, film, more. Also artistic aspects—landscape, portraits, fine art, etc. 281 black-and-white photographs. 26 in color. 176pp. 8⅜ × 11¼. 25128-4 Pa. $12.95

THE DORÉ BIBLE ILLUSTRATIONS, Gustave Doré. 241 detailed plates from the Bible: the Creation scenes, Adam and Eve, Flood, Babylon, battle sequences, life of Jesus, etc. Each plate is accompanied by the verses from the King James version of the Bible. 241pp. 9 × 12. 23004-X Pa. $8.95

HUGGER-MUGGER IN THE LOUVRE, Elliot Paul. Second Homer Evans mystery-comedy. Theft at the Louvre involves sleuth in hilarious, madcap caper. "A knockout."—Books. 336pp. 5⅜ × 8½. 25185-3 Pa. $5.95

FLATLAND, E. A. Abbott. Intriguing and enormously popular science-fiction classic explores the complexities of trying to survive as a two-dimensional being in a three-dimensional world. Amusingly illustrated by the author. 16 illustrations. 103pp. 5⅜ × 8½. 20001-9 Pa. $2.00

THE HISTORY OF THE LEWIS AND CLARK EXPEDITION, Meriwether Lewis and William Clark, edited by Elliott Coues. Classic edition of Lewis and Clark's day-by-day journals that later became the basis for U.S. claims to Oregon and the West. Accurate and invaluable geographical, botanical, biological, meteorological and anthropological material. Total of 1,508pp. 5⅜ × 8½.
21268-8, 21269-6, 21270-X Pa. Three-vol. set $25.50

LANGUAGE, TRUTH AND LOGIC, Alfred J. Ayer. Famous, clear introduction to Vienna, Cambridge schools of Logical Positivism. Role of philosophy, elimination of metaphysics, nature of analysis, etc. 160pp. 5⅜ × 8½. (Available in U.S. and Canada only) 20010-8 Pa. $2.95

MATHEMATICS FOR THE NONMATHEMATICIAN, Morris Kline. Detailed, college-level treatment of mathematics in cultural and historical context, with numerous exercises. For liberal arts students. Preface. Recommended Reading Lists. Tables. Index. Numerous black-and-white figures. xvi + 641pp. 5⅜ × 8½.
24823-2 Pa. $11.95

28 SCIENCE FICTION STORIES, H. G. Wells. Novels, *Star Begotten* and *Men Like Gods,* plus 26 short stories: "Empire of the Ants," "A Story of the Stone Age," "The Stolen Bacillus," "In the Abyss," etc. 915pp. 5⅜ × 8½. (Available in U.S. only)
20265-8 Cloth. $10.95

HANDBOOK OF PICTORIAL SYMBOLS, Rudolph Modley. 3,250 signs and symbols, many systems in full; official or heavy commercial use. Arranged by subject. Most in Pictorial Archive series. 143pp. 8⅛ × 11. 23357-X Pa. $5.95

INCIDENTS OF TRAVEL IN YUCATAN, John L. Stephens. Classic (1843) exploration of jungles of Yucatan, looking for evidences of Maya civilization. Travel adventures, Mexican and Indian culture, etc. Total of 669pp. 5⅜ × 8½.
20926-1, 20927-X Pa., Two-vol. set $9.90

DEGAS: An Intimate Portrait, Ambroise Vollard. Charming, anecdotal memoir by famous art dealer of one of the greatest 19th-century French painters. 14 black-and-white illustrations. Introduction by Harold L. Van Doren. 96pp. 5⅜ × 8½.
25131-4 Pa. $3.95

PERSONAL NARRATIVE OF A PILGRIMAGE TO ALMANDINAH AND MECCAH, Richard Burton. Great travel classic by remarkably colorful personality. Burton, disguised as a Moroccan, visited sacred shrines of Islam, narrowly escaping death. 47 illustrations. 959pp. 5⅜ × 8½.   21217-3, 21218-1 Pa., Two-vol. set $17.90

PHRASE AND WORD ORIGINS, A. H. Holt. Entertaining, reliable, modern study of more than 1,200 colorful words, phrases, origins and histories. Much unexpected information. 254pp. 5⅜ × 8½.   20758-7 Pa. $4.95

THE RED THUMB MARK, R. Austin Freeman. In this first Dr. Thorndyke case, the great scientific detective draws fascinating conclusions from the nature of a single fingerprint. Exciting story, authentic science. 320pp. 5⅜ × 8½. (Available in U.S. only)   25210-8 Pa. $5.95

AN EGYPTIAN HIEROGLYPHIC DICTIONARY, E. A. Wallis Budge. Monumental work containing about 25,000 words or terms that occur in texts ranging from 3000 B.C. to 600 A.D. Each entry consists of a transliteration of the word, the word in hieroglyphs, and the meaning in English. 1,314pp. 6⅜ × 10.
23615-3, 23616-1 Pa., Two-vol. set $27.90

THE COMPLEAT STRATEGYST: Being a Primer on the Theory of Games of Strategy, J. D. Williams. Highly entertaining classic describes, with many illustrated examples, how to select best strategies in conflict situations. Prefaces. Appendices. xvi + 268pp. 5⅜ × 8½.   25101-2 Pa. $5.95

THE ROAD TO OZ, L. Frank Baum. Dorothy meets the Shaggy Man, little Button-Bright and the Rainbow's beautiful daughter in this delightful trip to the magical Land of Oz. 272pp. 5⅜ × 8.   25208-6 Pa. $4.95

POINT AND LINE TO PLANE, Wassily Kandinsky. Seminal exposition of role of point, line, other elements in non-objective painting. Essential to understanding 20th-century art. 127 illustrations. 192pp. 6½ × 9¼.   23808-3 Pa. $4.50

LADY ANNA, Anthony Trollope. Moving chronicle of Countess Lovel's bitter struggle to win for herself and daughter Anna their rightful rank and fortune—perhaps at cost of sanity itself. 384pp. 5⅜ × 8½.   24669-8 Pa. $6.95

EGYPTIAN MAGIC, E. A. Wallis Budge. Sums up all that is known about magic in Ancient Egypt: the role of magic in controlling the gods, powerful amulets that warded off evil spirits, scarabs of immortality, use of wax images, formulas and spells, the secret name, much more. 253pp. 5⅜ × 8½.   22681-6 Pa. $4.00

THE DANCE OF SIVA, Ananda Coomaraswamy. Preeminent authority unfolds the vast metaphysic of India: the revelation of her art, conception of the universe, social organization, etc. 27 reproductions of art masterpieces. 192pp. 5⅜ × 8½.
24817-8 Pa. $5.95

CHRISTMAS CUSTOMS AND TRADITIONS, Clement A. Miles. Origin, evolution, significance of religious, secular practices. Caroling, gifts, yule logs, much more. Full, scholarly yet fascinating; non-sectarian. 400pp. 5⅜ × 8½.
23354-5 Pa. $6.50

THE HUMAN FIGURE IN MOTION, Eadweard Muybridge. More than 4,500 stopped-action photos, in action series, showing undraped men, women, children jumping, lying down, throwing, sitting, wrestling, carrying, etc. 390pp. 7⅞ × 10⅝.
20204-6 Cloth. $19.95

THE MAN WHO WAS THURSDAY, Gilbert Keith Chesterton. Witty, fast-paced novel about a club of anarchists in turn-of-the-century London. Brilliant social, religious, philosophical speculations. 128pp. 5⅜ × 8½.
25121-7 Pa. $3.95

A CEZANNE SKETCHBOOK: Figures, Portraits, Landscapes and Still Lifes, Paul Cezanne. Great artist experiments with tonal effects, light, mass, other qualities in over 100 drawings. A revealing view of developing master painter, precursor of Cubism. 102 black-and-white illustrations. 144pp. 8¾ × 6⅝.
24790-2 Pa. $5.95

AN ENCYCLOPEDIA OF BATTLES: Accounts of Over 1,560 Battles from 1479 b.c. to the Present, David Eggenberger. Presents essential details of every major battle in recorded history, from the first battle of Megiddo in 1479 b.c. to Grenada in 1984. List of Battle Maps. New Appendix covering the years 1967–1984. Index. 99 illustrations. 544pp. 6½ × 9¼.
24913-1 Pa. $14.95

AN ETYMOLOGICAL DICTIONARY OF MODERN ENGLISH, Ernest Weekley. Richest, fullest work, by foremost British lexicographer. Detailed word histories. Inexhaustible. Total of 856pp. 6½ × 9¼.
21873-2, 21874-0 Pa., Two-vol. set $17.00

WEBSTER'S AMERICAN MILITARY BIOGRAPHIES, edited by Robert McHenry. Over 1,000 figures who shaped 3 centuries of American military history. Detailed biographies of Nathan Hale, Douglas MacArthur, Mary Hallaren, others. Chronologies of engagements, more. Introduction. Addenda. 1,033 entries in alphabetical order. xi + 548pp. 6½ × 9¼. (Available in U.S. only)
24758-9 Pa. $11.95

LIFE IN ANCIENT EGYPT, Adolf Erman. Detailed older account, with much not in more recent books: domestic life, religion, magic, medicine, commerce, and whatever else needed for complete picture. Many illustrations. 597pp. 5⅜ × 8½.
22632-8 Pa. $8.50

HISTORIC COSTUME IN PICTURES, Braun & Schneider. Over 1,450 costumed figures shown, covering a wide variety of peoples: kings, emperors, nobles, priests, servants, soldiers, scholars, townsfolk, peasants, merchants, courtiers, cavaliers, and more. 256pp. 8⅜ × 11¼.
23150-X Pa. $7.95

THE NOTEBOOKS OF LEONARDO DA VINCI, edited by J. P. Richter. Extracts from manuscripts reveal great genius; on painting, sculpture, anatomy, sciences, geography, etc. Both Italian and English. 186 ms. pages reproduced, plus 500 additional drawings, including studies for *Last Supper, Sforza* monument, etc. 860pp. 7⅞ × 10¾. (Available in U.S. only) 22572-0, 22573-9 Pa., Two-vol. set $25.90

CATALOG OF DOVER BOOKS

THE ART NOUVEAU STYLE BOOK OF ALPHONSE MUCHA: All 72 Plates from "Documents Decoratifs" in Original Color, Alphonse Mucha. Rare copyright-free design portfolio by high priest of Art Nouveau. Jewelry, wallpaper, stained glass, furniture, figure studies, plant and animal motifs, etc. Only complete one-volume edition. 80pp. 9⅝ × 12¼. 24044-4 Pa. $8.95

ANIMALS: 1,419 COPYRIGHT-FREE ILLUSTRATIONS OF MAMMALS, BIRDS, FISH, INSECTS, ETC., edited by Jim Harter. Clear wood engravings present, in extremely lifelike poses, over 1,000 species of animals. One of the most extensive pictorial sourcebooks of its kind. Captions. Index. 284pp. 9 × 12. 23766-4 Pa. $9.95

OBELISTS FLY HIGH, C. Daly King. Masterpiece of American detective fiction, long out of print, involves murder on a 1935 transcontinental flight—"a very thrilling story"—NY Times. Unabridged and unaltered republication of the edition published by William Collins Sons & Co. Ltd., London, 1935. 288pp. 5⅜ × 8½. (Available in U.S. only) 25036-9 Pa. $4.95

VICTORIAN AND EDWARDIAN FASHION: A Photographic Survey, Alison Gernsheim. First fashion history completely illustrated by contemporary photographs. Full text plus 235 photos, 1840–1914, in which many celebrities appear. 240pp. 6½ × 9¼. 24205-6 Pa. $6.00

THE ART OF THE FRENCH ILLUSTRATED BOOK, 1700–1914, Gordon N. Ray. Over 630 superb book illustrations by Fragonard, Delacroix, Daumier, Doré, Grandville, Manet, Mucha, Steinlen, Toulouse-Lautrec and many others. Preface. Introduction. 633 halftones. Indices of artists, authors & titles, binders and provenances. Appendices. Bibliography. 608pp. 8⅜ × 11¼. 25086-5 Pa. $24.95

THE WONDERFUL WIZARD OF OZ, L. Frank Baum. Facsimile in full color of America's finest children's classic. 143 illustrations by W. W. Denslow. 267pp. 5⅜ × 8½. 20691-2 Pa. $5.95

FRONTIERS OF MODERN PHYSICS: New Perspectives on Cosmology, Relativity, Black Holes and Extraterrestrial Intelligence, Tony Rothman, et al. For the intelligent layman. Subjects include: cosmological models of the universe; black holes; the neutrino; the search for extraterrestrial intelligence. Introduction. 46 black-and-white illustrations. 192pp. 5⅜ × 8½. 24587-X Pa. $6.95

THE FRIENDLY STARS, Martha Evans Martin & Donald Howard Menzel. Classic text marshalls the stars together in an engaging, non-technical survey, presenting them as sources of beauty in night sky. 23 illustrations. Foreword. 2 star charts. Index. 147pp. 5⅜ × 8½. 21099-5 Pa. $3.50

FADS AND FALLACIES IN THE NAME OF SCIENCE, Martin Gardner. Fair, witty appraisal of cranks, quacks, and quackeries of science and pseudoscience: hollow earth, Velikovsky, orgone energy, Dianetics, flying saucers, Bridey Murphy, food and medical fads, etc. Revised, expanded In the Name of Science. "A very able and even-tempered presentation."—The New Yorker. 363pp. 5⅜ × 8. 20394-8 Pa. $5.95

ANCIENT EGYPT: ITS CULTURE AND HISTORY, J. E Manchip White. From pre-dynastics through Ptolemies: society, history, political structure, religion, daily life, literature, cultural heritage. 48 plates. 217pp. 5⅜ × 8½. 22548-8 Pa. $4.95

CATALOG OF DOVER BOOKS

SIR HARRY HOTSPUR OF HUMBLETHWAITE, Anthony Trollope. Incisive, unconventional psychological study of a conflict between a wealthy baronet, his idealistic daughter, and their scapegrace cousin. The 1870 novel in its first inexpensive edition in years. 250pp. 5⅜ × 8½. 24953-0 Pa. $4.95

LASERS AND HOLOGRAPHY, Winston E. Kock. Sound introduction to burgeoning field, expanded (1981) for second edition. Wave patterns, coherence, lasers, diffraction, zone plates, properties of holograms, recent advances. 84 illustrations. 160pp. 5⅜ × 8¼. (Except in United Kingdom) 24041-X Pa. $3.50

INTRODUCTION TO ARTIFICIAL INTELLIGENCE: SECOND, ENLARGED EDITION, Philip C. Jackson, Jr. Comprehensive survey of artificial intelligence—the study of how machines (computers) can be made to act intelligently. Includes introductory and advanced material. Extensive notes updating the main text. 132 black-and-white illustrations. 512pp. 5⅜ × 8½. 24864-X Pa. $8.95

HISTORY OF INDIAN AND INDONESIAN ART, Ananda K. Coomaraswamy. Over 400 illustrations illuminate classic study of Indian art from earliest Harappa finds to early 20th century. Provides philosophical, religious and social insights. 304pp. 6⅜ × 9⅜. 25005-9 Pa. $8.95

THE GOLEM, Gustav Meyrink. Most famous supernatural novel in modern European literature, set in Ghetto of Old Prague around 1890. Compelling story of mystical experiences, strange transformations, profound terror. 13 black-and-white illustrations. 224pp. 5⅜ × 8½. (Available in U.S. only) 25025-3 Pa. $5.95

ARMADALE, Wilkie Collins. Third great mystery novel by the author of *The Woman in White* and *The Moonstone*. Original magazine version with 40 illustrations. 597pp. 5⅜ × 8½. 23429-0 Pa. $7.95

PICTORIAL ENCYCLOPEDIA OF HISTORIC ARCHITECTURAL PLANS, DETAILS AND ELEMENTS: With 1,880 Line Drawings of Arches, Domes, Doorways, Facades, Gables, Windows, etc., John Theodore Haneman. Sourcebook of inspiration for architects, designers, others. Bibliography. Captions. 141pp. 9 × 12. 24605-1 Pa. $6.95

BENCHLEY LOST AND FOUND, Robert Benchley. Finest humor from early 30's, about pet peeves, child psychologists, post office and others. Mostly unavailable elsewhere. 73 illustrations by Peter Arno and others. 183pp. 5⅜ × 8½. 22410-4 Pa. $3.95

ERTÉ GRAPHICS, Erté. Collection of striking color graphics: *Seasons, Alphabet, Numerals, Aces* and *Precious Stones*. 50 plates, including 4 on covers. 48pp. 9⅜ × 12¼. 23580-7 Pa. $6.95

THE JOURNAL OF HENRY D. THOREAU, edited by Bradford Torrey, F. H. Allen. Complete reprinting of 14 volumes, 1837–61, over two million words; the sourcebooks for *Walden*, etc. Definitive. All original sketches, plus 75 photographs. 1,804pp. 8½ × 12¼. 20312-3, 20313-1 Cloth., Two-vol. set $80.00

CASTLES: THEIR CONSTRUCTION AND HISTORY, Sidney Toy. Traces castle development from ancient roots. Nearly 200 photographs and drawings illustrate moats, keeps, baileys, many other features. Caernarvon, Dover Castles, Hadrian's Wall, Tower of London, dozens more. 256pp. 5⅜ × 8¼. 24898-4 Pa. $5.95

AMERICAN CLIPPER SHIPS: 1833–1858, Octavius T. Howe & Frederick C. Matthews. Fully-illustrated, encyclopedic review of 352 clipper ships from the period of America's greatest maritime supremacy. Introduction. 109 halftones. 5 black-and-white line illustrations. Index. Total of 928pp. 5⅜ × 8½.
25115-2, 25116-0 Pa., Two-vol. set $17.90

TOWARDS A NEW ARCHITECTURE, Le Corbusier. Pioneering manifesto by great architect, near legendary founder of "International School." Technical and aesthetic theories, views on industry, economics, relation of form to function, "mass-production spirit," much more. Profusely illustrated. Unabridged translation of 13th French edition. Introduction by Frederick Etchells. 320pp. 6⅛ × 9¼. (Available in U.S. only)
25023-7 Pa. $8.95

THE BOOK OF KELLS, edited by Blanche Cirker. Inexpensive collection of 32 full-color, full-page plates from the greatest illuminated manuscript of the Middle Ages, painstakingly reproduced from rare facsimile edition. Publisher's Note. Captions. 32pp. 9⅜ × 12¼.
24345-1 Pa. $4.50

BEST SCIENCE FICTION STORIES OF H. G. WELLS, H. G. Wells. Full novel *The Invisible Man*, plus 17 short stories: "The Crystal Egg," "Aepyornis Island," "The Strange Orchid," etc. 303pp. 5⅜ × 8½. (Available in U.S. only)
21531-8 Pa. $4.95

AMERICAN SAILING SHIPS: Their Plans and History, Charles G. Davis. Photos, construction details of schooners, frigates, clippers, other sailcraft of 18th to early 20th centuries—plus entertaining discourse on design, rigging, nautical lore, much more. 137 black-and-white illustrations. 240pp. 6⅛ × 9¼.
24658-2 Pa. $5.95

ENTERTAINING MATHEMATICAL PUZZLES, Martin Gardner. Selection of author's favorite conundrums involving arithmetic, money, speed, etc., with lively commentary. Complete solutions. 112pp. 5⅜ × 8½.
25211-6 Pa. $2.95

THE WILL TO BELIEVE, HUMAN IMMORTALITY, William James. Two books bound together. Effect of irrational on logical, and arguments for human immortality. 402pp. 5⅜ × 8½.
20291-7 Pa. $7.50

THE HAUNTED MONASTERY and THE CHINESE MAZE MURDERS, Robert Van Gulik. 2 full novels by Van Gulik continue adventures of Judge Dee and his companions. An evil Taoist monastery, seemingly supernatural events; overgrown topiary maze that hides strange crimes. Set in 7th-century China. 27 illustrations. 328pp. 5⅜ × 8½.
23502-5 Pa. $5.00

CELEBRATED CASES OF JUDGE DEE (DEE GOONG AN), translated by Robert Van Gulik. Authentic 18th-century Chinese detective novel; Dee and associates solve three interlocked cases. Led to Van Gulik's own stories with same characters. Extensive introduction. 9 illustrations. 237pp. 5⅜ × 8½.
23337-5 Pa. $4.95

Prices subject to change without notice.

Available at your book dealer or write for free catalog to Dept. GI, Dover Publications, Inc., 31 East 2nd St., Mineola, N.Y. 11501. Dover publishes more than 175 books each year on science, elementary and advanced mathematics, biology, music, art, literary history, social sciences and other areas.